A History of
THE LIVERPOOL
WATERFRONT
1850-1890

THE STRUGGLE FOR ORGANISATION

The Steam Vessel Mystery, *Illustrated London News,* 1867.

A History of
THE LIVERPOOL WATERFRONT
1850-1890

THE STRUGGLE FOR ORGANISATION

DAVID JOHN DOUGLASS

FONTHILL

Fonthill Media Limited
Fonthill Media LLC
www.fonthillmedia.com
office@fonthillmedia.com

First published in the United Kingdom 2013

British Library Cataloguing in Publication Data:
A catalogue record for this book is available from the British Library

ISBN 978-1-78155-061-8

Typeset in 10pt/13pt Sabon
Printed and bound in England

A History of this History

The original work was written as a history of the Liverpool waterfront, but in the process, revealed the phenomenon of 'general strikes' in the city itself. This was a novel discovery: in the nineteenth century and doubtless in earlier times too, whole towns would turn out together in collective action, regardless of skills and trades. The general strike was not so much a national as a regional or city-wide action. It is a feature, which up until that time, as far as I could tell, had been largely ignored by labour historians. Why this should be so is related to another important feature of this book; the nature of pre-'new model' unions. These formations had been largely ignored or dismissed because they did not fit the tight proscriptions of what a union was, and were not as defined by the Webbs, the great labour social historians. These 'unions' were not unions in the Webbs' definition, not being 'continuous associations of wage earners'.

A quick canter through this history will show us:

1830: Liverpool Dock Labourers Society. Founded by John Finch, a socialist pioneer. He was, in the words of Harold Hikins, 'strangled at birth by the employers in 1831'.

1849: South End Dock Labourers Society; becomes the 'Old Dockers Club'.

1866: South End Dock Labourers Association, which under one name or the other lasts until 1911 when it merges with the National Union of Dock Labourers.

1850: Operative Dock Porters Society. It was already in existence by 18 February, but may have pre-dated this year.

1852: Clarence Dock Labourers Society, which existed into the 1890s and then, on amalgamation with the National Union of Dock Labourers, maintained its identity as a separate branch. Subsequently became the Vauxhall Road branch.

1853: Cotton Porters Association. By 1872 claims 6,000 members.

1854: Liverpool Dock Labourers Society. Societies merge, but exclude stevedores and lumpers.

1866: North End Dock Labourers Association, the descendant of the 1854 society. The north and south ends are in separate unions in the 1866 strike, but now include stevedores and lumpers, who had previously had their own unions. Membership given as North End Dock Labourers Society: 9,610; South End: 3,050.

1866: North Docks Railway Porters.

1866: Liverpool Seamen's Protective Society. Matthew Callaghan, chairman. Membership given as 1,212.

1866: Liverpool Mercantile Marine Stokers United Friendly Society. Friendly too, but distinct from, above.

1866: Liverpool Provision Porters Association.

1866: Coal Heavers Society. Mr Doyle, president. Sexton mentions a north end and south end Coal heavers Society. Total union membership, including small associations coal heavers, stokers, etc.; 16,260. The *Liverpool Mercury* (10 March 1890) had stated that the society had been formed in the mid-1870s. Taplin says, 'By 1890, it had some 1,300 members and rigorously controlled entry. Employers had been unable to break up this powerful body.'

1870: The Steamboat Labourers Friendly Burial Society, must have been more than that as it organised at least one strike on the Nelson Dock, although it may not have been confined there, having organised and negotiated an increase in wages among dockers employed by master stevedores, porters, and the shipping firms.

1872: Liverpool Seamen's Union. Oddly, it was formed on the advice of the Shipowners Association to ensure the quality of seafarers in return for redress of their demands on wages and conditions. It was confined to sail boat sailors of the south end. It is likely to have been highly localised and demand specific.

1876: Liverpool Seamen's Protective Society, still active and healthy since the 1866 society of Matthew Callaghan was founded.

1876: North End Dock Labourers Society, still functioning effectively, as is South End.

1879: Central Dock Labourers Club.

1879: (26 March) Birkenhead Amalgamated Dock labourers Union and Benefit Society.

1879: (Liverpool) Union of Stevedores Labourers and Quay Porters.

1879: Seamen's and Firemen's Union of the Bowl. Founded in February 1879, originally just in Liverpool, but probably also with a branch in Glasgow also by that month.

1879: Liverpool Seamen's Protective Society. J. Callaghan was still an official in this year.

1880: Liverpool and Birkenhead Stevedores and Quay Porters Union.

1880: British Seamen's Protective Society. This was a rival organisation and offspring of the Union of the Bowl. Taplin says it was founded in London in 1872 and concludes that, 'Liverpool Seamen's Protective Society' must be the Liverpool Branch of it founded in 1878. There was a South Shields Branch, presumably of the national organisation, still operating in 1930.

1888: National Amalgamated Sailors' and Firemen's Union of Great Britain and Ireland. A national Seamen's union founded by J. Havelock Wilson in Sunderland in 1887. The union gains a great coup with the election of Samuel Plimsoll, the great seamen's campaigner, as president in 1887. He held this position until diabetes caused him to resign in 1892. The union collapsed after 1894 and did not really revive until 1910, and from 1926, became the National Sailors' and Firemen's Union, and from 1926, the National Union of Seamen. It becomes infamous for being the only union in Britain not to join the general strike. There was a rival union, the British Seafarers Union, described as 'more radical' and with an obviously less cosy relationship with the shipowners.

1889: Merseyside Quay and Railways Carters Union.

1890: The National Union of Dock Labourers.

1890-1900: Liverpool Cotton and General Warehouse Porters Society.

1890: Fruit Porters Society.

Some of these organisations did of course last and are absorbed today in current unions of Dockers and Seafarers, but those that did not were to all practical purposes 'trade unions' nonetheless.

This history also challenges another central tenet of the Webbs' moulding of history, namely their classification of 'new unionism'; the theory that 'unskilled' or non-craft workers and labourers of all descriptions did not organise as a section of the working class until craftsmen in craft unions took their knowledge of craft organisation into the sectional organisation of the great mass of unskilled labourers in the 1890s. These central propositions are challenged by the history of struggle on the Liverpool waterfront and the quest for grass roots organisation revealed in this book.

Often, they were not preserved with organisational hierarchies and records, but instead were laid down or disassembled at the end of each epoch of struggle, only to be reconstituted anew when the need arose at some point in the future. In the heyday of rented accommodation; and in particular mass, working class council tenancy, tenants associations often acted in this way. They would be resurrected from some struggle ten or twenty years previously, usually around some surviving committee members who met on occasion and had safeguarded some small funds, and then re-established, perhaps with a new name because its area of recruitment had expanded, only to be laid down again following the next round of rent strikes or protests. The knowledge of what a tenants association was, was retained; and something of how it was organised was retained; a basic fabric of organisation laid aside for when it was next needed. Certain unions uncovered by this research probably existed in this fashion. Many of the organisations and non-organisational forms of action looked at in my history have been written out of history, or else regarded as inferior or primitive; not the 'real thing' at all. I take strong issue with such a view. Stripped down to the essentials, a union is simply solidarity. It is groups of workers standing out together in their collective interest. The union is the workers themselves in collective action. Indeed in 1879, we shall see that a general strike of the docks as a whole is conducted without any formal organisation. R. A. Sykes comments on a similar process among textile workers at the beginning of the nineteenth century:

> The phenomenon of periodic explosions of formal union membership, followed by periods of great weakness and often complete collapse of formal organisation was common. The Ashton Spinners' Union with, according to its secretary, twenty members at the start of 1830, had 2,000 on strike the following December, and collapsed in early 1831. It was not primarily a formal organisation, which provided the spinners cohesion, but rather those organisations, appearing then disappearing, but with significantly similar structures and policies, throughout the first half of the nineteenth century, which arose out of prior cohesion based upon the shared craft tradition. Similarly, the periodic federations of spinners' societies were in reality formalisations of underlying informal practice when the occasion demanded.

The process along the docks was similar. Some commentators would object that the dockers were not a craft; indeed, they would see them as an undifferentiated mass of labourers. I will argue such observers are unable to see the wood for the trees, and the dockers on closer inspection, other than at the casual and occasional fringes, were indeed skilled, often in the manner of a craft – at least to the degree that colliers of the same period were.

This is not to say that the aristocracy of labour did not exist. Truly it did, and this is why middle class observers were so enthralled by them. Skilled artisans often regarded themselves as further up the social ladder than the teaming mass of labourers, even when their wage levels were not particularly higher than formally 'unskilled' workers. Some of this is reflected by the absence of Liverpool Trades Council in the great events unfolding in this story. The council had been founded under a different name in 1848. For all its longevity, it was not widely representative of Liverpool labour. 'Its affiliated societies in 1887 consisted of engineers, printers, tailors, saddlers, bookbinders, railway men, gilders, cabinet makers, sawyers, brush makers, mast and block makers, and upholsterers. These represented 3,000 workers.' In part, this was not so much a rejection of dockers *per se*, but a strict implementation of a concept that rejected strike action and sought to promote arbitration. More often than not, the dockers confronted this perspective head on. This started to change only in the last year or so of the 1880s, firstly with the affiliation of the seamen, and then later the dockers. In 1889, the LTC had recognised the NUDL and invited its membership. However, they did not at that stage affiliate, although in the great 1890 strike, they selected five delegates to assist the dockers' negotiations, and in July 1890, NUDL affiliated. By 1891, Liverpool Trades

A map of Liverpool in 1851.

Council had the second largest membership outside of London.

In any case, craft aristocracy and fierce defence of skill demarcation must not be seen as completely blinding such workers to class identity and solidarity. Although it was an obstacle throughout the history of trade unionism, we find multiple expressions of mutual support to all groups, skilled and unskilled. There are very many examples of this class solidarity transcending trade differentiations.

The red flag and the black flag, along with the liberty cap, were common symbols of political rebellion from the early days of the 1700s and probably earlier. A dockers' leader in the great strike of 1879, Mr J. J. Baillif, asked the mass crowd, 'Who was it that built for the masters their mansions of houses and gave them their opulence and wealth? It was not the masters themselves, no it was the hard work – the sinews, blood, and muscle of the men I can see before me.' Turn outs of whole towns, not just whole trades, became a common character of nineteenth century industrial cities. The general strike was a term not applied to a country, but to a city or even a region. It was a call to resistance for all workers and all trades. I found it to be a breath-taking discovery, and again pardon my ignorance, but one entirely ignored by all the standard texts we were meant to read, as well as by most of the eminent labour historians at that time (although it seems to be getting a mention in passing in current research papers – see Sykes *op. cit.*).

The Origin of this Work.

Since I began this research, a recent resurgence in all things 'nostalgic', and therefore in black and white, has taken over many of our traditional working class centres. This is especially so where that particular industry is now dead and its radical proletariat safely disarmed, such as the mines, the docks, the foundries, and seafaring. Our history as part of our present day struggle has, to a large extent, been taken from us and sold back to us as a branch of the tourist trade or nostalgic time travel, rather than our radical class history joined root and branch to today's encounters. The heroic fight of the port's dockers in recent years, something of a 'last stand' of working class values in the port, will resonate back through time as people read this work. I defy the modern day historical iconoclast, debunker, and revisionist to tell me the fight of Liverpool's dockers in the 1990s has no historical, social, or genetic connection to their forbears described in this work. That they flow one through the other is no simple Marxist act of faith on my behalf, but an obvious, common sense conclusion in ethnic and ideological terms. When the miners in the great fight in 1984–85 talked of that struggle as being joined with earlier battles of their forefathers, middle class academics considered the miners were speaking figuratively. They were not, for the miners of 1984–85 were overwhelmingly linked to the miners of the 1920s and before, not simply by location, not simply by ethnicity, not simply by work and labour relations, not simply by ideology, but also by family and blood. I am quite certain that is also true of those in Liverpool's maritime and port trades, though doubtless the current academic trend toward hard-nose cynicism will find that fanciful.

I have not made mention of slavery as a trade in this work. Although great seaports such as Bristol and Liverpool established themselves on the back of it, it was declared illegal by 1807 in Britain. This work, although at times harking back to earlier cameos, runs from the end of the 1840s. It is therefore outside the formal period when human flesh bought and sold as chattels was itself a cargo, or when their unpaid labour fuelled the development of cotton and tobacco, the principle cargoes of the sea and docks. However, Liverpool was the unofficial 'home port of the American Confederate Navy' in the American Civil War. On the outbreak of war, the Confederacy had no fleet. As with the entire county's interdependence upon cotton and slavery, cotton and the fate of the South were likewise interwoven strands. Liverpool and Lancashire took sides with the South for reasons entirely motivated by self-interest and commerce. How far your average white wage-slave in the port and the county were also implicated in this is at least debatable. The workers of northern England, and its seafaring section in Liverpool and elsewhere, seem to have been early supporters of the movement against slavery, although there were undoubtedly contradictory pulls and pressures upon them, especially on Merseyside.

The completion of my 'histrilogy' on the British coal industry and miners union (Stardust and Coaldust) and the tragic death of my old tutor Raph Samuels in 2002 , prompted me to get my work down, lay it out, and try to bring it to life. The recent, two-year-long Liverpool dock dispute, the 2011 commemoration of the great 1911 Liverpool Transport General Strike, and occupation of the city by the state's armed forces may revive interest in the subject. In September 2002, Keele University advertised its UK Industrial Relations in the *Twentieth Century Weekend*. I sank with admitted disappointment, for there among the first session was a paper by Paul Smith, 'The Liverpool and District Carters' and Motormen's Union, 1889-1946.' Was this latecomer plodging in my water hole? Indeed, did he now own the water hole, and was this simply a chapter of a bigger work encapsulating all my previous, as yet undisclosed, discoveries? I chided myself for such academic *petit bourgeois* individualism; history belongs to the working class I reminded myself. Yet I was pleased this turned out to simply be a sample of a bigger work on the transport union aspect, and not on the port *per se*. His work at least gave me a few pointers to other work that had emerged in the years since mine had laid dormant, and suggested that nothing quite along the lines of this work had yet been put into print, although some of it has at least been turned over. As it was, if mine was a race to the Pole, the ice had decidedly melted by the time I got there. For there, already firmly in place these last decades, are the flags of Eric Taplin. Eric had written and published *The Dockers Union 1889-1922*, *Liverpool Dockers and Seamen 1870-1890*, and *Labour Unrest in Liverpool 1871-1873*. 'I'll get my coat then' seems appropriate. However, the story is large and the river is wide, and I am sure this area of history can stand at least two observations; a contrast of discovery might even be revealing and welcome. Having now thoroughly examined his work, our respective presentations, analysis, and focus of study could not be more different.

Way back in my distant Ruskin College days when I first started this work as a history workshop presentation in 1971, Raph Samuels, my long suffering tutor, warned me to watch out for a divided Liverpool workforce, for the spectre of religious/national sectarianism, and how it would impact upon labour organisation on the docks. Sexton indeed does at least mention it.

Paul Smith, in his study of the carters, states:

> The MQRCU (Merseyside Quay and Railways Carters Union) cannot be understood outside Liverpool's socio-economic structure, and especially its working class, which was permeated by entrenched ethnic divisions between Welsh, Ulster Scots, Irish migrants (with their distinctive religions, languages, and politics), and English inhabitants. Emigration from Ireland, escalating in the aftermath of the famine, had dramatically transformed the city's population so that 'by 1886, the sectarian geography of Liverpool was established'. Broadly, the north end dockside areas were dominated by Irish Catholics and the areas above in the north, Netherfield and St Domingo, and the Dingle in the south, were dominated by Protestants. The latter group comprised a number of distinct faiths and groups, e.g. Welsh Methodists and Ulster Presbyterians. Voluntary bodies were built on an ethnic basis. Debates on public order, health, and education were always imbued with ethnic overtones. The Irish constituted an easily identified ethnic group – marked by extreme poverty, a distinctive language or dialect, adherence to Roman Catholicism, and nationalist politics – which was regarded as inferior in a racial and cultural sense, and a threat to the political and social order.

The *Liverpool Daily Post*, near the end of the great 1890 dockers strike, reports:

> Until recently, the dock labourer's agitation has been conducted upon non-political lines, but at the meetings held lately, the question of Home

Rule for Ireland has been introduced, with a new watchword of 'success to the union and Home Rule'. This attempt to mix up politics with the labour dispute is, it is said, strongly resented by many members of the union, and if persisted in, may positively lead to a rupture.

I hear what they say, and I am aware that heavy historical enquiry has been made into the question of inter-working class sectarianism on Merseyside, and yet there is a strong sense in which I think it is oversold. Mr McHugh, the National Dockers Union leader of the 1890 Liverpool dock strike, in answer to attempts to undermine him on the basis of not being a Liverpudlian (he was an Ulsterman via Glasgow), replied:

There was a time when such an objection would have been important, but that had not been the case since the formation of the National Union. Since that time, all national, political, and religious hatreds and prejudices had been buried, and the employers might be assured that for the future they would not derive much profit from the attempt to stimulate bickering amongst the people of several nationalities.

Indeed, it became a point of principle with rule No. 19 of NUDL rule book: 'No member shall use unbecoming words or references to any other member's religious opinions, or nationality, or antecedents, it being a fundamental principle of the union that all men are brothers.'

I have read every single newspaper based in the city from every day over a forty year spread. The results of that study, at least how it impacts upon labour in the port, is produced here. At a time when newspapers were given to almost verbatim coverage of mass meetings and speakers at the centre of the labour storms, when hecklers, rouge leaflets, posters, and dissidence was widely covered, I can find little if any impact of this so-called sectarian tradition on the struggle of Merseyside in general, or Liverpool in particular. I am told it was there and I do not challenge that. What I say is, to all intents and purposes in strikes – in general and specific turn outs, large and small – it made no practical difference. Class blood seems thicker than religious/ethnic water when the chips are down, if that is not too many mixed metaphors. Platform speakers do not mention it, crowd hecklers do not use it, neither scabs nor strikers are motivated in either direction by it. On occasion where the Union Jack is carried on mass parade, so was the tricolour and the stars and stripes. That different groups of workers were organised around particular areas of the docks or trades according to religion of ethnic origin, I would take no issue with; that it affected their willingness to strike and support the class movement as a whole as one identity, there is not the slightest piece of evidence. It was rewarding to find that Eric Taplin also came to the same independent conclusion that sectarianism, alive and sadly well elsewhere in the town, did not flourish on the docks, and was absent from the effects of labour organisation in the port. In his words, 'The celebration of national or sectarian festivals such as St Patrick's day or Orange day led to some leg pulling that could degenerate into minor scuffles, but sectarian allegiance was unimportant at work.' It should be added that both Protestants and Catholics celebrated St Patrick's Day well into the 1840s. 'Irishness' was not at first challenged by Orangeism, only its allegiance and political direction. After all, there were Orange lodges in the southern counties of Ireland as well as the north. It was only later, as Ulster-British loyalism became more extreme in the face of all Irish Republican secularist propaganda, that sections started denying being Irish at all. Having said that, it cannot be simply left, and requires some explanation, awkward though this is.

The Orange Society was founded in Armagh in 1795. Its aim was defence of the Protestant faith and succession. However, from time to time its adherents attached far deeper purpose than this, seeing the pope as 'anti-Christ' and all forms of high church procedure and paraphernalia among Protestant churches as treachery. They vehemently opposed all forms of demand for Irish Home Rule. 'Home Rule is Rome rule' was their conclusion. Thus armed, most Protestants in Ulster came to see some form of 'Orangeism' as defence of Protestantism *per se*. This didn't mean they were members of the lodge or took part in the many excesses of sectarian violence against Catholics, but by community location, culture, and tradition they were linked, be it ever so tenuously, to Orangeism. For all that, religion made no essential difference to work on the waterfront. It is probably true that certain roles, trades, and locations became centres for one group rather than the other, but this history will show that that did not obscure any common identity as a single class and work force. What needs to be understood is that Orangeism is a *political* conclusion, it is not an inevitable part of Protestantism, as demonstrated by the fact that other Protestant communities did not come to this political adjunct. Indeed, it was not an inevitable part of Ulster Protestantism either. About the time of the formation of the Orange Order, Protestantism had another option in the form of the United Irishmen. This was the first Irish Republican movement, and was founded by Ulster Protestants seeking to unite Irishmen regardless of religion. Their brave attempts at rebellion were ruthlessly repressed. To uninformed readers it might seem odd, but the heroes of the IRA praised in songs and banners are all Protestants.

John Belchem comments:

Ulster Protestants, it seems, were the necessary catalyst that activated the latent anti-Catholicism of the native work force – without their presence, Orangeism failed to develop among native workers in other areas of Irish immigration. Even in Liverpool, the Orange lodges were initially restricted to Ulster ranks. Sectarian violence came to the fore however when Orangeism was appropriated and amplified by the local establishment. Incorporated into the Tory narrative of religious and constitutional freedom, Orangeism became the primary expression of allegiance; the symbol of inclusive national identity for all Protestants, native and immigrant alike.

Orangeism in Liverpool, linked as it was to Tory political agenda, had however absorbed positions quite hostile to the interests of dock workers, Protestant and Catholic alike. The Conservatives of those days were in favour of protectionism, and as such, vehemently opposed demands for free trade. Free trade was a liberal and radical demand, but it struck a chord with dock workers. Free trade meant more trade, and more trade meant more ships, more cargoes, higher demand for dockers' labour, and greater labour power. By contrast, the backbone of working class support for Orangeism, and often the actual proponents of violence and sometimes murder of Catholics, was the shipwrights. The artisans of this trade saw free trade as meaning trade from elsewhere, ships built elsewhere, and a diminishing demand for their skills. Orangeism mixed in with the Tory agenda did not confront their sectarianism, and in fact was grist to its mill. However, Kevin Moore urges caution:

One should be wary of interpreting all this as indicative of a high level of anti-Catholic bigotry among the shipwrights. The shipwrights had supported the Tories at the 1837 election largely for reasons other than religious, but had found themselves under attack from the Irish nevertheless. What was developing therefore was a 'grudge' or 'vendetta' largely independent of the religious issue, and which increasingly took on a dynamic of its own. It is also clear that those among the shipwrights who started the trouble were apprentices, and much of the blame for their violence can be put on the 'traditionally' violent behaviour of adolescent males. In addition, other youths, and not just shipwrights apprentices, were implicated in the disturbances, which in 1839 for example, were said to have begun when three shipwrights apprentices, followed by 'a crowd of blackguard boys', entered an Irish pub in Jordan Street. The general religious toleration of the journeymen shipwrights can be seen from the fact that there were *Catholics* as well as Protestants among them, and that these marched *together* in the parade that preceded the riots in 1839. At the end of the march 'the Protestant portion went to St Paul's church and at the same time … the Catholic members of the procession were listening to a sermon in the neighbouring chapel of St Mary in Edmund Street.'

Inman and Company SS *City of New York.*

Orangeism has always thrown up the most bazaar and extreme of characters, such as the Revd Ian Paisley in modern times, who in those bygone days had a predecessor in the shape of Revd Hugh McNeilie, 'the most militant, No-Popery crusader in Liverpool'. His organisation made little headway among Protestant working class ranks, and was largely middle class. Kevin Moore, in his chapter 'This Whig and Tory Ridden Town: Popular Politics in Liverpool in the Chartist Era' tells us:

> Orangeism enjoyed a significant upsurge in support in Liverpool in 1843 – probably primarily a reflection of events in Ireland itself. However, it is important to recognise that it remained organisationally small in numbers ... evidence suggests that there were in fact no more than 5,000 to 6,000 Orangemen belonging to 30 lodges. Given the large size of Liverpool's immigrant Ulster Protestant community (one-sixth of the Irish-born population in 1841), it is conceivable that the indigenous population were not involved at all.

The only 'Orange' presence we meet in dock labour comes in 1889–90 with the carters' leadership and their union's involvement with Liverpool Working Men's Conservative Association. Sam Davies describes the organisation as,

'Perhaps unique.' He comments, 'If the WMCA was effective in delivering working class votes for the Tories, it was hardly effective in delivering material rewards for its working class supporters.' That of course can be said of Orangeism and loyalism *per se* in Liverpool, Glasgow, and Belfast. However, whereas the dockers of those ports rejected sectarianism on the docks and organised together, the carters for a time were led directly to act against their own interests. They after all would benefit, along with the dock porter, from the radical demand for free trade, rather than the politics of WMCA who campaigned against it.

In the 1970s, the general tide of workers militancy was spreading nationwide, in length and breadth. It was leaping from skill to skill, plant and mine, dock and factory. Whole cities and counties once more began to mobilise in stark similarity to many of the general turn outs in this history. Occupations of work places were 'foreign' forms of industrial action; they took place on the continent, not Britain. Until that was the UCS shipyard occupation, which lit a fuse in industrial Clydeside that burned over all borders. In 1972, the largest single number of occupations to occur at any one time occurred in Manchester, with the greatest concentration of engineering factories in Britain. The workers at the GKN Bradbury steel plant decided to take action. Management threatened a lock-out, and the workers responded with an occupation of the plant on 16 March. This set the pattern, and by 8 April 1972, twenty-two factories were occupied; thirty-four occupations in the Manchester area in total that year. This was followed in Sheffield, Leeds, and London. Other major firms in Manchester staged traditional strikes, and once more the wildcat was loose everywhere at once. In France during May 1968, multiple strike actions and occupations came together in a general strike of revolutionary potential; only a fraction of the workers were members of unions. But workers have never needed unions to know they are workers, and that they belong to a class that is best able to respond when they respond together. Organisations, liketh the man can cometh with the hour.

This work attracted over 800 footnotes and source references too many for publication in a book of this size, however I intend to make the heavily referenced work along with the sources themselves available at one of the Liverpool Museums and failing that researchers should consult me directly.

Dedication and Acknowledgements

Dedicated to Bob Crow and the National Union of Rail, Maritime and Transport Union which absorbed the restless spirit of the seafarers union.

To Len McClusky General Secretary of UNITE who started his working life on the Liverpool waterfront at the Albert Dock, and the North West Region of that union who absorbed and now represent the Liverpool dock workers of today.

With thanks also to the staff of the Liverpool Museums.

Mersey Flats, (sailing barges).

CHAPTER ONE

Sailortown

1850s Liverpool had a larger Irish population than any across the water with the exception of Dublin, Cork, and Belfast. According to the commissioner of the *Morning Chronicle* in 1850, two-thirds of all dock labourers were Irish. Thousands arrived daily, swelling the ranks of the port's poor and flooding the labour market with desperate hands. But the docks were vast in this period, extending from the south to the north banks of the Mersey for a full four miles, providing fourteen miles and 119 yards of quay room. In the years following, they grew even more rapidly, with the coming of steamships and the ever-increasing cotton trade. By the 1870s, there was a nine mile stretch of docks – the biggest waterfront in the world. Already in the 1850s, Liverpool's trade had overtaken London's with a tonnage of 2,819,014 to London's 2,688,857. Liverpool was *the* maritime town, and an average of 8,490 sailors were in the port at any one time, exclusive of steamship crews.

Over the course of this exposition (1850-1890s), the number of steam vessels was to constantly increase in numbers and importance. With the beginning of the twentieth century, we can clearly see that the sailing vessel, the mast, and rope sailor had had their day. Large numbers of American steam vessels were arriving and departing weekly, mail steamers to Ireland and Scotland adding about another 500 sailors to those thousands of sail crews from 849 tall masters that lay in the port at any one time. The maritime population changed about fifteen times per year, based upon the assumption of three-and-a-half weeks for every vessel to arrive, discharge, transact the business, get fresh cargo, and depart. We would see from this that 135,000 sailors of various nations entered and left the port every year. It was said that from a distance, the port looked like a forest, so tightly packed were the ships' masts from hundreds of vessels.

The sea and Liverpool were inextricably linked, with constant interaction of cultures between seamen and the townsfolk. It was hardly surprising therefore that as struggles with port employers and shipping firms developed, the whole waterfront swung into united action.

Above: 'The Liverpool Forest'.

Left: On deck of a sailing ship at Liverpool docks.

It had been calculated that in the 1850s, the number of dock labourers winning their bread from unloading and loading vessels was 18,000; the average dock labourer's family in those days consisted of four people; therefore no less than 72,000 individuals depended directly upon porterage for a living. In the 1870s, 77 per cent of dock workers lived within one mile of the nearest dock, a walk from home to work of fifteen to twenty minutes.

Throughout the day, there was a mad rush of activity on the docks and quays; bales, boxes, barrels, and crates being tumbled and shifted from place to place by thousands of labourers and workers of all descriptions. There would be carters carrying heavy laden or returning at speed for new loads; the shouts of the dock masters and gangers; the chants of the sailors and their captains coming into moor or straining at the ropes. Foreign voices; heavy Irish, Scots, and other, more local accents.

On the street corners, but more particularly on the docks themselves, stood hundreds of jealous-eyed porters watching their colleagues at work and waiting patiently for the remotest chance of a job, even for one-third of a day. Their eyes too would jealously survey the great wealth being pulled along by huge horses on lorries and crates – the greater portion of these carrying cotton that would eventually end up in the mills of Yorkshire and Lancashire. Yet others would carry bags of corn and Indian meal to the town's warehouses. Trundling past the hungry would come great barrels of pork from New York, others of rum cakes and sugar hogsheads from West India. The largest vehicles rolling through the crowded streets and battling for room were the great carts pulling loads of timber from Canada and America, the wheels on which stood eight to nine feet in diameter. Great stores of wealth passed daily through the streets, not all of it left intact. In 1850, when the commissioner of the *Morning Chronicle* visited Liverpool, there were many half-starved people around, ready to pounce on whatever they could get. Although property was under the close scrutiny of dock police, the women and kids proved the maxim, 'Where there's a will there's a way.' Swarms of children were always on the prowl during the day and night. Grasping here and there the odd handful of meal, corn, beans, rice, and coffee. Cotton picking was also a principle source of plunder, in spite of the fact that even by 1850 standards, the police were very severe upon children who picked up cotton.

There were also copper nails, sheathing, old ropes, and other ships' stores that found their way back to the marine store dealers, who in turn would pay some measly sum for them.

One of the few legal jobs available for children was selling newspapers. On Lord Street for example, dozens of boys and some girls could be seen selling papers from 8 a.m. to 6 p.m. Their wages were 6*d* or 9*d* per week. Wilder ones, between eight and fourteen years old, would join into ragged gangs to drag cotton from the bales in the docks; the boys stuffing it into their pockets while the girls pushed it into the bosoms of their dresses. The older women also took corn, coffee, and other articles; cotton was however the main target. They wore dresses made for the purpose, with large receptacles or inner flounces that they stuffed with cotton.

Thieving was a sizeable trade in Liverpool, and a real source of livelihood. Thefts of cotton and other articles in 1850 amounted to some £100,000 per year. The situation was aggravated each week by the arrival of thousands more Irish exiles.

Women could be seen following lorries and carts laden with bags of Indian corn or bales of cotton. They would cut into the bags with knives or scissors and hold up their aprons to catch the contents as they were jolted out by the bumping of the cart. As the vehicle approached the dock gates, they would squat down and crawl under the vehicle with their aprons full, creeping out under the great feet of the horses to avoid detection by police at the dock gate.

At other times, up to a dozen lorries could be seen standing at the warehouse doors; during the confusion of drivers jostling for a place and shouting to get loaded and away, a rich picking ground was provided for the people. The drivers, fully occupied with trying to control the horses, would be unable to watch the women flashing here and there behind the carts. These women often operated in teams; one picked the cotton off the lorry and passed it to another, who in turn passed it on. The picker, if captured, could plead complete innocence, having nothing of value on her personally. Other poorer women, of the kind seen by Herman Melville when he visited, would be raking over heaps of soaked and stinking rubbish carried ashore from the holds of shipping. There would be crowds of them in tattered rags, armed with old rakes and picking irons. Their findings, we are told, were small, for as it is one of the immemorial perquisites of the second mate of a merchant ship to collect and sell on his own account all of the condemned 'old junk' of the vessel to which he belongs, he generally takes good heed that the buckets of rubbish carried ashore shall hold as few rope yarns as possible.

From 5,000 to 10,000 miscellaneous needlewomen, largely from the poor and near poor, worked day and night to furnish the sailors with canvas and cotton shirts, jackets, and trousers etc. Great and permanent distress fell on these women with the abolition of the slave trade among other things, for prior to the passing of the act, the slave masters supplied the Negroes with calico shirts that they were compelled to wear. A sizeable part of this trade was carried on by the city's women, and a decent wage could thus be earned. However, the huge portion of their work in this period was centred on furnishing sailors with their apparel.

This was the so called 'slop trade' in which many thousands of women laboured. There was great distress amongst the needlewomen of the town,

Landing cotton at Liverpool. An engraving by A. Boyd Houghton. *The Graphic,* 11 December 1875.

due to the daily increase of women employed or seeking employment; skills and standards diminished with the wage rate as all women in distress tried their hands at needlework. Of the slop sellers in Liverpool, there were three classes, namely: those in the wholesale houses who carry out the foreign and colonial trade in shirts, cloth, and flannel goods; the retail houses; and the so called 'slop tailors'. The slop tailors often employed a 'man catcher' whose sole business was to look out for emigrants and sailors and persuade them to buy outfits.

We are also told that the needlewomen of Liverpool:

Are very often the wives of sailors. If they get their husbands monthly money pretty regularly they do not care for needlework, but if there is any falling off in that they apply for the slop trade … Some of them are the wives of porters and dock labourers, who take to slop work when their husbands are out of employ, and leave it off as soon as the husbands get a few jobs to keep them going.

"From a distance the port looked like a forest"; Canning Dock from a nineteenth-century painting.

The town fed off the sea and the seamen. Much of the trade, in the form of dockers, carter's, sail and clothes makers was legal enough, but Liverpool bred another industry far less legitimate. The city abounded with every variety of illegal landlords, bar keepers, clothiers, crimps, thugs, and prostitutes, all aimed at snatching the homeward bounder's treasure.

To the town's parasites, the sailor ashore was considered 'fair game'. Some however, were easier prey than others. Generally, it was true that British sailors in foreign and colonial trade and crews of foreign ships were far easier 'got at' than the men of the coastal vessels who did not have the large accumulation of wages of the men coming home from long voyages. (When a ship docked after a long journey – in some cases eighteen months or two years – it had aboard a crew of twenty or thirty men, each with the accumulated wages of all that time, all eager to spend and forget the sea.) There would be many 'land sharks' as they were called, just waiting for their chance.

There were many varieties of land shark, but the three major types were the boarding and lodging house keepers of disreputable inclination (there were many honest boarding house masters), the slop tailors and outfitters, and prostitutes. When these three had finished, the fourth shark, namely the crimp, moved in. Of course, in certain cases, the crimp's business was but a branch of that carried on by the boarding house keepers. All of these sections played into each other's hands in tight collaboration. Only the prostitutes carried out their own business, although in certain circumstances they were in the direct pay of the crimps and outfitters. A seaman, after a fifteen month voyage to the coast of Africa, had fourteen months pay. Assuming that he had had an advance, this left him about £37 10s. The first clutches laid on him came from the lodging keeper who persuaded him to stay at his lodge. The keeper would recommend him to a slop tailor who might extract £15 for the sale of old clothes. The lodging house keeper would expect to receive some commission on every man he passed on to the slop dealer.

Along the docks at dinner time, thousands of beggars would line the wharfs and streets, beseeching the seamen for money. Every form of want and suffering was found there. Old and young, men and women, girls and boys; some starving, others incurably sick. Skinny, hollow-eyed women would hold up skinny, decrepit babies in the hope that some copper or coin might be given to them. Cripples and bandaged beggars stood side by side. Yards of ground would be covered with the writings of the penniless. Herman Melville said that as he walked these streets, he was beset on every hand by people catching at his coat, hanging on, following after him, crying 'for heaven's sake', 'for God's sake', 'for Christ's sake', beseeching of you but for just one halfpenny.

To a smaller extent, the lunchtime scene was found in the narrow streets of sailors boarding houses where the seamen met in great numbers before their evening revelry. Beggars and musicians with hand organs, fiddles, and cymbals clashed in tone with the voices of the seamen in song and the noises of the streets. Certain streets that were frequented by the sailors would have shocked a stranger who stumbled upon them by accident. Such places would include Rotten Row, Gibraltar Place, and Booble Alley.

The whole of the sailors' quarters was set aside for his bed and entertainment. Whall, in *Sea Songs and Shanties,* tells us that low-type concert saloons, brothels, pubs, and shanghaiing dives were in every street. Nearly every house would have a piano in the front parlour, and sell cheap liquor even if it was not a pub.

The prostitutes were an inseparable part of the scene. Some of them used a lodging house that catered for rooms rented by the hour; some had it away quickly up some dark alleyway. In many cases, the drunken sailor would be robbed and beaten by the prostitutes' assistants. The problem was linked most obviously to the port, where single men came to seek work. Juvenile

The Government Inspector's Office. *Illustrated London News,* 6 July 1850.

prostitution was led by poverty as well as clients' preferences. 'The workhouse and Lock Hospital annually admitted 1,000 persons with venereal diseases', but this was regarded as relatively few of those afflicted. By 1889, 443 brothels were 'known to the police', who did not intervene. 'An Englishman's brothel was his castle', observed the police surgeon Dr Lowndes.

In the bars and pubs, the better class of girls used little closets curtained off from the general saloon. Other girls lived in brothels managed by a madam who owned and ran the establishment, and whose profession was providing girls for the seamen. The madams played an important role, and the sailors called them 'Mother Judge' (of pricks). In Liverpool lived Mother Smyrden, who was infamous the world over. There was also Madame Anna of No. 18 Hotham Street, who introduced girls from Dublin, supposedly to go into 'service'.

In a report of 1853 focused on 1,123 Liverpool prostitutes, 44.2 per cent were born in Ireland, 26.3 per cent in Liverpool, 18.5 per cent elsewhere in England, 4.3 per cent in Scotland, 4.7 per cent in Wales, 1.3 per cent in the Isle of man, and 0.7 per cent abroad. Many of these operated from 'free and easies-pubs' with singing and dancing licences. Not all the girls played a double game with robbery or crime as an ulterior motive, and some had a different relationship with the seamen. While the sailors' girls themselves were often very different, this type of prostitute represented a long sought-after comfort to many of the sailors; a girl often dreamed about in the cold damp of the sea bunk after hours of backbreaking, wind-swept toil on deck. Olmstead, an American farmer visiting England in the 1850s, tells of how he was surprised at the quietness and decency of the waterfront girls. They were plainly and generally neatly dressed, and stood talking quietly and in kind tones to each other. They were not, we are told, as young as the same kind of girls in America, and in strong gaslight, their faces seemed expressive of a different character:

> Generally they were sad, but not ill-natured or stupid. As they stood, companioned but friendless – some with not even hats to protect them from the rain, others, with their gowns drawn up over their head, and others, two together, under a scanty shawl – it would have been difficult, I thought, for anyone not to have softened towards those abandoned thus to support of life that night. We could not but think the cheerful

The Emigration of distressed needlewomen 1850. *Illustrated London News*, 17 Aug 1850.

words with which the sailors recognised and greeted them, as the ships hauled near, were as much dictated by pity and sympathy as any worse impulses. They said, 'If nobody else is waiting for us, we know that you will be glad that we are coming to the land once more; so cheer up, and we will help each other again to enjoy a short space of jollity, excitement, and forgetfulness.'

The sailors' lodging and boarding houses were situated in every part of the dock, but the greater part of them were in the neighbourhood of the Princes, Waterloo, and Clarence docks. One street leading from the Waterloo Road, Dennison Street, was wholly occupied with lodgings and boarding houses, and of course pubs. There was however, a huge build-up of warehouses at the far end. There were more pubs in this street than anywhere else in the port. Out of forty houses, there were twenty wine and beer shops, nearly all of which kept lodgings for sailors. The other houses on the street were almost wholly devoted to the boarding of foreign crews. That particular street was almost entirely occupied by American sailors who claimed it as their own, even to the extent of operating a colour bar by not allowing black men down the street. We encounter few black seamen in this work, but in other ports, such as South Shields and Cardiff, Arab sailors, particularly men from Aden and Somalis, were a common feature of the ports. Arab boarding houses catered exclusively for this class of seamen, and ensured their dietary and religious needs were met. The boarding house master also acted as an agent to ensure that the seamen were reshipped, often granting credit until a ship and an advance settled the score.

The seamen's boarding houses were distinguished by gilded emblems outside an anchor or crown; perhaps a ship, a windless, or a dolphin. Some of them served as regular crimping houses, shipping inexperienced and destitute crews, and taking their rake off from the 'advanced notes' – the payment given to the sailor when he signed on.

Many famous crimps lived in Liverpool, their reputation became immortalised in the words of the black ballers, the crew who sailed the Liverpool–America fast packet ships of the Black Ball Line. One such crimp was Paddy West, who is said to have lived in Great Howard Street. He ran a 'school' for his potential ships crews; anyone bound for a ship could stay at West's house for a week and become an AB in that time. (The making of an AB usually took four years of hard experience.) It is said that he had a ship's wheel in the back garden to teach steering, with his wife coming out every now and again to throw a bucket of water over the would-be seamen. The passing out ceremony was to walk over a piece of string and three times around a table on which was placed a cow's horn – the seaman had therefore crossed the line and rounded the horn.

Dancing between decks. *Illustrated London News, 6th July 1850*

Oh, as I wuz a-rolling down Great Howard Street,
I strolled into Paddy West's house;
He gave me a plate of American hash,
An swore it wuz English scouse,
Sez he, 'look 'ere young feller, yer very just in time,
To go away in a big clipper ship, an' very soon ye'll sign'.
   Chorus. Then its put on yer dungaree jacket,
An give the boys a rest,
An' think of the cold nor'westers that blows,
in the house of Paddy West's
   Now he axed me if I had ever bin to sea,
I told him not till that morn;
'well, be jasus,' sez he, 'a sailor ye'll be,
From the hour that yoz wuz born;
Just go into the parlour walk round the ol' cow horn,

An tell the mate that ye have been, oh, three times round the horn!'
   Chorus
   When I got into ol' Paddy West's house,
The wind began to blow,
He sent me up to the lumber room,
The fore-royal for to stow;
When I climbed up to the attic, no fore-royal could I find,
So I jumped upon the winder-sill and furled the winder blind.
   Chorus
   Its paddy, me bhoy, he pipes all hands on deck,
Their stations for to man.
His wife, Sarry Ann, stood in the backyard,
A bucket in her hand –
His wife let go of the bucket, the water flew on its way;
'Clew up yer fore t'gallant, me sons, she's taking in a say'.
   Chorus
   To every two men that graduates,
I'll give wan outfit free,
For two good men on watch at a time,
Ye never need to see;
Oilskins me bhoys, ye won't want, carpet slippers made o' felt
I will dish out to the pair o' ye, wid a rope yarn for a belt.

Paddy West's boarding house had a terrible reputation. Seamen during the great seamen's strike of 1889 referred to men who were being shipped in their place as 'Paddy Westerners'. Another such character was John Da Costa, who had a certain kind of rough weather cloth, which was strung round the weather rail of the windy poop decks, named after him. He lived somewhere in the south end of Sailortown.

Yet not all boarding house keepers were land sharks. Many were retired seamen who aimed at setting up lodging houses of a decent sort to stop such exploitation. Many of these boarding house keepers considered that the sailors' home – set up by philanthropists as an alternative lodging for the seamen – practised many injustices, especially against those down on their luck without a ship. These men were often turfed out on their ear if they could not pay their score, whereas many honest boarding house masters allowed these men pay on credit, trusting that they would pay out of their advance when they eventually got a ship.

A mass meeting of boarding house keepers was held on 9 February 1872 to redress and discuss their grievances. This meeting, held at the concert hall, Lord Nelson Street, expressed the opinion that the sheer weight of seamen in the port could not simply be handled by the sailors' home, and therefore

Clippers at the dock-side.

boarding houses were an absolute necessity. To prevent sharks exploiting seamen, they called for the issuing of licences to all reputable boarding house owners, with the view of stopping malpractice and raising the standard of lodging. Many complaints were heard against the river police, who it was stated discriminated and victimised the seamen.

The demand for licences was clearly not an idle one, and by the end of the period, legislation made it an offence against the law for any private person or householder to accommodate a seaman. Seamen were required to stay in licensed seamen's lodgings.

Boarding house masters stood on both sides of the class divide. Some identified their interests with those of the shipowners, while others identified with the seamen. The former acted in the same capacity as the employer; he exploited the seaman as far as possible, robbing him, and when strikes developed, he worked directly against the interests of the seamen by importing scabs and shipping 'Paddy Westerners' in the striker's place. The other set of boarding house keepers were generally educated ex-seamen who had settled down to run a boarding house. These men identified very strongly with the actions and trials of their former shipmates. During strikes, they would house sailors for free, as would many sympathetic hotel and pub owners. When the seaman developed their unions, this class of boarding house keeper came very much to the fore, and on two occasions, the house keepers were promoted to leadership positions in the unions. The advantage of having a boarding house keeper at the forefront of a union was marked in his independence from the ties of shipowners, yet close proximity to the sailor and marine classes. The choice of such men was, in a sense, obvious. It has certain parallels with the early miners unions, a most notable leader for whom was Martin Jude, a Newcastle publican. Likewise, it mirrors the innovation of the checkweighman, having a source of income directly dependent upon the men he served, and having a lack of economic ties to the employer, rendering him free from victimisation and manipulation. Another advantage was in being there all the time, unlike the working sailors who were never in a fixed location long enough to serve as officers of the union. In coming to the forefront, such men were less afraid of defeat, for their livelihood remained more or less safe regardless of the outcome of the dispute or the work of the blacklist.

At all times, the presence of the boarding house master – for good or ill – was evident on the waterfront, and inseparably connected to the life and labours of the seaman, and this was never more evident than during the periods of mobilisation by the seaman, and of attacks upon them by the shipowners.

During the strike of 1889, the seamen were very incensed by the role of the boarding house keepers who had recruited scab crews. They were a prime catalyst in defeating the movement of the men. An infamous man in this capacity was Mr John Doyle of No. 6 Gibraltar Row. The seamen on strike smashed up his house in retaliation and terrified the rice out of his fellows who had played the same infamous game.

In the previous seamen's strike, many of the boarding house masters had made between £100 and £150 in providing shipowners with strike breaking crews. They tried to cash in on the 1889 strike on a far bigger scale. So keen were they to provide crews that they packed their houses to bursting point with men of all kinds, ready to be shipped. In one case that came before the courts, a Matthew Riley of No. 38 Dennison Street had managed to get ninety-eight people into his house, seventy-nine in excess of what the law permitted. A. T. Riley of No. 44 Dennison Street was got for overcrowding of the same nature, judging by the fines imposed on him.

Doyle, one the famous Liverpool boarders, also lived in Dennison Street. One of the classic Liverpool sea shanties, which rang from decks and masts on the oceans of the world, charged that they 'will hang Paddy Doyle for his boots'. During their strike, the seamen always made Dennison Street either the starting point of their mammoth processions, or else part of the route or its rallying point. Here, they would engage in booing and groaning the scab boarders. In one such incident, the police told the seamen that they could not block up the street. The men therefore commenced picketing, marching down one side of the street and up the other in a circular motion. Meanwhile, attacks were made on the various boarding houses. Marching up Gibraltar Row, a body of men attacked Doyle's house. The Gibraltar Arms was also hit; the widows were knocked out and the police intervened. The police then tried to force the strikers from the boarding house, but had considerable trouble dislodging them. Eventually, the mounted police were called in and the crowd dispersed.

The other kind of boarding house keepers supported the seamen in their strikes. In the great general strike of 1866, the leader Kavanagh was a boarding house master. He was at the founding meeting of the seamen's union, later called 'The Liverpool Seamen's Protective Society'. He was elected as chairman of the union and had been a seamen and an agitator for many years. He had been the chief agitator and strike organiser in the great 1851 seamen's strike in London.

In 1866, boarding house keepers played a definite part in organising the seamen's end of strike, and the enemies of the strike made much of this. As one of them wrote to the *Liverpool Mercury*:

> The public will be convinced who has made the greatest amount out of the sailors when another boarding house keeper states he will do all he can to obtain (strike) subscription, from boarding house keepers, publicans, outfitters and others. Who the latter are, the speakers do not state. It is possible that they are the 'unfortunates' who crowd round and infest the sailors' home. It is but too true that the boarding house keepers, crimps, publicans, 'Jews and unfortunates' get the greater part of the seamen's earnings. If the shipowners would be united and determined to abolish the advanced note system, a great evil would be removed. The boarding house keepers do not want it abolished, and will advocate its continuance. A good class of men would be obtained by giving them liberal wages and no advance, and no men should be engaged as able seamen unless they had been at least six years at sea. Desertions would then become a thing of the past. Preference should be given to British sailors, and ships would not be manned then, as they are now, with a sprinkling of Englishmen, Yankee-Irishmen, Swedes, Norwegians, Malays, Chinamen, Negroes etc. It is impossible that such a heterogeneous mass can harmonise together, hence the fearful losses and mutinies that are almost daily chronicled.

Such articles did not go unchallenged, and a seaman wrote back to say that the promoters of the Seamen's Protective Society were a few sailors who had family to support, 'I believe when we had our first meeting that scarcely a boarding house keeper in town knew of it, and we only admit them now when they prove that they are really sailors'.

Another sympathetic boarding house keeper crops up in the 1879 strike in a case reported as follows:

The labourers strike. Charge of intimidation this day. William Millard, lodging house keeper, Cazneau Street and London Road, was charged before Mr Raffles at the police court, Dale Street, this morning, under the conspiracy Act of 1872, with intimidation. The complainant was John Surridge, one of the labourers from Bristol who had been brought here to take the place of the men on strike, for whom Mr Walter Pierce appeared and Mr Bremner appeared for the defendant ... Mr Pierce then, after remarking that the statements he had attributed to Mr Simpson were a complete fabrication, and stating that he had his letters to show that the men knew there was a strike, said that the men who came from Bristol did not refuse to go to work because there was a strike, but they refused to go to work on an account of the intimidation they received from the defendant of the case. The lot of men in which the complainant came arrived here on Tuesday night to take employment with Mr Warren, by whom they were sent to Mr Millard's house. Mr Warren requested the defendant to provide them with food at night and in the morning, so that they might be able to go to work in the morning. Some time before twelve and one o'clock in the morning, the men had reason to leave the house, and when they were leaving, Mr Millard made use of words that they said intimidated them, so that on Wednesday, the whole of them went to Mr Warren's office and stated that they were afraid to go to work. The words were these: 'You are the west of England Men. You have come to rob your fellow working men. By heavens, look out tomorrow!' The men said that from the expression and the manner in which it was uttered, and from the fact that Millard had other men in the house, they felt that it was the intimidation that something would occur to them on the following day, and they went to Mr Warren and said that they were afraid to work. They would not go to work unless protection was offered them, and that protection was offered them, Mr Warren keeping them on board ship.

Joseph Surridge was then called and stated that he was a labourer from Bristol. After giving some evidence corroborative of Mr Pierce's opening statement, he said in reply to a question from Mr Raffles as to why he and his companions had left the house so early in the morning: 'Come bedtime we went upstairs. Before we got into bed we turned down the bed clothes; we found there was lice in the bed, and we did not wish to sleep in the house. Eleven of us came down, and Mr Millard gave us *6d* each to leave.'

Mr. Raffles: 'What had you paid him?'

A dock-side scene, *c.* 1890.

Witness: 'The money was paid for us. We went out of the house, and then Mr Millard said to us, "Look here, men; you are not in the west of England now; you are come here to rob your fellow men, and by heavens! Look out for yourselves tomorrow."' The witness further said that they did not go to work in the morning.

In the seamen's strike of 1880, the boarding house masters once more came to the fore. Mr E. Sinclair Battersby, a boarding master, stated that he assisted the movement by putting union men up free of charge for three of four weeks if it were necessary. Many other men acted in the same capacity.

Again in the strike of 1889, at a mass strike meeting of the seamen's union, a large number of boarding house keepers were present and agreed to assist the union. In this direction, they handed out their names and addresses to the leaders. The masters were to receive no money whatever from the union, although all of their homes were to be recommended to sailors coming to the port after the strike.

In the same way, waterfront concert hall properties and pubs came to the seamen's aid during the strike, offering them the use of their premises for committees and mass meetings.

To shield the seamen from the boarding houses, a sailors' home was built by local philanthropists. It was an austere, cold looking building, built in a sort of semi-Gothic style, and despite the number of its wash basins, one gets the strong impression that the seamen did not like it. Perhaps the regulations governing when one could use it and what time one had to be in put them off. Another reason could well be the fact that during strikes, union seamen were not allowed to shelter there.

The sailors' home, its governors, and its warders were often the centre piece of attacks at strike meetings.

The seamen's home played a clear, strike-breaking role in 1866. The strike-breaking crew of the *Spirit of the Age* was signed on there, and on another occasion during the strike, Captain Rankin of the home had come outside amongst the men and told the engineers and firemen, 'The strike has dropped off; the societies all broken up; come in and sign and go away.' This same man had advertised a notice to the same effect in the seamen's home. In the strike of 1889, the seamen actually raided and occupied the building, or at least a portion of it.

Scab crews had been signing on for vessels at the sailors' home, around which many union men used to congregate. On one occasion, a group of what was described as 'cattlemen' went to the home to sign articles to board the steamer *Virginia,* not it was said, to go as members of the crew, but for the purpose of obtaining their customary free passage back to America. At that time, over 1,000 seamen and firemen were congregated around the shipping office, and they declared that the men were actually going on board to scab. A union delegate wearing a rosette encouraged the men not to allow anybody to sign at the home. They then charged in and took possession of the waiting room and drove everyone else out. The cattlemen skedaddled very quickly. The union delegate insisted to the superintendent of the Mercantile Marine Office that he was allowing nobody to sign on. The police however drove the men from the rooms and mounted a guard on the doors afterwards.

It was in the 1850s that the seamen made serious attempts to organise. That is not to say there was no strike action before then, as there frequently had been, and riots, 'the continuation of industrial relations by other means' let us say, had been 'the spirit of rebellious, direct action implanted by seamen in the eighteenth century'. In 1775, after seamen's wages had been reduced by one third in the depressed state of trade following the war with the colonies, mariners on Captain Yate's ship *The Derby*, being fitted for a Guinea voyage, unrigged the ship. A riot involving 2,000 to 3,000 seamen spread into the town. The Exchange was besieged, and after several rioters had been killed by gunshot, the building was bombarded with cannon. Several merchants had their houses ransacked.

The War of American Independence had caused a crisis in the British shipping trade, and there was a reluctance to send out merchant shipping in such grave times. Additionally, an embargo on the export of gun powder – a staple commodity of Liverpool's trade with Africa – was being enforced, and the 'market' for slaves from Africa to America was likewise at a standstill. Ships were coming into the port and being laid up. By late August, 3,000 additional seamen had joined the port's unemployed. It was in such a time that the port's merchants thought they could get away with a bit of hard-nosed wage cutting. After the work on *The Derby* had been completed, the merchants would pay only half the usual rate. Later, the arrests of some of the militant seamen led to 2,000 to 3,000 armed seamen surrounding the goal and releasing the prisoners and their supporters. Events after that took on their own momentum, with thousands marching on the Exchange:

Preceded by a red flag and followed by a large crowd of men women and boys, to make a proclamation stating their demands for increased wages … they elected two leaders (a bo'n's mate called Jemmy Askew and a pseudonymous 'General Gage'). The merchants then hired a gang of hundreds of armed men. These were posted around the Exchange with a view to arresting the strikers leaders. When they were confronted by the seamen's mostly unarmed demonstration, they let fly with a volley of shots, killing and wounding many of the strikers and demonstrators.

Harold Hakins takes up the story:

Next morning naturally enough, the mood of the seamen had become much more gruesome, and they set about collecting arms, declaring their intention of pulling down the Exchange to the ground. With this in mind, they brought canon ashore from the ships, and put them in position to bombard the building. Other parties of seamen meanwhile visited the warehouses and gunsmith shops, and amassed a variety of weaponry in preparation for the attack. Then all marched, their hats bedecked with red ribbons, to surround the Exchange once more; and at one p.m., they raised the red flag and began a systematic bombardment of the building, which continued until nightfall.

If the use of cannon was somewhat extreme, armed resistance was not itself uncommon. Ships' sawyers were also said to be:

Particularly noted for extreme individual violence, including murder and arson. Other trade associations tended toward collective violence.

The most serious riots were among shipwrights, but rope makers, shoemakers, iron founders, and builders used similar methods during these years.

Armed resistance to impressment aboard His Majesty's Navy was later to become a source of widespread violent resistance. Such violent resistance and rebellion was not of course the prerogative of Liverpool; it was a common feature to most mass industrial areas. What is perhaps surprising is that despite evidence of violent class resistance both in unions and as communities, from the mid-nineteenth century through to the present day, such armed or violent episodes are presented as 'un-British'; not the 'English' thing one does at all, quite foreign to our supposed industrial and class natures. It is a fact that many well-heeled union bureaucrats and labour politicians tried their damnedest to make such a view a reality throughout history, but frequently failed.

The first, real general strike in the port happened some time outside of the parameters of this work, in 1791. It appears to have been remarkable in both scope and duration. It involved the seamen, ship repairers, and carpenters, and very likely included many other related trades not mentioned in the contemporary reports. It sought to establish a general improvement in wages. Hikins tells us this was no spontaneous uprising or flash in the pan, but a planned campaign, 'Distinguished by the fact that some sort of organisation (or organisations) had preceded it.' Troops were called in, and bounties offered for the arrest of both leaders and pickets.

As far as sailors were concerned, the chief feature of the mid-Victorian times was the rise of the big Liverpool shipping companies, and the fierce rivalry between them.

The Clipper

Boats powered by sail reached the height of their development in terms of speed with the advent of the Clipper, and the greatest impetus to this was the tea trade. The term 'Clipper' was originally a general term for any vessel capable of making a fast passage, but was soon evolved with a particular sleek, yacht-like cut in mind.

Tea had become a much valued commodity over the preceding 150 years; East India ships carried it round the Cape of Good Hope *en route* to Britain. The Chinese had sought to restrict its export to the port of Canton, but following the Anglo-Chinese war of 1839–42, China lost control of her own destiny and a number of great ports opened to the trade (Hong Kong, Foochow, Shanghai, and Hankow). This in turn had broken the East Indian monopoly on trade and routes, and smaller ships and companies started to vie for the trade. During times of war and restricted trade, tea had been stored and kept in stock often for twelve months and more. 'New tea' now entering the country was said to be of better flavour and quality. It gave rise to a clamour for fresh tea. Tea was gathered in May and ready for shipment by June and July. But this was when the south-west monsoon was blowing straight through the China Sea. Ships were forced to battle against it before passing through the Sundra Straights between Java and Sumatra out into the India Ocean. To best deal with these trials of nature, ships capable of sailing at faster speeds and beating to windward were demanded. By the end of the 1840s, a number of ships of around 400 tons had been specifically designed for the purpose.

In 1849, The British Navigation Acts were repealed following pressure for 'free trade'. This permitted ships of any nationality to bring cargoes to Britain, including tea from China. The change coincided with the discovery of gold in California. To supply the explosion of trade around this, considerable numbers of large Clippers were being built on the east coast of America. Delivering their gold-crazed masses to San Francisco, they discovered a newly emerging market in shipping tea to England. Tea for London was being loaded at rates of £6 and £7 per ton at a time when British shipowners were only achieving £2 to £3. This gave rise to a rivalry that lasted for years, until firstly, the ebb of the Californian gold rush, and secondly, the American Civil War ended all competition from that quarter.

American Clippers had often been far bigger than their British counterparts. Large ships, although delivering a heavier load, were not necessarily quicker. The *Oriental* had been the first American ship to enter the Thames, in December 1850. At 1,003 tons, she was double the size of her nearest British rival. However, the *Aberdeen,* built by John Bunyan, had earlier that same year made the passage from Shanghai to London in 101 days, only four days longer than the *Oriental*. Aberdeen became the shipbuilding port of choice for the British Clippers. From these yards came the *Cairngorm*, generally acknowledged as Britain's fasted Clipper at this time. On her maiden voyage, the *Cairngorm* made seventy-two days from Lisbon to Hong Kong (1853), and her fastest homeward voyage was from Macao (China) to Deal in ninety-one days. Her reign did not last long, as the speeds quickened and the passages shortened. The American *Eagle Wing* took eighty-three-and-a-half days from Deal to Hong Kong. We should perhaps recall that at this time, very much in the age of sail (1850–60s), American Clippers were achieving speeds of twenty to twenty-one knots, while British ships such as the famous *Cutty Sark* and *Thermopylae* were achieving speeds of seventeen knots and covering distances of 300 miles in 24 hours.

Ultimately, it was the opening of the Suez Canal in 1869 that stole the tea market from the Clippers and gave it over to the steamers. They could make a faster passage through the canal, with freights at prices the Clipper could not compete with. By 1875, tea was loading at £1 10s per ton, too low for the sail ships to compete with, no matter how much swifter they were on the high seas. Their total reign was something in the order of twenty-five years. This was not yet the end of the Clipper or sail. During the last twelve years of the nineteenth century, large, four-masted ships and barques were being built. Ships such as the *Liverpool*, 3,330 tons fully rigged and 333 feet in length, could stow 26,000 bales of jute and were fast and powerful in strong winds.

Coal for steam took up much of the space that would otherwise have been used for cargo or passengers. The amount of coal carried in turn dictated the amount of cargo or passengers, and the profit that could be earned from the voyage. So too, the boiler and the amount of coal might not last the distance of the voyage. For all these reasons, most early steam ships carried many yards of sail in order to cut down on using coal for power, and also to back up the engines. Ironically, it was the question of cargo space and ship construction that firstly took boat builders away from wood as the only form of major construction. These had required vast baulks of timber to give longitudinal strength, and the huge beams were supported by numerous wooden pillars, all of which occupied precious cargo space. *Cutty Sark* and her ilk were trend-setters in working a matrix of steel and wood hulls. She had been built in 1869 to the order of Captain John Willis. She was constructed of wooden planks over an iron frame, with copper sheathing covering the bottom and bulwarks, and fore and main lower masts made from iron. She was built rather too late for the Clipper tea trade, and five years after her construction, she was carrying wool from Sydney to London, recording her fastest time of seventy days. Later, all metal hulls and the space occupied by structural members was negligible, 'To the infinite delight of stevedores and dockers.'

The years from 1850–1875 were hard years for the seamen, when competition between sailing ship lines became fiercest, and the companies tried to cut back on expenditure (particularly wages) to face the ever growing threats from steam. Companies found it harder to find crews for their floating factories, and it was in the period of the 1870s and 1880s that the crimping profession found its fullest market. As the days of sail drew to a close, we find in the phrase of A. L. Lloyd that the seaman '… became conscious of himself as an exploited, floating proletarian rather than a proud if battered sea-dog'. Slowly but surely, the iron steamer took the place of the sailing packets. Not without a struggle however, and for many years while the fight was on, the chief looser was the seaman. His wages, conditions, and even food rations were cut down, as the sail companies stripped to the buff everything that seemed like additional expense. The pressure of the work needed to outstrip the steamers made seamen not the least bit willing to venture to sea in the floating sweat ships, and this gave rise to the *shanghai* system of employment.

An early Inman Line advertisement showing a typical steam/sail clipper.

Many of the sail companies, in their haste to turn to steam, poured in everything they had and went bust; others still in the inter-steamship combat went in for floating palaces years before even the smaller vessels were secure in their freight.

A man not to be stampeded into the rashness of steam vessels was James Baines, sail-ship owner. Baines was confident of fighting the steamship on his ground, and for many years must have raised grave doubts as to the superiority of steam over the fast Clipper. James Baines' company the Black Ball Line ran fast packets to Australia. However, its name sake, another Black Ball Line, ran across the Atlantic in the American–Liverpool trade, and this was a most famous line. I first heard of it in songs when I was fifteen in far-away Tyneside during the swinging sixties. The line had been immortalised in the songs of her seamen, 'black ballers' and 'packet rats'. They were a distinct group of Liverpool, Liverpool-Irish, and Irish-American and black American seamen (often a mix of all four groups). They gave rise to a group of work and sea songs that have survived in greater numbers than any other shanty or for'biter in the country. These vessels carried a black ball painted on the foot of the fore topsail, a custom practised by many firms in those days. The American Line was the pioneer, and had been established in 1816, and at first consisted of vessels from 300 to 500 tons. These little ships, with their full bodies and bluff bows, made wonderful passages, averaging twenty-three days outward and forty-three homeward. One exceptional run made by *Canada* took only fifteen days, eighteen hours on the New York–Liverpool run. One of this fleet, the *Fidelia,* did the New York–Liverpool run in the record breaking time of thirteen days, seven hours. The Black Ball Line was pledged to sail on the first of every month between Liverpool and New York, irrespective of weather or the amount of cargo loaded. She flew a crimson, swallow-tailed house flag, with the black ball painted on the fore topsail. A. L. Lloyd tells us that these were emblems of hardship for seamen. The sailing schedules were of unprecedented tightness and the discipline was merciless; the skippers were well known as hard-cases who cared nothing for the weather or the weariness of their men. The seamen usually lived in the forecastle, which was cold and damp. The chain cables passed through it to the chain lockers below. The hawser ports often had ill-fitting wooden plugs, and when the ship plunged in a head storm, the forecastle was flooded. There was no place for the men to dry their clothes. Their food was 'salt tack' with the odd enlivener of rum. The *Morning Chronicle* of 1850 reported that, 'Of crews of American ships out of Liverpool, twelve or fourteen out of twenty-four are Englishmen or Scotsmen.' American ships were a preference for British crews because they received better treatment.

The Australian–Liverpool Black Ball Line was started by James Baines, whose mother kept a cake shop on Duke Street, where he was born in 1823. He was running his first ship by 1851, and was to progress to eighty-six ships flying the black ball with a compliment of 4,000 men. His first ship was the *Marco Polo,* built for the Australian trade, of 1,622 tons. His ships dominated the emigration trade for many years, flying off the fore topsail the emblem of the black ball. The impetus of the Clippers was the California gold rush in 1848, and then the discovery of gold in Australia in 1851. A rush of emigrants looking for a fortune through hard work and good luck filled the vessels.

His most famous ship, the *Marco Polo,* had been sold to him by Paddy McGhee, a junk merchant, who bought her from an American for a mere song. She was in turn followed by four splendid Clippers built by the famous Donald Mackay of Boston. The *Marco Polo* was captained by the well-known Bully Forbes. She went to Australia in sixty-eight days from the Salthouse Dock, and back from Melbourne in seventy-six. He is credited to have told his terrified passengers, scared at the way he piled on the sail, 'It was hell or Melbourne.'

Some of the most famous transatlantic fliers best known to Merseyside were ships like *Red Jacket, Flying Cloud, Dreadnought,* and the *James Baines.*

The Bibby Line was established in 1850 by John and James Bibby, who had operated for many years a line of sailing vessels trading to Italy. Among the

The Inman steamer *City of Richmond. Illustrated London News,* 2 May 1874.

sailing shipowners, the firm of T. & J. Brocklebank Ltd., was a leader. Their ships, distinguished by a white band, seemed to monopolise the Albert and Salthouse docks. They were the biggest shipowners and merchants carrying mainly their own cargoes, and for too many years they resisted to move to steam.

The rush to the Australian gold fields in the early 1840s also made the demand for emigrant vessels, and here the American shipbuilders scored heavily. The founding of the White Star line, started by two young Liverpool shipbrokers, John Pilkington and Henry Threlball, was owed to that fact, and began in 1869. They owned the *Red Jacket* and *White Star*. In 1867, they sold their flag to T. H. Ismay. It was taken over by the American International Mercantile Marine in 1902. Thomas Henry Ismay (1837-99) was born in Cumberland; his father was a shipowner and shipbuilder. His White Star Line was the first real competitor to the Cunard and Inman lines on the Atlantic.

When the Australian gold rush came to an end, a number of sailing packet lines also went out of business, but other lines used the profits from that trade to develop other routes, such as the triangular routes based upon Liverpool and Australia. These would run Liverpool–Australia–San Francisco–Liverpool, or Liverpool–Australia–Far East– Liverpool. These became the classic routes for Liverpool's sailing Clippers.

American Clipper, *Aryan.*

Steamship ocean routes from Liverpool were developing throughout the period, and it was Liverpool ships that pioneered the first steamship services to the Mediterranean and to the West Indies. Until around 1869, steamships were not really in a technological position to compete with sailing ships in the passage of goods in bulk. However, after this time, with the development of the compound steam engine and the introduction of the high pressure steel boiler and the triple expansion steam engine in 1885, the death knell of the bulk freight Clipper was sounded.

Later, as the threats from sail diminished, there came an equally cut-throat competition between steamship owners to establish their rights over particular runs. The competition led to the creation of vast fleets, 'build or bust' being the maxim of the owners as they tried to crowd each other off the oceans. 'Any port in a storm' became a real maxim to the shipowners. They sailed anywhere and everywhere, indiscriminately picking up every sort of cargo. This was greatly assisted by the utility of the telegraph, which increased the speed of communications. Then, one shipowner finding a small paying port in Iceland or Madagascar immediately brought three or four of his competitors swooping in to share the small carcass. A vessel would be reported arriving in Boston; next time you heard of her, she was at Singapore or Bombay, then turning up again in an American port.

Cutty Sark, running before
the wind.

This was the birth of the 'Tramp Steamer', so called in popular understanding
because these ships wandered from place to place without regular route or
destination. More particularly, the term referred to nature of the contract;
the charterer rather than the shipowner provided the cargo, and there was no
advertised times of sailing or schedule of the voyage. The cargo was carried
under the terms of a 'charter party'. The charter party took one of three forms:
the voyage charter; the time charter; and the bare boat charter. This charter
party was a contract between a merchant or a charterer and the shipowner to
carry their goods.

Prior to 1914, the main tramp trade was known as 'the eternal triangle'
– coal out from Britain to Italy or the Eastern Mediterranean ports, ballast
to the Black Sea, and then grain home from Ukraine. Liverpool was not one
of the main tramp-owning ports during this period, those being Newcastle-
upon-Tyne, Glasgow, Cardiff, and London (and nearby associated ports).

The Cunard Line, founded by Samuel Cunard in 1839, never went in for
sail, but had banked everything on a belief in steam. The most outstanding
figure among shipowners of 1850-1880 was Charles MacIver of Cunard. He
built up the Cunard Line, which in the 1850s paid one-third of Liverpool Dock
dues. Colonel MacIver used to march down Water Street at the head of 1,000
men who he had drilled and trained; it was one of the first volunteer regiments
raised in 1858 when fears of Napoleon III were rife. Tales of MacIver's iron

Red Jacket.

discipline abounded. One of his captains was granted permission to take his wife to sea, but when the captain turned up on the day of sailing, he found he had been issued with two passenger tickets and his command had been superseded. Although the master builder of the line, he was not one its founders. These had been Samuel Cunard, George Burns, and David MacIver.

Ten years after the Cunard Company was established, William Inman, in conjunction with the Richardson Brothers of Belfast, founded a line of steamers to Philadelphia. Their first steamer was the *City of Glasgow*. Shortly afterwards, they made New York their headquarters. It was Inman's policy to cultivate the emigration trade, which had hitherto been the preserve of the Clippers. Inman had launched into the Atlantic steamship arena to fill the vacuum created by the advent of the American Civil war; a war that had seen the withdrawal of the trade from American companies. Inman was quick to take advantage and ordered three new ships, the third of which was to be the ill-fated *City of Boston*. On 8 February 1865, she had her maiden voyage from Liverpool to New York. Her final voyage came five years later as she cleared New York on 25 January for Liverpool via Halifax and then Queenstown, Ireland. She safely reached Halifax by the next day, and loaded mail passenger luggage and naval packages shipped by the naval storekeeper. In clear, cold weather, she steamed out of Halifax harbour *en route* to Liverpool. That was the last anyone ever saw of her or her passengers and crew. Years later, a message in a bottle, allegedly from one of the passengers called Thompson, thrown over the side before he died, asked for his son be looked after, and reported the ship sinking on 21 March: 'Be gone in two hours'. Inman died in 1881, but before doing so, pride of place had already been wrested from his hands by the White Star Line.

The White Star Company was founded in 1845 by John Pilkington and Henry Threlfall Wilson, and originally operated wooden sailing ships carrying immigrants to the New World. By the 1850s, the wind was in the company's sails as thousands of prospective miners headed for the Californian gold fields. When Pilkington retired, Wilson took on James Chambers as a new partner and the named changed to Wilson and Chalmers, although it was still known popularly as the White Star Line. When the Californian gold fields dried up, the rush next turned to Australia, and the Company was at hand to transport the eager miners. It seems to have been fool's gold for both, as in 1867, the company went into liquidation with vast debts owing to Royal Bank of Liverpool. Thomas Ismay bought the company for a mere £1,000.

The struggle for the Atlantic passenger trade went up several notches when Thomas Henry Ismay (father of Bruce) formed that White Star Company in 1869. Cunard hitherto had been unchallenged. In 1873, just four years after the founding of the line, the sixth White Star vessel, the *Baltic*, set the transatlantic (eastbound) speed record. In the same year, they claimed another,

The New York ship, *Oriental*, 1850. *Illustrated London News*, 21 Dec 1850.

more dubious title, as on 1 April 1873, White Star claimed the title of the worse shipping disaster in history: the *Atlantic* had left Liverpool on 19 March to cross to New York. She was carrying 966 people, including the crew, fourteen stowaways, and 200 children. The vessel ended its days on Mars Rock, Newfoundland. 565 men, women, and children died, either drowned or dashed to death on the rocks. Despite this, by 1880, White Star had become the most prominent steamship company operating the transatlantic service. Two years previously, John Burns, head of the Cunard Line, had suggested a merger of the two companies, but that development would not come for another half century. T. H. Ismay died in 1899 and was succeeded by his son Bruce, who remained chairman until the infamous loss of the *Titanic* just thirteen years later.

Much has already been written about the *Titanic*, and that story is broadly outside the time period of this book, but the crude class injustice illustrated by it is not. The magnificent ship had carried almost 3,000 passengers in three parts of the ship divided by classes. Only 868 survivors had made it to the lifeboats, it being now well known that the haughty shipowners had vetoed a full complement of boats for fear it would damage the look of the ship and inhibit the first and second class walkways. 'Women and Children first' was said to have been the order enforced by the crew, at times ordered at gun point, but this did not mean *all* or *any* women and children first. Of women and children surviving via the boats, the overwhelming majority were from first and second class; the smallest minority being from third. The poorest men, women, and children were held below decks until all the higher class women and children who wished to board life boats had done so. Even men from those higher classes were given the precious places before the third class women and children had been allowed onto the decks, by which time the angle of the ship, as she rose with her stern out of the water and bows submerging, made the few boats still available almost impossible to reach from the poor accommodation quarters.

Bruce Ismay was a shy and sensitive man, but being head of a major shipping company, sought to disguise his nature and adopt a mannerism that presented him as short tempered and irascible. Such a manner caused people to take an instant dislike of him, at least until they broke through his façade. He was for all this a shrewd and capable business man.

For twenty years, the company continued to rival and often surpass the Cunard Line. A 'follow the leader' race in breaking new technology marked the epoch struggle. In 1889, with the launch of the *Teutonic* and the *Majestic*, the modern ocean liners—vessels without sails, luxurious and spacious—was born. By the 1890s, the Germans had entered the race and the competition became even fiercer. Huge profits were up for grabs, and this came to the attention of the American financier J. Pierpont Morgan. He began buying up shipping

Cutty Sark from Astern.

companies under the name 'International Mercantile Marine'. By 1902, he had added the White Star to the consortium. Bruce Ismay retained his directorship of White Star, but also became chairman and managing director of IMM. The company was to carry the process into the construction of the world's largest, most luxurious vessels, the *Olympic* and the *Titanic*. The latter would make them world famous for nearly a century, but not as they would have envisaged.

By the end of nineteenth century, fierce competition for the North Atlantic passenger trade fares had fallen to an all-time low. Morgan's vision was to buy up and absorb the competition with a view to establishing more profitable returns. He began buying up shipping companies under the International Mercantile Marine name. The Leyland Line, founded by Fredrick Leyland, was one of the first to be absorbed. It had been largely engaged in the cotton trade, and its vessels were marked by cavernous holds to house the bulky cargoes. The company was infamous for overloading vessels and squeezing the juice out of their ships and masters. It was the butt of jokes: 'A ship at sea passes another so heavily laden that almost the entire hull is below water. The captain radios, "Have passed four funnels heading west, presumed Leyland steamer."' At the same time, Morgan took over Dominion. By 1902, he had added the White Star to the consortium. By the turn of the century, he had also taken over American Inman and Red Star lines.

In the Mediterranean fleet, the situation was the same. No less than six shipping companies operated, or attempted to operate the Mediterranean. They scoured every island and back water for freight, only to return with some 700 to 800 tons in a steamer of 2,000 tons, the rest being made up from ballast.

Sometimes, the people benefited from the competition, even if the sailors did not. In the 1860s, one of the lines that ran from Liverpool to Ireland found itself confronted with another company. The result of this brief period was a benefit to the passengers. The fare for deck passengers, which had been 4s, dropped to 6d each. Eventually, the fare was abolished and one of the companies started offering a 2 lb loaf to each passenger in order to drive the other company out of business. It did not, and both companies started heading very heavily for the rocks. At length, the original company offered a glass of whisky in addition to the loaf; this finally proved the last nail in the coffin of the competitor and he gave in.

In this great scramble for freights, only the most resourceful were to survive. But it wasn't simply the biggest vessels; some who banked their money on these, such as the *Great Eastern,* were to be sorely disappointed. Others remained conservatively to their sail ships, like Baines of the Black Ball Line, only to be ruined and sent back to an impoverished existence away from the lofty heights of capitalism. The resulting effect upon the seafarer and docker alike were even more cruel and despotic. In the same way that particular employers of dock labourers had particularly bad names, so the seamen have infamous employers. During the 1866 strike, Inman and MacIver were stated by the workers to be the biggest company, and they yet paid their workers the worst wages.

The Cunard Line had been started by Charles MacIver in 1849. Cunard and Burns joined him in 1851. Six years later, its name was changed to the British and Foreign Steam Navigation Company. Lastly, in 1878, the name was changed to its present title, The Cunard Steam Ship Co. The line did very fast voyages. From 1886, it ran two ships a week in the summer and three a fortnight in the winter times. Cunard's was one of the most consistently anti-union antagonistic firms. From an early time we can see it stubbornly resisting any efforts the men made to improve their living standards. The Cunard Line usually employed a big team of dockers on a permanent basis. During the great strike of 1879, they had some 700 permanent dockers who did not join the permanent turn out, probably because their wages had not been affected. The Cunard Line also took the lead in importing blacklegs, and was responsible for most of the Glasgow men who arrived in the port during the second week of the strike.

During the seamen's strike of 1889, the Cunard Line were determined not to give in to the men's demand, and shipped men for their vessels from other

The magnificent *Great Eastern*; a commercial disappointment, but eventually the first ship to lay a trans-Atlantic cable.

ports. The Warren Line was also highly antagonistic to the union, and shipped scabs at the rates demanded by the men just to rub salt into the wound. Nearly all the other shipowners gave way. On 25 January, the seamen's delegates at a union meeting stated, 'With regard to the Cunard company, they [the members of the union] were determined to keep clear of them.'

Cunard's dividends, which became a barometer of the North Atlantic passenger trade, averaged no more than 23 to 24 per cent between 1883 and 1911. From 1883 to 1886, and from 1894 to 1895, no dividends were declared. The tight margins clearly must have influenced the hostility toward union demands and workers' organisation.

In the same way as the dockers who regularly worked at a single cargo or dock became characterised by it, so it was with the seamen. Sailors who sailed regularly with the same line became known after the company; 'black baller' for example. He would also be named after the voyages he took: 'western ocean packet rats', 'flying fish sailors (Hong Kong)', etc. It was, in fact, men such as the black ballers who were amongst the most highly paid. The western ocean voyages were rated by both shipowners and seamen to be worthy of a higher wage than the other voyages, although they often disagreed about the rates. The western ocean men were always paid at the very least 10s per month, sometimes as much as £1, more than the voyages next down the scale.

Of course, the transatlantic voyages were the longest and most dangerous, and if the weather was bad, there was no port or refuge to restock food or water in the middle of the ocean.

Losses at sea in ships, and more importantly men, during the period of this study are truly shocking. Using Norman Middlemiss' book on the twenty most important tramp fleets operating out of the four major tramp ports of Britain, and confining the search simply to those operating during the period of this study, while excluding those destroyed in the First World War, throws up an interesting snapshot of ships' and seafarers' life expectancies in this period.

Company	Ship Name	Date Built	Fate
Moor Line	Harefield	1871	Lost in collision 6-11-1893
	Levant	1865	Missing 1893
	Buteshire	1887	Wrecked near Landsort Lighthouse 16-11-1897
	Abbeymoor	1890	Wrecked at Renews Island, Cape Race. Sailing from Shields to Baltimore
	Edenmoor	1894	Gutted by fire off Gibraltar, Red Sea, sailing from Boston to Bombay with case oil 25-11-1897
	Hazelmoor	1894	Lost by Strandling 1920
	Kylemoor	1896	Lost by Collision with March off Sulina 8-1896
	Pearlmoor	1897	Wrecked on Kuria Muria Islands, sailing from Karachi to Port Said 11-1904
	Olivemoor	1897	Left Quiberon and disappeared 1918
	Spennymoor	1899	Floundered near Oran, while sailing from Smyrna to London 1903
Sutherland SS	Coventina	1893	Wrecked at Porman, Spain 15-5-1900
	Laughton	1893	Left Newport Ness for Copenhagen and disappeared

Hall Brothers SS	Mercury	1864	Floundered near Cape Bon 27-7-1878
	Heaton Hall	1864	Lost after striking rock 15 miles from Bizerta 8-8-1872
	Bywell Castle	1869	Left Alexandria for Hull and disappeared 15-1-1883
	Commander	1871	Left Quebec for Britain and disappeared 4-11-1872
	Dilston Castle	1871	Lost in collision 4-6-1897
	Raby Castle	1871	Wrecked near Pantellaria 11-3-1872
	Durham Castle	1872	Left Holyhead for Suez and disappeared 15-1-1873
	Chillingham Castle	1872	Passed Dover while on voyage from the Tyne to Odessa and disappeared 20-11-1872
	Royal Crown	1874	Foundered after striking a rock off Ushant 6-9-1890
	Cilurnum	1874	Abandoned on fire in South Atlantic on route from the Tyne to San Francisco 20-8-1885
	Tiara	1874	Abandoned off Finisterre 29-11-1879
	Trident	1874	Sunk in collision 13-12-1879
	Renown	1874	Stranded 1889
	Asdrubal	1877	Abandoned in ice south-west of Cape Race 21-6-1882
	Bretwalda	1881	Wrecked off cape St Vincent 31-8-1897
	Bosphorus	1883	Lost in collision off Start Point 12-8-1888
	Ambassador	1888	Wrecked off Start Point 19-9-1891
Denholm Line	Mount Park	1884	Lost 12-1887

	Cathcart Park	1894	Wrecked 1-1887
	Cathcart Park II	1897	Wrecked 4-1912
	Mountpark 3	1897	Sunk by collision 12-1911
Monarch Steam Line	Caletea	1880	Foundered off Sale 12-1899
	Miramam	1880	Foundered 1884
	Marbella	1882	Wrecked 11-1896
	Dilsberg	1883	Wrecked 12-1892
	Seraglio	1883	Foundered 1885
	Abydos	1884	Lost 12-1894
	Abington	1885	Lost in collision 3-1892
	Lamington	1885	Stranded 2-1896
	Kremlin	1885	Wrecked 1887
	Memling	1887	Wrecked 1889
	Holyrood	1889	Lost in Collision
	Buckingham	1891	Wrecked in 1904
	Linlithgow	1894	Abandoned 12-1896
Evan Thomas Radcliffe	Kate Thomas	1884	Lost near Ceuta 21-10-1895
	Walter Thomas	1884	Sank off Europa Point, Gibraltar, after collision with Romney 12-7-1907
	Clarissa Radcliffe	1889	Lost off Cape St Vincent after grain cargo shifted 30-12-1897
	Douglas-Hill	1890	Lost 30-1910
	Wimborne	1898	Lost off Polperro 7-11-1910
British Steam Shipping Co.	Ruby	1874	Wrecked 1878
	Rothwsay	1874	Foundered 1877
	Ravenshoe	1876	Wrecked 1883
	Raglan	1877	Wrecked 1882
	Ruperra	1877	Wrecked 1880

	Rokeby	1879	Wrecked 1888
	Rhiwabon	1880	Wrecked 1883
	Rhyl	1880	Lost in collision 1893
	Rumney	1880	Foundered 1883
	Redbrook	1880	Lost by collision 8-1890
	Ross	1881	Wrecked 1906
	Resolven	1882	Wrecked 2-1893
	Rheubina	1882	Lost by collision 9-1898
	Rougement	1882	Lost by collision 6-1893
	Rhiwderin	1883	Wrecked 9-1893
	Reading	1883	Wrecked 11-1913
	Mark Lane	1887	Wrecked 6-1912
	Ravenshoe II	1889	Foundered 4-1-1895
	Goimungding	1890	Wrecked 5-1898
	Ravenshoe III	1899	Wrecked 12-1919
BSSC Watts Watts and Co.	Dunholme	1883	Sunk in collision off Dover 7-1891
	Highbury	1877	Ashore near Marabout, Alexandria
CLT	Brentford	1885	Wrecked 1888
	Wandsworth	1888	Stranded of Spanish Battery, Tynemouth while inward from Benisaf with iron ore 1889
	Hounslow	1890	Wrecked 4-1906
	Windsor	1890	Wrecked 2-1908
	Kilburn	1893	Wrecked off Ethel Reef Fiji when on a passage from Newcastle upon Tyne to NSW, Guaymas
	Woolwich	1893	Sank off Maasluis after collision 25-2-1903
	Anarley	1881	Wrecked 20 miles from Fusan, Korea 1-8-1904

	Finsbury	1880	Sailed from Kobe for Vladivostock and disappeared 22-9-1903
	Chatham	1898	Sunk in Suez Canal to extinguish fire in cargo, blown up 5-9-1905
J. & C. Harrison Ltd.	James Southern	1865	Sunk in Collision 12-1905
	Benamain	1878	Foundered off Mumbles when on passage from Swansea to Treport
	Harborne	1893	Lost in collision 3-1894
	Harden	1894	Stranded 1-1897

Early steamships were no more safe and reliable than the windjammers they sought to replace, and frequently were less so.

We should remember that this is a mere snapshot from the tramp steam companies of the four major tramp ports. It gives us but a hint that the advent of steam over sail did not bring new era of safety and longevity. Life aboard the windjammers in the last two decades of their final stand against steam was raw and harsh, but deep down in the bowels of an iron ship, working to feed a volatile, blazing boiler in a cauldron sea, as demonstrated above, offered little more by way of safety. The miner's anthem *Miners Lifeguard* tells us that a 'miner's life is like a sailor's'. While this reads something like a subliminal understanding of how dangerous pit work was in this era, perhaps the calamitous nature of maritime work in this period is not yet fully comprehended.

In Liverpool, it was 'the packet rats', the seamen of the fast western ocean packets, who were the most militant section of the seamen. Most strike movement and unions centred on such men, and their demands were always the centrepiece of any wage claim. Other sectors, indeed all other sections of the seamen, would ultimately be recruited to the union, and attach respective claims and conditions, but in almost every case it was the western ocean men who blew on the embers of discontent and fanned them into a flame. At the other extreme were the seamen of the coasting trade. These men might make as many as two or even three voyages a week. They were paid a lower rate, since in essence their work was fairly regular and usually less dangerous (so it was said). Irish and Scottish steamships ran from the port, as did the Isle of Man vessels. Coastal vessels were lost, for instance the *Ellan Vannin*, which sank with all hands in the Irish sea:

> Then a monstrous wave and *Ellan Vannin* was gone,
> Oh, *Ellan Vannin*, of the Isle of Man company,
> Oh, Ellan Vannin, lost in the Irish sea.

She was the only peace-time loss from the Isle of Man's United Steam Packet Company Ltd., although the coast of Britain is littered with wrecks of coastal vessels.

We get an idea of the sort of distinctions they recognised between crews and voyages by looking at the rates of pay the seamen were demanding in 1889. In the case of the mail boats, the fast steamers (and earlier, the clippers) that sailed the western ocean, the seamen at first demanded £4.10s per month, and the firemen £5. For all the other vessels sailing the western ocean, they demanded £4 for sailors and £4 5s for firemen. Later however, the union changed its demand to that of £4 10s and £5 to all men sailing to the west, regardless of whether they carried mail or not. Men who sailed southward were demanding that their rate be £3 per month. These men were often away for over a year, the southern voyages being longer, although much more comfortable than the

The Clipper 'Mersey' from astern

western ones, hence the huge differences in pay demands. Although later we read that, 'At the Brunswick, two steamers bound southward shipped crews at the demand rates of £4 and £4 5s' So it seems probable that the union upped the demand of the southern voyages at a later period of the strike.

The Liverpool shipping proletariat was at any one time composed greatly of native Liverpool and Liverpool-Irish stock. At other big ports, one could say that the maritime community would be made up in great numbers of foreigners and strangers. In Liverpool however, this was less so; more than any other port of its size in the country, Liverpool managed to keep the shipping lines for her own men. On the Tyne, at Hull and Cardiff in the 1880s, the percentage of foreign seamen was over twenty-one per cent, at London nearly fourteen per cent, while at Liverpool it was only nine per cent.

However that the Liverpool men dominated their own lines was certainly not owing to the preference of the Liverpool shipowners, as we see from a statement of Messrs. Frederick Leyland and Company:

Whenever we can get [foreigners], we decidedly prefer them to British seamen, because they are more amenable to discipline, are generally more sober, and can be relied upon to join their ships on sailing. One very serious and growing evil with British seamen is their habit of signing articles for a voyage, and afterwards not joining their ship at all, or joining her then leaving her before she gets through the ship gates.

Because a man was a seaman, it did not mean that all of his life was spent at sea; large portions of time may well have been, but long periods of time ashore were the breeding ground of joint actions of dockers and sailors. The sailors ashore were rooted and part of the Liverpool community. A sailor being paid off did not always spend everything he had earned after years away and then go right back to sea after the money was gone. Even a very consistent sailor might take a break for a year or two between the long passages. In many cases, the sailor settled for a long period of time, taking up shore work. Sometimes, he might travel inland and take up work that was hardly related to the sea, for example, farming or even pit work. However, the life at sea suited him best if he was applying for a dock job. His experience with ships, cargoes, weather, ropes, blocks, and tackle, etc. made him a very good candidate for waterfront employment.

Stan Hugill comments:

Packet rats considered themselves deep water sailors only – they hated dock labourers' work. As soon as a packet docked, many of them jumped ship and headed south as fast as possible. Others left to avoid hauling frozen ropes and wading waist deep in icy water. They found plentiful employment in Gulf ports as 'hoosiers' or cotton stevedores. This job was very arduous, usually done by Negroes or Creoles, but from the 1830s and 1840s, white sailors began to do it. Originally, they worked side by side, but in later years a system was developed with white in one hatch and black in another. They used jack-screws, and Negroes sang purely Negro songs as well as adapted ones.

Some of these white sailors never reached port again – ships (often called 'coffin ships') often floundered in deep water – too much load and before the days of the Plimsoll line. Obviously, these white seamen would bring home new Negro songs they had picked up and also exported Irish songs to the Negroes.

James Sexton says that, although the docker was classed merely as casual labour, he would have to be an all-round man, knowing as he did everything from the keel below to the gantling block aloft.

Often, especially in the early days, ships were weather-bound for months on end. Such occasions would necessitate a man seeking employment in the vicinity of his ship. Dock work was an obvious forte. A sailor joining his ship for a long voyage as a young lad might spend fifteen or twenty years at sea, broken up occasionally by shore work in his own port. He would obviously not be able to keep up sea faring until death; at some stage, he would take up other work.

Many men returned to become boarding house keepers or publicans. At every stage of the seaman's life, he would associate with his home port, usually returning to the same boarding house trip after trip, falling into the same casual employment, or returning to his family. Many seamen upon getting married did not wish the long periods of separation that resulted, and as such took up a job at home to which they were best suited. That the sailor kept a strong bond with his home port is demonstrated in the wealth of shanties that the Liverpool men, more than any others, centred on the life and culture of the port. A very good example of this process is shown in the trade of the riggers, who would swap work very easily from sailing vessels to actually rigging them. By the 1890s, all riggers coming into the trade were ex-seamen.

Dockers and seamen in certain jobs worked side by side. In the timber trade for example, the ship's capstan would help with hoisting and discharging the cargo through a hole in the bow of the vessel, as well as hoisting the blocks and tackle from the masts and dock. The seamen and dockers worked the ropes and capstan together, singing the same shanties:

> Where yi's ever in Quebec
> Stowing timber on the deck.
> Watch the lion and the unicorn,
> Riding on a donkey...

Hey, ho, away we go
Donkey riding, donkey riding.

On the waterfront, the vessels could be seen getting ready for sailing; sailors and dock workers toiling side by side at their respective tasks, and the boarding houses and docklands streets running side by side, with bars and places of entertainment bringing the two together. It is not surprising in the light of all this that the industrial unrest and subsequent strikes of the port saw both groups operating in unity.

The sailor and docker were in many cases one and the same man. Certain dockers had been injured at sea, or had been sailors who had got married and settled ashore. The work of the ships gave a good grounding for dock work, providing experience in stowing, hoisting etc. In the early years of the timber trade, many sailors' jobs were the same as those of dockers in many ways. When work was slack on the docks, many dockers would jump at the chance to go to sea. In other trades, the similarities between jobs was more marked. Riggers, as we have seen, were experienced seamen of many years standing. The work of the coal stower, packing loads for the steamer's voyage, was in many ways similar to the ship's fireman who fuelled the boilers. Both of these classes of men were often courted by employers to break the strikes of either one as they developed.

The connection between the seaman and shore work is typified by the life of James Larkin, the great Liverpool-Irish socialist. He had been born in Liverpool in 1876, and throughout his childhood, crossed between Liverpool

The 'transatlantic flier' *Red Jacket*, a star of the White Star Line, founded in 1869.

and Ireland many times, alternately living in one place then the other. At six years old he had already started working in Liverpool, carrying milk every morning and evening, and working in a butcher's shop all day Saturday and half of Sunday.

At nine years of age he started a full time job with a jobbing painter and paper hanger, and became quite a good worker with a brush. From there, he went to serve his time as a French polisher. However, although his employer was a Catholic, he would not allow James to go to mass. This led to a disagreement, after which he quit and took the road to London. During the following seven weeks, he passed through the depths, slept in fields, barns, and dyke-sides everywhere between Liverpool, London, and Cardiff. Eventually, he went to serve his time as an engineer in Liverpool and started at 3*s* a week with the same firm as his father had worked for for many years.

Before long, Larkin got a job on relief work at 4*d* to 8*d* per day, also working odd days at the docks. He made his way to Cardiff in search of work, and in the meantime took his share of open-air agitation in the ranks of the SDF (Social Democratic Federation). By the time he was fourteen, Larkin's father had died: 'My mother and self fought along for some time to keep the house together.' Faced with the problem of staying alive, he threw up his trade and went down to the docks where money could be earned and his brother might be kept serving his time. Another brother Peter worked at the north end as a coal heaver, and was active among the ports anarcho-syndicalist groups. Larkin worked at everything: stevedoring, portering, carting, coal heaving, carrying bags, bushelling – everything aboard ship and ashore. When dock work became slack, he decided to stowaway to the River Plate. Consequently, he drew his wages, sent them off to his mother, and stowed away aboard a vessel. However, his first attempt was aborted, as his ship was run into and was brought back to dock. Next time he tried it, he had the cooperation of a fireman on the ship, who opened the hatch for him every now and again. Larkin explains:

> During the following two days, no less than eleven other stowaways were found. The voyage out to the Plate was relieved by a little dispute over grub. By the way, stowaways were not objected to at that time on these boats at all events. They had been used to carry coals in the fore-hatch, and brought down amid ship's bunkers. The mate, who knew me on account of working at the boats loading them, give me charge of the crowd.

After a fantastic period of struggle against exploitation on the ship, he ended up at St Lucia and lived by beach combing. He shipped from there as a fireman on a steamer. On arriving at Galveston, he refused to re-sign and ended up in jail. Later, he joined an American cruiser as a marine, which was

Searching for Stowaways. *Illustrated London News,* 6 July 1850.

in commission and ordered to Valparaiso to demand satisfaction for the death of some American sailors who had been assaulted on a tram car. He then joined a schooner trading between the Windward Islands. Then he got a job as a coal passer on an American Revenue cruiser on patrol between Galveston, Texas, and Key West, Florida, watching for gun runners between the mainland and Cuba. This was, according to James, a good job, other than for a 'big slouch of a lieutenant, who was half Chinese. His amusement consisted of watching you dump ashes. If any of the men spilled any he would maul them on the bare skin with his side arms'.

From there, Larkin worked his way down the coast; Pärnu, Rio, Santos, then back to Buenos Aires where he joined a revolution, then 'skimmed out for Eusanada up to Rosario and back to Compagru'. After many such voyages, Larkin returned like many before him to the Liverpool docks, where he restarted his work and agitation among the dock labourers.

James Larkin became an organiser for the NUDL in 1905, which was organising dockers in its home base of Liverpool, as well as Humberside, Ireland, and Scotland. His policies were those of class militancy, swinging the whole of the union's finances into support of local action and sympathetic strikes. These tactics were in head-on confrontation with James Sexton, who had become general secretary after the ousting of McHugh in 1893.

Sexton's vision was one of bureaucratic paternalism: accumulation of funds, conciliation, and peace with the employers.

Larkin's finest hour, although there were many of them, was in the Belfast dock dispute of 1907. For his actions in Ireland, he was to be suspended from NUDL in 1908. Larkin stood at the centre of a huge, united dock front dispute. Despite the entrenched sectarianism of that city, a united, non-sectarian militant battle broke out, and it is not too much of an exaggeration to say that at times it posed revolutionary potential. Police mutinied, troops were called in, and men were shot dead, but the union stood firm. Later attempts to form a sectarian Protestant union on the back of the dispute ran aground on the rock of class solidarity. Larkin founded the Irish Transport and General Workers Union in 1908 following his suspension from NUDL, and most of the Irish branches supported him, but Sexton's influence over the Irish membership soon collapsed. In 1909, Sexton sued Larkin over his handling of the finances of the former NUDL branches in Ireland. He was charged with conspiracy to defraud the NUDL. He was convicted in the Dublin Assizes and sentenced to one year's hard labour. Of course, the funds had not been used by Larkin to line his own pocket, but rather to fund the militant programme he and the Irish branches were pursuing. What looked like a 'class trial' using the bosses' laws to suppress a working class militant led to widespread protests from the labour movement. It certainly cannot have done Sexton's standing any favours. Larkin wrote what was described as 'a virulent answer to Sexton's use of the law against him', which was published by the Anarcho-Syndicalist International Club. He was released after serving three months following massive protests from Liverpool and Ireland to the Lord Lieutenant of Ireland. James was later the centre of the Dublin workers' epic transport strike in 1913, and a firebrand in America from 1914-1923, where he was imprisoned for two years for treason and later deported.

An earlier Liverpool example was James Sexton himself, the dockers' leader of the 1890s. He was born in Newcastle-upon-Tyne in 1857. His parents were both of Irish decent. He had gone to sea as a young man, stowing away on a ship bound for San Francisco. However, after his father died at the age of forty-three, it became necessary for him to come to look after his mother. He had been used to many parts of the world and his first attempts of settling ashore were not very acceptable to him. Getting a job in St Helens, he found that he could hardly earn enough to feed himself. Subsequently, he found himself landed on the Liverpool waterfront. He tells us:

> My experience in rigging and handling ship gear generally had made me a handy man, and for a considerable time I got fairly good and steady work. Apart from the needs of my belly, I wanted little for myself, and most paydays found me able to send something to my mother, who certainly needed all

the help I could give her. And right glad I was to be able to do so, as many another man has discovered on return home after years of wondering.

The discharging and loading of sailing ships utilised primitive methods, for mechanical appliances were scarce and relatively ineffective, and called for a considerable amount of skill and knowledge. The square-rigged ship, equipped with both sail and steam, which had not then entirely ousted the windjammer, was hardly threatened by the modern craft, with its bare poles and complete dependence on steam for power. She had need for a rigger's skill, and Sexton was paid well for his work.

Sexton, like other major leaders of the dockers in the late 1880s and early 1890s, had been a member of the Knights of Labour, and a founding member of its Bootle branch. He was to join the Bootle branch of the NUDL, and became involved in their first great strike in 1890.

Although Larkin was a contemporary of Sexton, and indeed the two men may once have been close friends, they were soon to part company, as we have seen, in a bitter feud over the direction of the union and working class organisation. Larkin became an industrial unionist, while Sexton became a very embittered, moderate bureaucrat, frequently at odds with the rank and file despite his early militant credentials.

So we would see then that the relationship between docker to seaman, in work proximity, tradition, and often in the holding of duel trades, deemed that the waterfront, from an industrial standpoint welded the whole community into a complete body. A federated, loosely-knit body maybe, but inseparably bound one to another. The strike of any one section might immobilise the whole port, so closely did they depend on each other's labours. This explains the degree of solidarity shown in strike situations; the strike of one sector being self-same impulse behind the strike of the whole body.

Perhaps the most fundamental point held in common was the fact that in many cases, the sailors and dockers were employed by the same shipowners. Certainly in the case of the dockers, the shipowners hired subcontractors, 'the masters', who in turn were the dockers' direct employers. Yet in the later period, we will find the seamen and dockers engaged in meetings with the employer of both of them, namely the shipowners themselves.

This was particularly true of the 1879 strike. It was almost entirely the big steamship companies at the north end who launched the reduction attempt on the dockers. Once locked in combat with the dockers and others who had struck in sympathy, the seamen realised the relative weakness of the shipowners and choose that time to strike for an increase in wages.

In a similar way, we find the seamen and docker out in general strike together in 1866, as we can see from a poster that called upon, 'All mariners, mercantile marine stokers, dock labourers, coal heavers, and quay porters …

not to go near a vessel on Monday morning.'

In case of the 1866 strike, the whole waterfront had been seething with discontent. With one section after the other striking or returning, it was not surprising that the logic of the general strike eventually broke through. While previously there had been separate strikes for most of the waterfront, it was but a short step to close ranks and weld the sections into one body; seamen and dock labourers of all kinds united. As a direct result of the pressure of the 'packet rats', large bills were posted all over the port urging everyone to 'strike, strike, strike'. It called upon mariners, mercantile marine, stokers, dock labourers, coal heavers, and quay porters not to go near any vessels, and to take all measures necessary to obtain justice. Not one of the sections turned up for work. A united strike was constructed by all the sectors, standing up one with the other. In this strike, due to the inter-changeability of labour, the employers attempted to utilise the labour of the riggers to take up the various work of the other men. The riggers however refused and joined the general turn out.

In the strike of 1879, the coal trimmers, who had previously not joined the strike, found that their labour was being used not to stow coal for the ship's boilers on its voyage, but in the holds as cargo. They were being used to break the labourers strike. As soon as they discovered this, they turned out with the rest.

There is an exception to the rule of solidarity between the two groups of workers in the 1890 labourers' strike, where the seamen would not come out in support. I think it is largely true that the solidarity and close identities between the different trades operated much more clearly in the heyday of sailing vessels, and that the increasing intrusion of steam tended to specialise the workers apart. The jobs involving ropes, tackles, and rigging was diminishing. There is also the suggestion that the seamen had not been asked to assist the strike until it was too late. As it turned out, although the dock union held together and maintained its national structure (albeit greatly weakened), the National Amalgamated Sailors' and Firemen's Union actually collapsed in 1894. Despite spectacular gains and dynamic internationalist perspectives, it did not fully revive until 1910. The years after the First World War were the most shameful for the seamen's unions. In response to falling trade and mass unemployment, they adopted a thoroughly racist policy, campaigning against the employment of black, mainly Arab seamen – British as well as foreign – whether they were members of the union or not.

However, on at least three occasions there is simultaneous joint action, more frequently backing action, and on others, tactical delays in actions to maximise the length of time that shipowners or employers were under pressure; first action by one group, then the other.

CHAPTER TWO

Dockland

One should not think of the docks as one totality, as particular traits and characteristics will emerge that distinguish one dock from the other, and the north side from the south side. In the mid-nineteenth century, they were divided into three categories: enclosed docks, surrounded by walling; enclosed docks with warehouses; open wharfs and quays. The enclosed docks included the Sandon and Wellington, the Bramley Moor, the Nelson, the Stanley, the Collingwood, the Salisbury, the Clarence, the Trafalgar, the Victoria, the Waterloo, and the Princes docks. The docks with warehouses included the Albert Dock, and the open wharfs included the older docks of Georges, Canning, Salthouse, Kings, Queens, Union, Coburg, and Brunswick.

At the south end, three docks had been constructed without the benefit of warehouses, these being the Toxteth, Harrington, and Herculaneum docks, and most of the south docks were unenclosed. At the other side of the river there developed the Wallasey Dock, Morpeth Dock, the East Float, and the West Float. The Birkenhead docks tended to specialise in the export trade. The north docks dealt with the lucrative North American trade – cotton, grain, and passenger traffic; the south with South American; and the central docks with the coastal trade. These docks, who some had compared with the building enterprise of the pyramids, were built by Welsh quarrymen and miners.

The docks grew from handling 4.4 million tons of shipping in 1858 to nineteen million by 1914. Up until the First World War, thirty per cent of Liverpool's total imports was cotton yarn; piece goods and other cotton textiles accounted for half the total exports. Apart from cotton and grain, the other major transatlantic trade was passenger traffic, particularly emigrants. Between 1860 and 1900, three quarters of a million British emigrants to America left from Liverpool, which was also the major port from which to embark for Europe. Cargo and passenger work were complementary to cotton, which peaked in autumn, while the passenger trade peaked in spring and summer.

In earlier days, slavery had been a major feature; by 1792, the town engrossed five-eighths of Britain's total slave trade, and helped to build the town and the fortunes of unscrupulous merchants. Between 1820 and 1850, cotton was becoming dominant, with four-fifths of England's supplies coming through the port. Later, cotton dominated passengers, food, and live cattle trades.

Each dock had its own dock master, custom house superintendent, and police force. The nature of this force was such that even the fiercest ship master was a submissive lamb before them. They also had their specialities – tobacco at the Kings Dock, for instance – and definite sets of men, more or less firmly attached to them.

In the 1850s, three docks were set aside for the use of steamers. The American steamers were often too large for them however, and could be seen lying in the stream. Later on, new docks were built at the north end to accommodate them. By 1900, forty Mersey docks covered 1,600 acres, with 35.5 miles of lineal quay space.

Labour on the waterfront was not an amorphous mass; there was a variety of skills and trades embodied in the general term 'dock labourer'. In theory, a man could pass from job to job, but in practice, each of the different waterfront jobs required a particular skill and experience. Workers would attempt to keep to the class of work they were used to, although when these jobs were scarce, they would try anything that was available. The men of one class often formed themselves into societies to protect their particular interests, and even when a general union of the waterfront was formed, each of the sectors retained their particular identity. Different rates of pay were demanded for particular jobs in recognition of the fact that they were particularly hot, hard, or irregular. According to James Sexton, who worked as a labourer on the docks in the 1870s and tried to organise them in the 1890s, there was a 'caste system' on the docks, and 'almost innumerable' little clubs and societies, 'all hostile to each other'. It has not been the evidence of this work however that such 'hostility' prevented joint solidarity action.

Some of these were sick and funeral clubs, dividing the available funds amongst their members at Christmas time, trusting to luck and the generosity of members, with perhaps a 'tarpaulin muster' at the pay table to meet any emergencies that arose before the society was again in funds.

Sexton claimed that religious and political differences frequently kept these bodies apart, and indeed alive. Thus, the coal heavers had one society at the north end, another at the south. The leader of one was a Northern Ireland Orangeman, the leader of the other an equally perfervid, Irish, 'Home Rule' Catholic. The League of Nations itself could not reconcile two such organisations. The only point on which they were united was a mutual objection to mere cargo hands handling coal. However, we have

City of Rome, a graceful combination of coal and sail power in the majestic line of the clipper.

found throughout the course of this study nothing but close cooperation and solidarity, regardless of such 'castes'.

The carters too, played specialised and different roles. The biggest group was the traffic section – men employed by firms of master carters, hauling between the docks, warehouses, railways, and canals. There were also timber carters, coal carters, and 'short carters' who carried materials for building, road making, and excavations etc. Carters were paid on rising scales according to how many horses they were responsible for.

Salt heavers took up the same attitude as to the exclusiveness of their job; if you were not one of them, you could not touch bulk salt. Similarly, those whose work was the loading and discharging of railway bars to and from barges and steamers – in which there were at that time enormous traffic – had their two societies. Sexton tells us that one was the 'Cabbage Club', though how it got that title heaven alone may know. The other the 'Clarence Dock Club', which was for men engaging only in the coasting trade.

All these clubs and societies had their own rules and conditions of employment. The north end was described as 'distinctly Irish and Catholic'. Cultural provision was less cohesive in the south end, 'An area of more mixed social and ethnic composition, including a significant Ulster Protestant presence.' 'By the late nineteenth century, Great Netherfield Road was the acknowledged boundary between Catholic and Protestant Liverpool with the most partisan Orange district running north of Netherfield Road. Other borders were less clearly defined...'

In his report on the Liverpool–Irish in 1848, George Smyth observes:

The Irishmen in Liverpool perform nearly all the labour requiring great physical powers and endurance. Nine-tenths of the ships that arrive in this great port are discharged and loaded by them; and all the cargoes skilfully stowed. Out of 1,900 shipwrights, 400 of them are Irish, or of Irish parents; and although Liverpool is a port rather for repair than building vessels, there is one Irishman of the three or four master builders of the town, and many Irish foremen. In almost every branch of trade, Irishmen, notwithstanding the many prejudices with which they have to contend, have risen to the highest promotion ... a large majority of the boot and shoemakers and tailors of the town are Irish, and I know that Irish skill is recognised in the various foundries. Many Irishmen are distinguished for their ability as architects, draftsmen, and clerks of the works.

Work on the docks for the great majority was irregular, depending on how many vessels were in dock to unload, where they had docked, and what their cargo was. It was said during the 1879 strike that 75 per cent of the men only averaged 2.5 to 3.5 days per week. Returns published by one firm at this time, relating the nine weeks of December 1879 and January 1879, show the following lumpers and stevedores:

30 men working six days and overtime earned 43s 10d
27 men working five days and overtime earned 35s 3d
28 men working four days and overtime earned 27s 11d
35 men working three days and overtime earned 21s 9d
25 men working two days and overtime earned 14s 0d
25 men working one days and overtime earned 8s 2d

The porters who worked on the quays are paid after a somewhat lower standard, and of course their wages are proportionately less; but for the same nine weeks, the analysis presents much the same features as is the case of the lumpers and stevedores. Among the porters the pay was as follows:

46 men working six days and overtime earned 30s 3d
26 men working five days and overtime earned 24s 6d
18 men working four days and overtime earned 19s 5d
35 men working three days and overtime earned 14s 3d
48 men working two days and overtime earned 9s 7d
48 men working one days and overtime earned 5s 7d

The most common way of gaining employment was via 'the stand', either in the road outside the dock wall, or inside by the sheds, close to the berth of the ship that was to be worked. It was not as casual as it seemed. The labourers knew the respective places where the different employers held their stands and grouped themselves accordingly; the shipmen in one place, quay porters in another. The foreman and wharfinger for each branch, or in the case of small firms the employer himself, would pick as many of the men he thought he would need. Over the years, the foreman would get to know the faces of the men who attended his stands most regularly and whom had worked to his satisfaction. It would be such men as these that he would take in preference to any strangers who turned up, unless he was pressed for men, in which case he might hire the whole lot. It was within the interests of the employers to prevent their regular men from drifting away, therefore even in the slackest of times, he would try to take on as many of his regulars as he could. Once lost to another firm, he would find it hard to win them back when trade picked up again.

In large firms, there was usually a bigger nucleus of permanent or semi-permanent employers. All the firms gave brass tallies or notes with the number of each week on to their men. These served to identify the men when claiming payment at the end of the week. In the smaller firms, the tallies were given to their best men that bore the lowest numbers in a crude order of preference from lowest upwards. Week after week, according to the lowness of their numbers, a particular group of men would be maintained.

However, whether the numbers were given out or not, nearly every firm had a certain body of men who followed its work as long as it had any work for them. The wharfinger or foreman would refer to such men as 'our men', and he would know their ways of work and character very well. Such a situation did not present itself to most dockers however, and the majority of men moved around a great deal in search of work. If their regular stands had no work for them, they would ascertain from enquiry or newspaper when the ships were due in and where they were due for. As a rule, the men of the north end of the quay did not seek work at the south, nor *vice versa*, except in the case where they were 'following the work' of their regular employers. On most occasions, the south and north were different labour markets, and rarely, if ever, crossed.

The Princes Dock ran as a border line between the north and the south end docks. There were many differences between them in terms of size, cargoes, types of vessel, the nature of employment, and working class organisations.

Firstly, the north end was very much bigger and very much more developed. The Mersey Dock's Board and Harbour spent most of its attention upon improving it, whereas the south end was a poor relation. The north end always was the most prosperous, and as the years went on it became more so; it had something like six times more shipping tonnage than the south.

We can see this very clearly by looking at some simple statistics. Firstly, the total tonnage entering the north end of the Liverpool docks:

    1851: 3,095,000 tons, with 166 acres
    1880: 6,621,000 tons, with 273 acres

Secondly, the proportion that went to the south end of the port:

    1851: 180,000 tons, with 66 acres
    1880: 202,000 tons, with 82 acres

The north end principally dealt in deep sea vessels, while the south had the predominance of coasting and smaller sized ships. Most of the unemployed would make their way to the north end, which being the greatest portion of the port, offered at least a chance of a job. Most of the large American and Mediterranean steamers had berths at the northern docks, and there were many more casual workers taken on there when one of the big steamers arrived in port. The trade of the south end was smaller and more specialised.

> The cause of this attraction to the north end of our dock estate is readily explained. The majority of the large American and Mediterranean steamers have permanent berths in these docks, and as they arrive, when they arrive at all, pretty punctually, there is always a chance – and, unhappily just now *only* a chance – of temporary employment.

In broad terms, it was the south end of the port that steadily became the most organised, often it did not feature in strikes simply because the port's rates became so far advanced and its union so strong that it did not need to. In the later years when we find them striking, it was almost always in support of the men at the north end. The South End Dock Labourers Association outlasted all of the others that arose in the port, even in the 1880s when the trend was towards the building up of mass national organisations, we find it maintained its own identity. It was still in existence in 1903. By that time, its chief membership were coal heavers, although earlier it controlled the whole southern dock for decades. The two local societies of coal heavers referred to by Sexton earlier may well have been around as long as The South End Dock Labourers Association, as they did not merge with the National Union of Dock Labourers until 1911.

The north end unions were of a generally transient nature. In the south, once the sparks had been kindled, they were kept alight for generations. The South End Dock Labourers Association was founded in 1849 and remained in existence for over fifty years. In 1855, it was strong enough to attempt to enforce a closed shop.

The society was stable enough to support its own burial society, known in 1866 as the Liverpool South End Dock Labourers Sick and Burial Association. In the strike movement of the same year, the South End Dock Labourers Association, meeting at Toxteth Hall, drew up a whole scale of wages to be increased, and in so doing, told us of the area of membership they included.

An advance of 1s per day on the existing rate (4s)
1d per hour on overtime, from 6 a.m.
2d per 100 stacks of salt
2d per ton of ballast
1s 4d per ton on coals
1s per day to a 'leading' man in the holds of a timber or cotton ship
1s per day to Stevedores
1s extra for night work; and all men working throughout the night at salt or coals to be paid an advance of 6d from 6 to 12 p.m.

The South End Dock Labourers Society had stood the test of time, although it had not been the first. John Finch, a self-made man of impeccable, working class origin, and a socialist pioneer of the Owenite school, had made the first attempts not simply to found a dock workers union, but actually to undermine capitalism in the port and install a dockers cooperative. McHugh, leader of the Liverpool dockers strike of 1890, also had such a plan, although one to be pursued with a little more vigour than Finch's. He envisaged a militant trade union struggle that would make or break the shipowners. Those who failed would be bought out by the workers, who would run the enterprise themselves. Clearly, this was not a plan simply for the docks. A docker of the period saw it thus:

When a company failed, each member (of the union) would be called upon to pay 1s per week into a fund that would enable the union soon to possess the defunct companies' ships ... The project is to give each labourer £2 per week, work or no work to be obtained, and at the end of the year divide equally among themselves what now goes into the employers pockets ... Every class of trade is to be attacked in turn until everyone shall be brought to the same level. All work will cease at 6 p.m., after which time the shops will shut and the parks will be filled with happy families going there by tram and cab to listen to music.

A not dissimilar plan of Finch's emerged after the defeat of the great Liverpool dockers 1890 struggle, with the victimised men attempting to become a dockers cooperative able to compete for the work as contractors.

Finch, a Temperance Society member, in work among the dockers to wean them off the evil brew, had been shocked to find a system of contracting work that robbed the men blind while pushing them to the ale house. He told a parliamentary committee of 1834:

> I made a particular enquiry into the situation of the dock labourer, and I found that there were about 120 of those persons called 'lumpers' in Liverpool – men who take the jobs of loading and discharging the vessels from the merchants for a certain sum, and then go out upon the quay and engage a number of labourers to do the work for something less, living themselves on the profits ... I found that there were not more than 1 or 2 out of all the 120 lumpers who did not pay the workmen at a public house.

At this time, the wage was reported to be 2s per day for a three or four day week. In September 1830, in a large room over the store of a cooperative society in Greenland Street with 200 dock labourers present, Finch outlined his plan. The first step was to found the Dock Labourers Society. The docks were divided into three groups, each with a branch office, one for the Kings and Queens docks, another for the Salthouse and Dry docks, and a third for the Georges and Princes docks. The offices were supplied with winches, barrows, chutes, and all other necessary mechanical equipment. Together with this were libraries, and plans by which literate dockers would instruct the illiterate in periods when they had no work.

It seems quite remarkable, but some 6,000 dock and warehouse workers were recruited and the society began to operate the scheme, presumably bidding for the work directly themselves and passing on the lumper's share of the fees to the workers. We are told the scheme 'had considerable initial success'. 'At each branch office, a secretary was elected to keep the books and look after accounts, while the president canvassed for work and exercised general supervision.' The branch societies were divided into gangs under a foreman, who after paying his contribution to the society, divided the wages equally among the workers. The fixed rate was 3s per man per day, and 6d per week was deducted for membership fees. The new system was estimated to have raised dockers' wages by half, so the 6d would hardly be resented.

It seems an ideal system, the very essence of workers' control and self-management, and to an extent it was. That being the case, it required quite a degree of political and social consciousness to maintain itself. Such levels of self-discipline and class responsibility were at a high premium on the waterfront of the 1830s. There had been quarrels, and there had been disputes with the employers, who of course were not under the control of the dockers. Books were stolen from the libraries, as were many of the tools and even desks from the workers schools, mostly to buy ale without the chore of working for the money. In the end, however, the death blow was delivered not by the men but their class enemies, who exercised a 'strike of capital' by not hiring the societies' dockers. That anyway is the implication of Finch's reflections:

> The employers looked on the society with great suspicion as a combination of labourers against their employers; some objected to giving a fixed rate of wages; others thought 3s per day too much, not considering that labourers employment is extremely precarious, that they have not six months work in the year on average. Thus, their friends were not sufficiently numerous, and therefore the society could not get sufficient employment to enable them to pay the salaries of their officers and their other expenses; they exhausted their funds, became dispirited and heartbroken.

The men of Clarence Dock, who handled the coasting trade, were remembered by Sexton as being particularly clannish. They followed the work in the coasting trade and worked under somewhat different conditions of pay and hours to the other docks. The system of employment was peculiar, as the cargoes took less time to clear. At the Clarence Dock, men were taken on for only a quarter of a day at a time.

The coasting firms' wages in 1879 were 5s per day and 9d overtime. However, on average, only three boats per week came in for discharge and loading, which gave the worker an average of 17s 3d per week.

The Clarence Dock Labourers Society was an ancient society, and along with the South End Dock Labourers Society, was one of the last to go. The Society makes an early appearance in 1852, when the dock labourers claimed that it was simply a Friendly Society. But it took part in organising a strike when the Clarence men joined with the timber workers and Albert dockers behind the banners of the Dock Labourers Society, demanding a standard rate. They added their own particular demands, and one of their special grievances was the system of employing men for a quarter of a day. The Clarence men complained that the steam boat agents, by engaging them only for the two longest quarters in the day, got 6.5 hours labour from them for half a day's wages; they wanted 3d to 6d for their work, and the quarter day regulated. The agents on their side complained that the men were trying to charge them at the rate of half a day for three hours labour.

In 1880, the Clarence Dock Labourers Society was still a very strong, small, and highly localised union that controlled the workers employed on the coasting vessels. The newly formed National Dock Labourers Union was attempting to 'court and marry' it, but the society was not prepared to be swallowed up by the new giant. After persistent wooing in the 1890s, it eventually affiliated to the Nation Union of Dock Labourers.

As well as particular docks, there were also distinctive groups who stood out for their greater cohesion and ability to earn higher wages.

Timber work was different from the other work, as the dockers required tools when few others did, or needed tools that were nowhere near the same price bracket. The cant bar was used for turning the timber over, while the shod bar assisted in the operation of canting. These tools might cost 16s. Timber work was also harder than others and required skill, whereas in cotton work for example, any man who was strong enough could do it. But although timber work needed special strength and a certain knack to work the cargoes (and as such received a special rate), the men were not maintained as timber workers all the time. When no timber work was available, they would pass to the other cargoes with the rest of the men. The timber season was a very short season. While it lasted, most men who wanted it could find work at the south end of town at the Brunswick Timber Dock. The timber season usually extended from the beginning of April to August. When it was over, the regular timber hands were laid off for about six months of the year; they would then try their hands at other work, for instance in cotton cargoes.

The grain workers were a distinct section. They ranged over numerous tasks and rates of pay, but generally, they were better paid than other workers. Working in the grain was either dangerously dusty, excessively heavy, or both. These men were specially chosen for this particular class of work because of their great strength and endurance. We can see why both were essential when we read that in 1889, these men were required to start work from 7 a.m. until 5 p.m. (One hour was allowed for dinner break.) The men worked all day carrying sacks of grain on their backs, which weighed anything from 2 to 2.5 cwt., all of which had to be humped up an inclined plain to be deposited in a stack dome twelve feet high. Under these conditions, a man might carry 45 tons of wheat on his back in the course of a day.

Not all of the ships carried the grain already bagged. In certain ships, particularly in the 1880s and 1890s, the grain was in bulk in the hold. The task of unloading this cargo was no easier, and it was in many ways more dangerous, since great clouds of dust thickened the air (and lungs). If the dock did not use an elevator (a mechanical device for conveying the grain from ship to shore, of which the south end had very few in the late 1880s), then the bulk would have to be broke by hand. Men would shovel or 'bushel' the grain into bags, which would be held by a 'bag holder' or 'bag man', who would sling these to the stevedore to take from the ship. With the introduction of the elevators, which I assumed to be similar to a mining conveyor chain, the grain would be 'skipped' by men called skippers. In other words, the grain would be shovelled onto the elevator that transported it either to the quay, or else in passages to the warehouse. The trimmers would be employed to reload all the grain that would be continually spilling off as it went along its way. All of these men would be working in confined spaces with clouds of dust rising from the loose grain in the thick clouds. The grain workers claimed that the men who worked on the elevators could not work one day after another because of the effects of the work, and many men died prematurely as a result. Grain carrying was proved to be a speciality when the bag carriers of Henderson Brother's Anchor Line struck in 1889 and had to be replaced by a double team of workers to take over their work. So skilled were the regular bag men that the job had to be split into two sections for the new men, one set taking the bags from the hold and onto the quay, the other to truck it then pile it in the sheds. We see here why only specifically chosen men normally did the work of carrying these bags. The work of these men was such that even a corn merchant himself had to admit, 'Their work is very hard; it is indeed laborious, and within my experience, I scarcely know of any man who had not been used up in ten years.'

The grain porters took a leading role early in the strikes of the 1880s. This seems to have been because their jobs were threatened by the introduction of a new mechanical unloading device – the elevator. These elevators in other parts of the country had caused considerable trouble among the dockers and there had been strikes against them in Bristol. In Liverpool, they had been introduced slowly, but by July 1888 there were sixteen or seventeen elevators, which the men had termed 'devils'. Up until that time, the Wellington Dock had not used them. As soon as they appeared at the dock, the grain porters struck work, followed by the Wellington porters who came out in sympathy. The technology for the 'devil' probably came from the coal industry. The endless line of overhead 'buckets' that carried waste to the pit tip, and the underground 'scraper chain' dragging coal and stone underground from the coal face, would have posed an obvious application to grain and coal in holds. The elevator began as a sort of chain of wide mouthed 'buckets'. In later years, it progressed into a 'sucker', similar to a large vacuum cleaner nozzle.

These devils were to cause considerable trouble in the years following the strike of 1888, as we shall see. They had been increasing in their numbers, and since they discharged the grain quicker and cheaper, company after company was introducing them. The unrest of the men against these machines is perhaps not surprising when one realises that one 'devil', with the aid of between six to twelve men, was doing work that fifty labourers had been well-paid for previously. When the elevator eventually reached the Wellington Dock, the men found that the employers, in spite of the strike, were determined to use them. In the face of the walk out, they had simply sent for another machine to do the work. However, it seems clear that men could not be found to work either of them, since later we read that the ship was moved from the Wellington to the east Waterloo Dock where it was eventually discharged by the dock board's employees.

A year later in 1889, we find the grain workers at the heart of the waterfront unrest in Liverpool. A strike that started among the grain carriers at the Harrington Dock was later to catch the imagination of grain workers along the length and breadth of the dock. Not simply the grain workers either, but also many other sectors.

The unrest started at the south end when about 100 grain carriers at the Harrington Dock struck work and marched as a body to Toxteth Dock. They were demanding 1s extra on their existing rate of 5s. They also claimed an increase from 8d to 1s per hour overtime rates. At Toxteth, there were three grain ships being discharged, and it was the intention of the Harrington men to call them out. Unrest was such that all three vessels were left almost as soon as the Harrington men had put the case. It was largely the grain carriers at the south end that joined the strike. One dock struck at the north end, but the employers gave way to them immediately and the men returned to work. The grain carriers were left more or less in isolation with the exception of the dock labourers on their own docks who stood out from them. Nevertheless, they won. One or two firms had come forward with an offer of an extra sixpence, but this the men did not even consider. Within a week of the strike being started, it was finished with a resulting victory for the grain men.

It was the men working in the grain trade who started the movement of 1890 that lead eventually to a general strike. It started when 100 grain men at the Langton Dock struck work. The bushellers – those who were the bag fillers and weighers – took the lead, asking for 1s per day. When this was not granted, they struck. All the other men who depended upon them were subsequently thrown out of employ. The bushellers had been working on kurrache grain, which was exceptionally dusty and had the same effect as coal dust upon the lungs. A day later, the northern portion of the Langton Dock was affected. The skippers came out, and ultimately some 100 quay men refused to work unless a further 6d per day was paid.

On 20 January 1890, we are told that the strike at the south docks was over, the grain carriers having resumed work at the old rate of wages. At the north end however, the men remained out. The trade was becoming disorganised as large quantities of loose grain accumulated, the employers being unable to get the labourers to load it into the bags.

The strike spread next to the grain carriers at the Toxteth Dock, where the bushellers came out demanding 5s a day and 6d per 100 sacks, and the skippers 5s per day. The classes of workers that got what they were after, returned to work, but other classes of grain men came out.

An effort was to be made by the Corn Trade Association to deliver East Indian wheat in bags and thereby do away with skipping and bushelling. The weighers were holding separate meetings in support of their claim for 6s per day, up from 5s, and the scalers marched along the line of the docks in support of their wage claim.

On 28 January, the men employed by the Liverpool Grain Storage Company went on strike for an increase of 6d per day, their wages being 4s per day at the time. A great deal of dissatisfaction had been displayed, owing to the fact that their work was more dangerous and trying than ordinary labourers. The grain was brought to the warehouses through subterranean passages by machinery from the docks. When it got to the warehouses, the men were almost choked by the clouds of dust that it raised.

The strike now became general, and in the course of it, the elevator question came up again. On 28 February, the grain men at the Huskisson Dock struck work for an advance of wages, demanding 7s per day. The strike originated among the few men who were trimming the elevators in the hold. The strikers then spread the strike to another ship lying in the same dock. The union officials told the men that they were acting on their own initiative and were pursuing a very unwise course.

Previously, the men had been paid for feeding the grain onto the elevator 6s per day and two pints of beer on some ships, and 5s and a drink on others. The employers next offered to take the hazardous machines out of the holds to allow the men to bushel the corn, paying them piecework at the old rate. The men however wanted a written guarantee that the firms would not use the elevators in the future, but they were refused this. A delegate from the union who visited the Huskisson Dock to advise the grain porters to resume work faced the threat of being thrown into the dock if he did not 'clear off'.

Another small group of workers with a very arduous task were the coal heavers. Like the men who worked in the grain, the job had various components. The coal heavers carried great bags of coal from the quay aboard the vessel, while the coal trimmer worked in the holds stowing the coal so that not an inch of room was lost. The coal had to be stowed tightly so that enough fuel could be carried to sustain the ship in its long voyage; if the coal was not tightly packed, it could shift in heavy weather and cause the vessel to list.

James Larkin tells us that in his time the coal was stowed in the forward hatch, while the bunkers that fed the engines were amidships. As the bunker became empty, the coal had to be carried from the forward hatch abaft.

Due to the heavy nature of such work, both trimmers and heavers were very well paid. Their work must have been one of the very hardest on the waterfront, and as such, their wages were quite astounding compared to what other workers were receiving. In return, they had to work flat out. The largest steamers carried 750 tons of coal, while others carried between 600 and 650 tons. When men had to meet turnaround deadlines and tides, they often worked for two or three days without any sleep.

Coal trimmers worked with their heads bound in handkerchiefs, probably to act as sweat bands to keep their eyes clear. It generally took two-and-a-half days to load an average steam vessel in the 1850s, but when rushed, it was possible to do it in twenty-four hours. These men were employed by master lumpers. With a good master, a man could expect to earn 16s 3d for two-and-a-half days

Cunard sailing four times per week 'come hell or high water' New York to Liverpool and back, 1870's.

employment in loading a vessel, but then would not expect to get another vessel that week. The foreman of the gangs earned 2s 6d extra per week over the actual trimmers. Like colliers, these workers were said to drink a great deal of beer.

At the time of the strike of 1879, when all other sections were receiving reductions, we learn that not only were the coal heavers and trimmers unaffected by reduction, but were earning on average the fantastic sum of £3 a week.

There was another section in the coaling fraternity. These were the wheelers, who would take the coal from the warehouses (probably in barrows) and quays to the heavers, who in turn would carry it to the holds for the trimmer. All in all, the crew, including all three sectors, would number seventeen men on average, although when rushed, extra workers would have been taken on. In the days before the steamer was the chief vessel of the port, these men would have been chiefly employed in stowing coal aboard the American, Dublin, and Glasgow steam packets.

The coal heavers sometimes operated in their own societies. At other times, they joined with the other classes, but they never relinquished their independent identity. The nature of their work, their pay conditions etc., set them in a different class than the other men, but they still had a high degree of class solidarity consciousness.

Coaling a large steamer through coal chutes into her bunkers.

These men, employed by coal lumpers or directly by the steamship companies, were more often than not striking in support of other sectors when they themselves were not in an industrial dispute. Their strike of 1879, in solidarity to the north end dockers fighting the reduction, was typical, as was their participation in the strike of 1866. At one of the first mass rallies of the general strike, Mr Doyle, the president of the Coal Heavers Society, addressed the meeting thus:

One question might be asked of them – what had brought them there that day. It might be said that they had no business there under any circumstances, for they were not in union with other men. But they intended to support them as they had done to the very last, and whether the movement rose or fell they meant to stand by it. (Applause.) When their employers asked them what it was they were looking for, it was a very hard and crooked question to answer, and it would be useless for him to attempt to answer all the arguments that might be put forward by the masters. It might be said that they were getting what they asked for, but let the question never be asked again – namely, that they were joining in this movement because their fellow unionists had not got the same rights as they enjoyed. He believed the coal heavers of Liverpool were a body of men that no-one could despise, and when it came to the point of their manhood, they had the coal heavers to depend upon.

The coal heavers remained a strong, unionised sector for many decades. In 1904, we find that at the south end, they were virtually the only dockers left in the old South End Dock Labourers Union, the other men having left and joined the National Union. The coal heavers probably found that the local nature of the South End Dock Labourers Union suited them better than the big national amalgamation of all the skills on the docks.

The coal heavers on the other side of the Mersey were equally militant, and in 1855, we find that the Birkenhead coal heavers were the culprits of 'a disgraceful riot' when they were fighting against an attempt to reduce their wages. Some blacklegs had been introduced from Liverpool, but the Birkenhead men put pay to them with volleys of stone, and were not deterred even when a master turned a revolver on them.

The biggest single group of workers on the docks were those involved in the cotton trade. Cotton was, after all, Liverpool's chief import and the very cornerstone of its trade. In the old days when the cotton sailing ships docked, it took six weeks to unload a cargo. (This was of course before the advent of steam winches.) The ships would pull into the Georges and Princes dock and have all their three decks unloaded by hand. By 1883, most of the American and all of the Egyptian and East Indian cotton arrived in steam vessels and was unloaded by steam. No sooner did the cotton ship come alongside of the docks, the lumpers would take over. They clambered up the rigging and out upon the derricks that hung over the hatches. Men would be seen perched on the extremity of the derricks, making fast the blocks and tackles and roving 'falls' (lifting ropes) threaded through the pulleys. One end of each rope was then wound around the driving wheels of the steam winch on the deck. The other end would be left dangling over the mouth of the hold. These men would be termed 'riggers', and while they were aloft, another gang would be laying down the stages to connect the vessel to the quay, while the porters hurriedly fetched weights, weight boxes, and scales. Unloading the bales was a difficult task, more so than the effort that the Americans had used in wedging them in. Strong hooks, wedges, and crowbars were required to prize the bales free. This process was called 'breaking out'.

In the 1880s, the cotton cargoes were discharged with great speed day and night. The master porters were faced with an avalanche of bales teaming out of perhaps five hatches at a time. He had the task of finding room to stow them. The master carters and the consignees of the goods very often grumbled that the goods could not be found. Often the carts had to wait for hours before they could get their loads. One of the chief bones of contention was the fact that the consignees had to remove all their goods within seventy-two hours, or else pay a fee of £6 per day. On the day that the goods arrived, there was consequently a rush of carts towards the evening to get the cotton away. The masters often found themselves unable to supply gangs of men to load the carts. In the morning, the master would put approximately five gangs from 7 a.m. to 9 a.m., which kept the men busy. But later, until about 3 p.m., the work would die off and the men were kept hanging about (although still getting paid). From 3 p.m. until 5 p.m. there was a glut of carts and a great demand for loading gangs. The scene can be well imagined, with one or two vessels discharging at one of the Alexandra Dock berths, while at the dock immediately opposite, other large vessels would also be discharging cotton. If there had been rough weather, there would often be a whole batch of cotton steamers entering the port at the same time. It was practically impossible for merchants to get their orders off the docks in time, despite the cursing of the carters and the toil of the labourers. Often, the goods could not be got at amid the industrial chaos of cargoes that blocked up the sheds, streets, and passages along the entire range of the berths.

The job of stowing cotton was also a very dangerous one, owing to the great heights to which the cotton was stacked. Men often fell from the top of the piles and were killed. We must remember that during this period, the bulk of 8,000,000 bales came to the port every year. These bales were often twenty feet high, but men could be, and often were, killed due to falling some fifteen feet from the tops of bales.

Even by the 1890s, the boundary of this research, Mr Tom Frank Parr of the Liverpool Cotton and General Warehouse Porters Society stated that the warehouses were not inspected in any way, shape, or form, and hoisting machinery and sanitary arrangements, and in some places light and floors, suffered from this neglect. Men were cut to pieces through unguarded machinery. In general, the warehouse porters' job was regarded as a dangerous occupation. There is little focus in this work on the danger of dock work, but it was endemic. *The Lancet* reckoned that no-one could be a docker for five years and escape disfigurement. One docker interviewed by the Royal Commission on Labour was without a toe, and grain bags had beaten Sexton's face 'into a mummy'. Certain cargoes, such as cement, bulk guano, bleaching powder, sulphur, pitch, and hides always spelt a special danger.

The cotton porters, to all intents and purposes, seemed to have been the chief catalyst of the strike movement of 1853, as their association issued placards urging their fellow workmen to remain out for an increase. They appeared again as a separately organised force in 1872. In the middle of June, a Cotton Porters Association registered itself. Out of a work force of some 15,000, it claimed to have recruited 6,000 members and intended to test its strength almost immediately. They demanded a rise from 4s per day to 4s 6d per day, or else they were to strike. Members were to pay 1d per week to keep a paid secretary, medicine, and medical attention for sick members, and 8s per week for men disabled by accident.

Despite this, their industrial position was not strong. Many of them were employed only for six months of the year throughout in the winter, and left the docks during the summer. In 1854, the cotton porters complained that they received only 3s 6d per day, while the dock labourer received from 4s to 6s per day. They held themselves to be the worse paid class of worker in the ports.

In 1872, it seems that the cotton porters were still somewhat backward in their wage compared to other trades. In May, they put forward a claim for 6d extra per day to make up their wages to 4s 6d. Other waterfront workers at this time were demanding 5s per day.

In the same way that workmen along the waterfront were not a faceless, indistinguishable gang, neither were the employers of the port. The conditions of life on the waterfront were dominated by not one employer, but by a host of various masters and shipowners. Labour on the docks was employed by four different sets of employers:

A: By the master stevedores and master porters who contracted with the shipowners and merchants to do the loading or unloading of their ships and cargoes.

B: By the shipowners directly, who did their own stevedoring or porterage or both.

C: By the merchants who did their own porterage.

D: By the Mersey Docks and Harbour Board, who alone employed labour in the six closed docks of Stanley, East Waterloo, Albert, Wapping, Birkenhead, and Birkenhead grain docks. To these might be added the London and North Western Railway, which had its own docks at Galston.

There was another class of employer, who although not figuring greatly in my exposition, deserves mention. There were the owners of the warehouses; the privately owned store rooms that were leased to various companies. These employers often employed their own gangs, as did the shipping companies who owned their own warehouses and those that came under the control of the Mersey Dock Board.

In the 1830s, most warehousemen were Welsh: employers tended to think that by custom, tradition, and culture, Welshmen were more reliable than the Irish. We are told by P. J. Waller that since warehousemen hired porters, Welshmen got the best places. Welshmen, Irishmen, and Englishmen (and some Scotsmen) each constituted one-third of porters, but under-warehousemen and regular porters were rarely Irish. Waller also tells us that little change occurred in the nineteenth century. The Warehouse Porters Union was founded in 1890.

The master stevedores were commonly called shipmen, stevedores, or stevedores' labourers. These did everything connected with loading the ships, including the bringing of the goods from the sheds, carts, or decks to be stowed in the holds. They also unloaded or 'broke out' the cargo as it was called. They then landed it onto the quays, or else 'overside' into the barges.

The master porters, commonly known as quay porters or simply porters, received the goods on the quays. They then either dealt with it there or in the sheds. Dealing with it would include counting, sorting, weighing, marking, and finally packing it into the consignees carts, trucks, or barges. The quay porters had nothing to do with outward cargoes in the 1890s. The master porters were in perpetual competition with each other, always trying to offer the lowest rates to the shipowners, and in doing so of course, reduce the wages of the dockers.

At the beginning of the period I am writing about, 1850, the most important dock employers were the master stevedores and porters. Under the Mersey Docks Act, their numbers had been restricted to a number of licensed masters and firms.

Before the new method of master porterage, each consignee of goods on board, although there may have been twelve, or twenty, or any number, employed his own porters to weigh, weigh off, mark, sample, and remove his consignments to the warehouses, meaning that if there were twelve consignees, there were twelve different, independent gangs of porters employed in discharging the cargo. This system, the merchants argued, impeded the trade of the port. They further argued that nothing short of legislative enactment could change the situation, and they demanded that a clause be included in the new Docks Act, demanding the employment of only one set of porters for discharging the cargoes of any vessel unloading at the Liverpool docks. This clause, which became law, effectively meant that all firms had to employ the master porters.

Later, with the growth of the big steamship companies that started to take over the direct employment of work on the docks, the role of the master porters and stevedores diminished. This is reflected in the strikes. The big strike of 1866 was fought against the master porters; in 1879, the steamship companies led the employers, and they were responsible for importing blacklegs into the docks.

One of the most hated employers in the port, and one who consistently held out the hardest resistance to the workers, was not a private contractor in fact, but the Mersey Docks and Harbour Board. The dockers at the other docks knew that by striking, they had a good chance of forcing their masters into defeat. The masters would see their money going down the drain, while perhaps masters who had conceded were raking in the profits. With the Board however, no such pressure could be brought to bear, as the individual members of the board lost nothing through the strikes of the workers. It was for that reason that between 1850 and 1890 they alone defeated their workers time after time.

A Royal Commission of 1853 had recommended the formation of a new body to take over the Mersey docks, and in 1857, an Act of Parliament took away control of the docks and harbour from Liverpool borough and created a new body, the Mersey Docks and Harbour Board. The 1858 Act stipulated that the board should consist of twenty-eight members. Twenty-four of them were elected by the dock rate payers and four nominated by the Mersey Conservancy Commissioners.

Previously, the docks had been governed by a corporation who had in their possession only one dock, the Albert, which the new Mersey Docks and Harbour Board inherited.

The Albert Dock was opened with great pomp and ceremony by HRH Prince Albert in July 1846. It was surrounded by its own sheds and warehouses, all within the dock premises, both bonded and free. Neither lumpers nor master porters were employed in the same capacity as the other docks. The trustees of the dock assumed all responsibility of the discharging, landing, and warehousing of cargoes, alongside the employment of all porters. Such trustees were appointed by the town council of Liverpool, who in turn kept a permanent body of porters, averaging about sixty men. If the docks were full, extra workers were employed; as many as 1,200 men have been employed on such occasions on just one day. In all, the appearance and running of the dock sounds like a modern corporation, although we shall read that these masters were the most stubborn and cruel of all the waterfront employers. Immediately after its founding, the board took steps to construct new dock space, and the first important space they constructed was the Canada Dock in 1859. This dock was situated to the north of the Huskisson Dock. A smaller one at the extreme south end was the Herculaneum Dock. Later, the board constructed a much greater dock on the Cheshire side near Birkenhead. This dock, the Great Float, was the largest dock on the Mersey, and was opened in 1860.

However, the only docks that came under their direct management were the closed docks of Stanley, East Waterloo, Acbere, Wapping, Birkenhead, and Birkenhead Grain Dock.

The men who worked for the Mersey Docks and Harbour Board on loading and unloading the vessels were paid at a lesser rate than those operating elsewhere. The dock board labourers at the Albert, Stanley, and Wapping docks always received 6d less wages than the standard dock rates paid everywhere else. The men at these docks claimed that they worked longer hours – considering winter and summer hours together – than the other docks.

Even the officials of the dock were badly paid. The foreman ship worker, for example, was paid 1s less per week than labourers 'over the hatch' at the outside docks. The housing foreman in charge of warehousing received only from 4s to 8s per day. The ganger in charge of a much smaller area at the other docks was receiving between 30 to 40s per week.

The board was particularly hard on losses. If a foreman or labourer made a mistake, he had to pay any and all of the expenses, or else leave the job.

In the big strikes of 1852, the board argued (as they did afterwards) that the regular nature of employment offered by them was worth a little less wages. They also argued that the porter on the quays had to work from 6 a.m. to 6 p.m., while hours of the Albert Dock porters were (in winter) from 8 a.m. to 4 p.m. There was therefore four hours less labour. In addition, these men were sheltered from the elements. In 1852, the men of the Albert Dock were successful in winning their parity claim, along with the men of the Clarence and Timber docks. This was not usually the case however, and in the strike of 1854, when the dockers were demanding an increase to 4s per day; they were the only group not to win.

The same outcome awaited the board's dockers when they struck along with the other men in 1866.

The Wapping Dock men, particularly those known as shipmen, had put in for the same increase as they had demanded twelve years earlier, i.e., from 3s 6d to 4s per day. They also added a claim for a one hour dinner instead of twenty minutes. The board replied by issuing notices offering employment at the old rates to whoever would take it. Sufficient labourers were obtained at the old rate, and the Docks Board Warehouses Committee, in true style, issued strict instructions to its superintendents that none of the men who had struck for the increase should ever be employed again.

Much the same fate befell the strike movement of the board employees in 1872. On that occasion, the strike was at their grain warehouses on the Waterloo Dock, but spread to include all the grain workers of the docks. Before the strike, men had been paid 4s 6d per day, with 6d per hour overtime. They demanded 4s 6d per day with 7d per hour overtime, and the bag carriers (heavers) wanted 5s per day instead of 4s.

On 4 July, a deputation of dock warehouse porters, ship workers and porters on strike waited upon the docks and quays committee of the Mersey Dock Board, but had no joy. The last we hear of this strike is that the men were still out. The defeat of the dock board employees at the Albert and Wapping was to be a recurring feature. In striking against master porters, the labourers were hitting the employers directly in their pockets; a most tender spot. However, since the dock board committee was not directly losing (in essence any loss would simply come out of the rates) they could be much more stubborn to the movement of the men. Time and again we find the Wapping and Albert

Steam and sail ship *Strathleven*, 1875. *Burrell, Mitchell Library.*

dockers courageously turning out with the other men, only to be left isolated
after the others had won. Even when the others lost, mostly with one or two
exceptions, they got back to work without victimisation. The dock board
however always made a point of locking out strikers

CHAPTER THREE

Waterfront Strikes 1850-1890

The first dock agitation opening the period came on 16 February 1850 when a meeting of operative porters was called at the popular working man's meeting place, the music hall, Bold Street. The meeting was against the hated system of porterage that involved the dockers in so much hardship. The dockers were complaining about a clause in the Dock Act, which 'restricted the free disposal of labour' and put them at the mercy of the master porters. Local MPs in the hall promised to fight for the repeal of the clause when the bill came before Parliament. It was proposed that every operative porter in Liverpool be levied 3d per week to support the battle. Given the strength of such a resolution, it must have been confidently predicted that such a levy would have the widespread support of the porters, and that this body of men had the capacity to organise and collect such a levy. Such abilities take time to extend, so we could conclude such widespread organisation had been growing for some time. The meeting as such had attracted not simply the labourers, but also corn and fruit merchants who added their objections to the working of the Act.

The first mention of this organisation as a *formal organisation* came a little later in September 1850 when the Operative Porters Association is recalled as meeting at its clubroom in Marylebone. Basically a routine meeting, it had involved the election of its officials. It was also proposed at this meeting that a room or 'house of call' be established in the neighbourhood of the Exchange buildings so that porters out of employment could be within easy distance if a job should come up, and yet at the same time have some protection against the elements.

It was to be the seamen however who were the first to be discovered striking. Like the dock labourers, the seamen were agitating against a piece of new legislation that was changing their conditions of employment – The Mercantile Marine Act – and which was to be the cause of seamen's strikes and protests all over the country in 1856. Before the strike was many days old, a striker found himself before the courts. Dennis Carrol, 'a conspicuous agitator', was had up for assault outside the sailors' home. 21 February 1851 saw a mass meeting of the port's seamen at the music hall in Bold Street. Captain Palmer was in the chair, and many captains expressed their hatred of the new bill. One such man proposed that the meeting see the bill as 'an attack on the rights and privileges of seamen, and an encroachment on the civil and religious liberty of the people of Great Britain and Ireland'. An attack was made upon the *Shipping Gazette* amid roars of support, and a letter from a seaman who described the seamen's home as the seamen's gaol was read to loud cheers from the crowd; a delegate from Shields spoke and a telegram from Gateshead was read out. With the cry of 'no surrender', the men resolved to stick to their guns. This was a national protest, and the Liverpool men had resolved to do their part in spreading the movement. About 300 of them arrived in Manchester to agitate, gain support, and collect as many contributions to the funds as possible. Most of them arrived in what was described as a large vessel by canal; the rest walked in line along the towpath. They all gathered at Hulme Church and then walked off in, with flags flying boldly and a band in front, to a mass meeting at the People's Institute, Heyrod Street. Many of the seamen were to subsequently sleep here, being unable to find rooms to accommodate them elsewhere. Around the town, placards appealing for support were posted, and leaflets were distributed. Huge crowds of people turned out to watch the Liverpool men march. This could not be tolerated by the local magistrate and Chief Constable Wills; he charged the men to stop all noise and take down the banners. With this done, they carried on to their meeting in orderly file. It had been done before the eyes of thousands to maintain their support among the public. Meanwhile, a further 400 seamen were rumoured to have left Liverpool for Manchester to reinforce the men already there.

By 22 March, Chief Constable Wills and his ilk were desperate to stop the highly successful collections being made. Wills ordered the seamen to give up the collections on pain of arrest for vagrancy. The reply of the men was borne on placards all over the town. The placard was signed by order of the sailors' committee, with J. Adams as secretary:

Citizens: Having received in statement from his worship the mayor to the effect that he could not permit any more subscription boxes for the sailors now on strike to be carried about after yesterday; therefore, the following resolution was passed at the sailors' home, or people's institute this morning, resolved that, under our present circumstances, we forego one of the two meals from this day and that we make an application to the sympathetic public of Manchester to stand by us in this our present struggle with the enemies of our country, and for the rights of man: and that subscription boxes be left at the various shop keepers and publicans and other places, some of whom have generously offered to take charge of the same for the purpose of receiving any contributions that the public may voluntarily give ... It is the intention of the sailors to stand out to a man in this struggle and we trust that, since the boxes are forbidden, that you will not forget us in the hour of trial. We are now 417 and have never had but two meals a day since we came here, but those were far better rations than double the rations at sea. We are truly thankful for the support we have received from the public last week, as well as the private subscriptions from the soldiers, to Saturday night amounting to £112 altogether.

On the Thursday following, fifty of the seamen marched to Ashton-under-Lyne and processed through the town. They held a public meeting at Councillor Grundy's music hall saloon. Charges of 1d or 2d entrance were made, the money being gained being passed to the strike fund.

One Year Later

In 1852, we see the re-engagement of the dock labourers in battle with the masters. The labourers at the south end timber docks went on strike. They demanded from the master stevedores that a uniform rate of wages be paid to all of them, namely 3s 6d for ordinary work and 5s for discharging from the ships hold. The result of this strike was a 99 per cent victory, with only one master resisting the claim.

After the timber workers, other porters took up the demand for a standard uniform rate, 3s 6d being the collective demand. A general meeting of the port's labourers was held at the concert hall, Lord Nelson Street. Its object was to explain the cause of the dispute with the masters. The porters at this time denied that their society was a trade union and claimed it was a simple, mutual benefit society. The complaint of the men was similar in character to that expressed by some miners under the 'butty system'. They claimed that the money paid on their behalf by the merchants was being plundered by the master stevedores who then passed on a lesser sum to the men. They demanded to receive 3s 6d per day, which in fact was paid per man to the contractors who never received it. A secondary issue was that of overtime, for which they were often not paid.

The men employed in discharging the steamers at the Clarence Dock harboured a special grievance, that being the system of employment by quarter of a day only, which kept large numbers of men running after the few jobs, while also cheating them of wages. There were 'short quarters' at evening time, from 6 to 8 a.m. was one quarter; most of the work was done in the 'long quarters' in the middle of the day. The strike caused a meeting of the agents, at which some thirty steam companies were represented. They agreed to pay 3s 6d per day and 4s per night, but only on condition that the men kept to the quarter system.

Near the end of November, the strike started to warm up, although most of the steam packet companies, with the exception of the Bristol, Waterford, and the Newry steam packets, had given way. A Large number of union men, or 'club men' as they were called in the press, were still out in support of a total victory. On 19 November, a non-union gang with a collection of other blacklegs went to unload the steamship the *Glendower*. When these men started work, the union porters came onto the dock quay unobserved by the scabs. While one man was on his knees passing stuff into the hold, he was suddenly thrown in head first, receiving a fractured skull and internal injuries. Another scab jumping off the ship to inform the police was struck in the face by a union man who forced him back onto the ship. Extra police were to be drafted in as a consequence.

The strikes of 1852 were piecemeal, with sections of dockers fighting their own respective battles. One year later, they had got themselves organised on a far wider and more effective front, and every ship in the port was to come to a standstill on 6 June 1853, as 5,000 porters and lumpers struck in support of a strike call made in the name of The Cotton Porters Association. A public meeting had been called some five days before the start of the strike, at which it was unanimously decided to strike on the following Monday. The union men were fighting for 4s a day as standard rate, and for this they had united the whole port. At first some sections declared they were satisfied with the 3s 6d won previously, but the pressure of the strike forced them to join in.

During the course of the strike, blacklegs once more took advantage of the shortage of labour, and as they took up the employment, tempers began to rise. As the dockers waited to unload a ship the *New World,* most of them, true to resolution, came forward and offered themselves at the union price of 4s One man however, a Mr Murphy, offered himself for 3s 6d. A union man named Finnigan whipped round, and with a shout of 'black sheep', stabbed him in the arm. When Finnigan was brought before the court, nobody would give evidence against him. Another similar incident at the time involved a 'black sheep's' wife. One evening, the wife of a dock labourer reported to be 'not a member of the society' was standing at her door when a cotton weigher, being in the same street, went up to her and asked if her husband was at work. She replied that he was. 'Ah,' retorted the weigher, 'A black sheep.' 'No,' she replied, he was not a black sheep, he was working for the usual 3s 6d and '[that's] pretty money'. The man then threatened to find someone to put her husband into the dock. He was subsequently apprehended under this information and was placed before the magistrate that morning. The facts having been proved,

Mr Mansfield said that it was evident the prisoner had done all in his power to intimidate the complainant and prevent him from following his lawful calling.' The most valuable possession of a working man in this country was the free disposition of his labour. With that right unimpaired he might raise himself to a higher position in society.'

The employers gathered up their forces, and at a meeting of all the commercial associations, decided not to employ any members of the union. In the meantime however, the port remained silent. By 11 June, many of the employers had given in, and the men were back at work in those places. In response to a series of resolutions against the union issued by the Liverpool Chamber of Commerce, the Cotton Porters Association published a resolution urging the men to stick out. But with more and more black sheep being introduced to the already crowded port, the strikers lost heart and the union had to yield its general claim. The *Liverpool Times* gloated on the employers victory, preaching the old maxim, 'No reasonable operative can expect that they [the employers] will be bullied by threats or forced to yield to the dictation of trade unions, which have ever proved injurious to the interests of all connected with them.'

The union did not disappear; it moved its offices from Union Street to Lamb's public house in Tithebarn Street, and declared that although it had given way this time, they were determined to conduct the strike again at a later stage. The newspapers treated this as mere bravado, but the following year saw a general strike movement in Liverpool with the dockers as its central component. In one month, joiners, ships' firemen, rail porters, and coopers came out.

General Strike

On Monday 8 May, a general strike spread across the waterfront. The rate of wages was still more or less at the old figure of 3s 6d per day. The dockers once more raised the demand for 4s per day and 7s for night work if the full shift was worked; if not, it should be paid at a rate of 7d per hour. They demanded extra weekend payments such as 8s for Sunday work. The men had chosen their time well, as the docks were full of work and the employers wanted the men back as quick as possible. The labourers' new society, the Dock Labourers Society, had extended its scope to take in a wider membership. It claimed 5,000 members, and called a strike meeting almost a week beforehand to give the employers a chance to concede to the demands. The strike call was very effective. Not more than a dozen vessels had enough hands to work on them. The ordinary labourers were joined by 450 extra hands working at the Albert Dock; even sections of the 'regular' hands came out with them. Many masters came forward to sign an agreement with them.

A meeting was held to give the masters a chance to concede, with Edward M'Mahon, the union chairman, presiding. Mr Murphy, the secretary, put the strike demands to the crowd, who expressed determination to stick out against the few masters who had not yet given way, while working for those who had. The dock labourer Murphy said he was helping keep everyone, even the King and Queen, out of his measly wages. Richard Burns, one of the leaders from the Albert Dock warehouses, took to the platform. He announced that his men were as good as any porters in the town and that they intended to organise a union like the Dock Labourers Association.

At the end of the meeting, it was announced that almost sixty masters had given in, meaning that by far the majority of the men had gained the increase. Only 200 men turned into the Albert Dock for work. The dock committee threatened that if the Albert's strike committee did not surrender, the goods would be removed from the Albert to another dock. A mass meeting was held of the labourers in front of the customs house, where they voiced their determination to continue the fight.

Hitherto the strike, and therefore the victory, had been largely of north end labourers. Seeing the success of the movement, the men at the south end turned out with the same demands. The masters however had learned their lesson and conceded completely.

At the Albert Dock, things were less successful, and the extra dock porters, 900 in all, were facing defeat. Vessels were leaving the Albert Dock to be discharged at other ports in greater and greater numbers. The employers were bringing in large numbers of Irish, and Scottish black sheep, and on 17 May, the men had to admit defeat. The victory of so many others had left them isolated.

Just one year later, the previously quiet Birkenhead men showed that they were not placid. Owing to heavy frost in March, nearly all outdoor work had been suspended at Birkenhead. The Coal heavers however had managed to retain 5s and 6s per day. The company of Messrs Laird decided to cut the rates, in keeping with others, to 4s per day and 6d per hour overtime. They sent to Liverpool for their master stevedore Edward Howard to hire men and load one of the ships. The men refused to work for such a reduction point blank, whereupon Howard returned to Liverpool and gathered a crew of fourteen heavers along with seventeen barrows and a winch. When he reached the Morpeth Dock with the intention of loading the ship, they were met by 150 Birkenhead men, 'Nearly all Irishmen.' The wage cutters and the master were driven back. Howard drew a revolver and threatened to shoot the striking coal heavers, but unafraid, they simply dropped out of range and let fly with a volley of stones. Severe wounds were inflicted, especially upon the master. The Liverpool men were driven back to the ferry, abandoning some of the barrows, which were quickly seized and thrown into the river after the retreating ferry. A body of police were drafted to the ship, but these Liverpool men were not called on again.

The Birkenhead coal heavers asserted that they would not allow anyone who was not a member of their society to work ships. A similar struggle for the closed shop seems to have been going on on the Liverpool side. In 1855, the local newspapers were full of complaints about workmen intimidating non-unionists. In 1855, Peter Brady, a dock labourer, was charged that he, along with twenty others, threatened men employed by a stevedore on the ship the *Woodman*, which was lying in the Queens Dock. 'A number of men unlawfully usurped the right and power of dictating to others how they should dispose of their labours, and combined to prevent others from labouring at all unless they agreed to the wicked rules laid down by lawless men.' Peter Brady received three months hard labour for being such a wicked fellow. Further proof of the active life of the union came on April of that year when the South End Dock Labourers Society held a public meeting at the concert hall, Nelson Street, to propagate their society; the meeting was well attended. Another section, although one that emerges little during this history, makes an appearance one month later when the Woodside ferrymen staged a wildcat. The strike was a response to a reduction in wages of some 2s per week. The men manning the *Monks Ferry* joined in sympathy, and in just over an hour the reduction was withdrawn. The strike of such a small and apparently unimportant section such as the ferrymen shows the high degree of collective consciousness that existed at this period, which was clearly passing from one section to another.

In 1862, the 'Lancashire cotton famine' arrived, caused by the total suspension of the cotton trade, which Lancashire and much of Liverpool had depended upon; a consequence of the American Civil War. The northern forces had shut off all trade to and from the Confederate States. The desperate plight of much of the working population had sparked a major riot at Stalybridge and smaller ones across the country. A massive relief effort by the state probably forestalled widespread hunger riots.

The General Strike of 1866

The first signs of the unrest that was to break out in 1866 came when the cotton porters, late in 1865, put forward a parity claim to bring their wages into line with the other dockers. These workers had not in fact joined in the earlier strikes, and as such found their wages of 3s 6d per day well below the rates paid to the Dock Labourers Society members.

The year broke early with a wave of strikes in widely different sections of the Liverpool working class. Highly sectionalised and skilled workers were seen striking in and around the same months as the very lowest categories of workers in the docks. This was perhaps best characterised by the strike of the 'night soil men', the workers who cleared away and dumped the human effluent from the densely populated quarters. They went out for an increase from £1 and 24s to 30s per week. The highly specialised sail makers and carters struck a little later. These sail makers, who had been unionised for some time, had been asked to accept a reduction in wages, and an alteration of their practice with regard to the number of apprentices taken on by the employers. The workers refused the reduction of what would have been 12s per week. The carters had struck for an increase in wages that had not in fact been specified in the press of the period. These strikes, coming from broad areas both highly and lowly rated, were symptomatic of the period to follow.

The coal heavers, whom we saw earlier were a tight-knit body, were found on strike at the same time as the night soil men. These particular heavers worked on the Leeds and Liverpool canal, and were demanding that they should receive 7s per day instead of their customary 'drink money'. In a short time, they were to be successful.

On 23 April, the lumpers, the men engaged in loading and discharging cargo, struck for an increase in their wages, as did the shipmen at the Wapping Dock. The South End Dock Labourers were busy formulating a whole programme of wage demands, and so one after another, and very often at the same time, whole areas of workers started mobilising. These sectors, although independent from each other, were highly affiliated, both in obvious class terms, and in simple physical and social terms.

The lumpers, who had previously been receiving 4s per day, the rate they had won in 1854, struck for an extra 1s a day with 9d overtime and 10d extra on night shift. The first out had been the men of the Princes Dock, from where it spread rapidly southwards along the more militant areas. The shipmen, who had been a lower paid section, turned out for rise from 3s 6d to 4s per day, thus keeping their proximity of earnings with the other labourers' demands.

That evening, a meeting of the South End Dock Labourers Association was convened to formalise the demands of the workers. The meeting was packed to capacity and several hundred dockers waited around outside Toxteth Hall, Mill Street, being unable to get inside to the gathering. One of their leaders, John McClarery, presented the demands:

Advance of 1s per day on the present rate of wages
1d per hour on overtime from 6 p.m. to 6 a.m.
2d per 100 sacks of salt.
2d per ton of ballast.
1s 4d per 100 tonnes of coal
1s per day to a leading man in the hold of a timber or cotton ship.
1s per day to stevedores.

All labourers to have an hour break for breakfast and leave work on Saturdays at five o'clock.

The suggestion of five o'clock seems to have been a misjudgement that incited the crowd. 'Four o'clock! Four o'clock' was chanted again and again throughout the hall. The chairman tried to restore order and pleaded that the weight and numbers of cargoes would necessitate the employers engaging more men if the afternoon was so short, thus endangering the jobs of the workers already employed. His words fell on deaf ears and the crowd restarted the chant of 'four o'clock! Four o'clock!' At length, the motion was amended to include four o'clock on Saturday. At this stage, several employers went forward to sign the demands.

Mr Gregory, secretary of the North End Dock Labourers Association, took the platform, and after extending his fraternal greetings to the body, he went on to speak about the various differences between the two associations. He spoke of the advanced nature of the demands and the militancy of the South End Dock Labourers Association, and how they were in advance of his own association. He called upon all workers to stand by the meaning of the resolutions they had just passed. The crowds stood packed to the doors throughout the course of the meeting.

By 26 April, it is becomes clear that the south end men had won and the strike was spreading. The shipmen of the Wapping Dock struck for an increase of 6d on their 3s 6d rate, which they had failed to secure in their last strike. They were followed on the Friday by the shipmen at the Albert Dock – another group of men working in an enclosed dock and directly employed by the Mersey Docks and Harbour Board. On the same day there was an interesting extension of the overall movement with the railway porters engaged at the Great Howard Street and North Dock's Merchandise Station of the Lancashire and Yorkshire Railway Company, i.e., the railway station directly serving the docks. The men had previously been receiving 3s 6d per day, which was a total of thirteen hours. They entire body of porters struck for an advance of wages and a reduction of hours. They were now demanding 4s per day at twelve hours, from 6 a.m. until 6 p.m., and 6d per hour after that time; also they should leave work at 4 p.m. on a Saturday, and if requested to work after that time, they should be paid at a rate of 6d per hour. The strike was a wildcat, and took immediate effect. All of the yards where the goods were loaded, as well as the whole of Great Howard Street, Oldhall Street, and the other minor streets in the vicinity, were entirely blocked with large wagons and carts, some top-heavy with cotton waiting to be loaded and unloaded. The action of the porters threw the managers and owners into the utmost confusion, and they gave away almost immediately to the men's demands. The men started work at three o'clock after being out for only a few hours. It was soon announced that the London and Western Rail Company's porters were also intending to strike for wage increases like those of the Lancashire and Yorkshire Railway unless it was to be offered to them without recourse to strike.

Men in the skilled trades were also sensing their advantages. On Thursday 26 April, the Liverpool house joiners met and determined to strike on 1 May unless their employers came forward with a 3s rise to bring them from 28s to 31s in conformance with the association's rules.

The saddlers and bricklayers held meetings on that Thursday too, announcing *their* intention to strike in support of wage claims in a few days' time. In fact, other groups of workers wishing to hold strike meetings may have found the search for vacant venues quite difficult given the range of work groups holding such meetings.

Next came the Liverpool foundry workers. One of the largest iron works in Liverpool, the Mersey Iron Works, were already solidly out. Other groups of skilled workers were being affected by the growing spirit of combativity rife in the port. The operative bakers of the town were out in an attempt to reduce their hours of work to twelve per day. Around the central ring of their open air meeting stood members of the union committee bearing wooden peels (used to extract bread from ovens, each carrying a motto of their trade).

On 1 May, the workers of the North End Dock Labourers Association struck work for a pay and hours deal the same as their south end counterparts. However, the example set by the south end dockers had been sufficient enough to assure the northern master stevedores that resistance may be a good idea; they conceded to the demands straight away. They seemed to have developed a similar intention to pass on the wage rise to the merchants. The masters however were not simply rolling over. Indeed, the north end and south end masters associations called a joint meeting at the Clarendon Rooms with the view of merging their two societies. The topics of debate were not disclosed, but one can imagine that ways and means of passing on any future wage awards to the merchants and strategies to combat the high tide of unionism in the port were high on the agenda. At its conclusion, the meeting had produced a common scale of charges and loads to be presented to the merchants.

Next came the seamen, holding the first of their meetings on Friday 4 May at Mr Leatherbarrows', Regent Street. This meeting was to formulate a Seamen's Association and put forward an advance of wages. The meeting was crowded and the reasonably sized hall had been unable to hold all the seafarers who had turned up. Mr McGregor explained the objects of the meeting and suggested the course of proceedings. Speeches were then given in support of the formation of a union, and it was subsequently agreed that the society be formed, and that it be called the Liverpool Seamen's Protective Society. Mr Matthew Callaghan was elected president and Mr William Chase the secretary; a committee was also appointed. The subject of wages was next considered, and a resolution was put forward announcing that since the cost of the bare necessities of life had risen beyond the scope of the seamen and that they could no longer support themselves or their families, the wages be advanced to the following extent:

Instead of £4 per month, a rise to £5 per month for New York, Boston, Philadelphia, and the Gulf of St Lawrence.

Instead of £3 per month, a rise to £4 per month for voyages to the Mediterranean and ports south of New Orleans.

5s per day for shore work, instead of 4s now paid, and 8d per hour overtime.

Prior to this demand, no remuneration was given for overtime. One speaker stated that he had known seamen kept at work the whole night on the shore and received nothing for it. The meeting demanded that the merchants and shipowners should concede the advance requested, and that it should come into effect at once. This was met with unanimous approval of the meeting. After many impassioned speeches, the meeting concluded with large numbers of seafarers coming forward to join the union.

8 May dawned to another crowded seamen's meeting, to which merchants and others directly or indirectly involved in the welfare of seamen were invited. The meeting was held at the Alexandra Assembly Rooms, Duke Street, and the purpose of the meeting was to consider new rules for the recently formed Seamen's Protective Society, and also to hear further statements of reference to the claim for an advance of wages. In some papers, Mr J. Kavanagh, a boarding house keeper who had been a seaman himself for many years, was voted to the chair. It is not uncommon for seamen of this period to put such men into office as a block on blacklisting and victimisation. This particular man, Mr J. Kavanagh, had been the chief agitator and strike leader of the great seamen's strike in the city of London earlier in 1851. After internal matters of finance, benefits, and rules were discussed, they progressed to the question of their wage demand. Mr Baldwin stated that the seamen of the south end had complained that at the recent meeting, an increase scale of wages had not been proposed for sailing vessels. This matter was then discussed, and arising from this, it was decided to press for increases for sailing vessels crews, these being £3 per month for voyages round either Capes; £3 10s per month on this side of the Capes, including the Mediterranean, with the exception of what was known as the Western Ocean trade, which was to be £4 10s per month with no advance, and £4 per month with half a month's advance. The rate of pay for voyages in steamships engaged in the western ocean trade was to

be £5 per month, no advance; to all ports south of New Orleans and in the Mediterranean, £4 per month. All steamers lying in port, including tug boats, 30s per week, not including Sunday. If employed on Sundays, men were to receive 5s. Men belonging to any vessel along the line of docks to receive 5s per day and 8d per hour overtime. The scale of prices was unanimously agreed to.

The meeting was next addressed by several seamen and boarding house keepers. Mr Campbell, a boarding house keeper, said that all of the many boarding house keepers in the room would stick with the seamen through thick and thin. He went on to say that the only way of winning would be to keep away from ships, and that since the ships had to be manned, if the men refused to go in them at the present rates the demand would have to be conceded. The system of crimping and dumping non-seamen on ships to pass off as experienced men was attacked; a seaman told of how he knew a notorious boarding house keeper who kept a capstan in his house on which to practice completely inexperienced men. Mr John Collins, another boarding house keeper, said he would do all in his power to collect subscriptions from boarding house keepers, publicans, outfitters, and others, and further to that, he would start it off with a subscription of £5 from himself.

On 9 May, the movement spread to another group of workers closely connected to the waterfront – the women cotton pickers. The task of these (mostly young) women was an arduous and boring one, comprising of picking out soiled sections and foreign bodies such as seeds, spelks, etc. from the freshly arrived cotton. For this they were paid 1s 2d per day or else 7s per week working a twelve hour day. They had struck in furtherance of a demand for either a 4d per day or 2s per week rise. Gangs of girls, 'bonnet-less and bared armed', went from factory to factory calling out their sisters; very few stayed at work. The women showed a great maturity of strategy by striking at this time, which was soon after several cotton fires when their labour was badly needed by the employers to salvage the undamaged from the damaged cotton. By Saturday 12 May, the cotton pickers had won their demands and returned to work almost in every case.

The strikes continued to spread. The coopers were asking for an increase of 6d per day; the tailors who had been on strike had won their advance of 1s 2d per hour. Meanwhile, cooks and stewards in the mercantile marine service were agitating for increases in keeping with the general labour movement.

On Friday 11 May, another overflowing meeting called by the Seamen's Protective Society had accepted the earlier suggestion of not going near another ship until the new rates were met. This meeting was held at the Alexandra Assembly Rooms, Duke Street, in connection with the pay claim. Mr J. Kavanagh, being the chairman, announced that it was proposed to initiate friendly benefits for the Society's members. These benefits would provide for shipwrecked seamen when they returned home, to recompense them their loss of clothing, wages etc. He gave examples from the north of England where such funds were already flourishing and kept up by the weekly contributions of 6d each member. If a sailor was shipwrecked and lost all his goods, he received 7s. If he lost his life, his widow received £10. This fund would also help seamen and their families in cases of sickness. It was joyously heard in a statement from Mr Campbell that the seamen in London had demanded an advance of wages in consequence of the example set by the seamen of Liverpool. Subsequently, they voted to continue the strike against all companies who refused to pay the wage rate worked out by the union. It is perhaps worth mentioning that several of the companies had in fact conceded and were paying the rate demanded, and the ships of these companies were accordingly untouched.

Another section of seamen now came out: the stokers and firemen. This section was obviously not included in the general seamen's Society, feeling themselves and their conditions too individual and different to be swallowed up in a union of general character. The terms of their demands were laid before the eyes of the shipowners and merchant to add to the other reading materials received from the Seamen's Protective Society. The strikers and firemen then joined their brother seamen in 'hanging around the dock', which was one way of watching the ships and developments, and also a means of being available if and when the employers were to concede.

On 15 May, the stokers and firemen formed a society. This, like that of the seamen, had listed its objectives as being to raise the scale of wages and provide for its members and their families certain support in cases of sickness or accident. The society was to be called Liverpool Mercantile Marine Stokers United Friendly Society. At their meeting, which was held at North Store Vaults, Boundary Street, Vauxhall Road, Mr James King presided and presented the proposed rules to the meeting, all of which were duly accepted. The secretary Mr Michael Clare stated that they had made a good start with membership, it being 500 strong with more and more joining each day. The stokers, once more like the seamen, had special rule books and membership cards printed, and resolved never to go to sea with a man without a union card. Thus, we see the duel effect; on one hand protecting the trade and their jobs from unskilled outsiders and blacklegs, and on the other hand, of increasing the bargaining strength of the union by taking 100 per cent control of the labour force.

In many respects, the firemen and ships' coal trimmers were different from normal seamen. They were more of the 'floating proletarian'. Their job was shovelling coal into a furnace or stowing and re-trimming coal aboard the vessel, not clambering up rigging or stamping round the capstan. Frank Bullen gives an excellent description of their work:

It must however be remembered that pitching coal into the furnace, though it is the principle work of the firemen, does not by any means complete his work. After he has been 'firing' for a certain length of time, he perceives the necessity for 'cleaning fires'. He has been carefully raking and poking his fires at intervals so that no clogging of the bars shall hinder the free upward draught, and this operation, performed with long tools called a slice, a rake, and devil, is very severe. The operator must stand very close to the furnace mouth and peer within at the ferment glow, while he searches the vitals of his fire as quickly and deftly as may be, lest the tell-tale gauge shall reveal to the watching engineer that the pressure of steam is lessening, bringing him to the stokehold on the run to know what the 'all-sorts-of-unprintable-words' that particular fireman is doing. But this is only the merest child's play to cleaning the furnace or furnaces. (Each fireman has two or three under his charge and must be at the top of their blast, doing their very utmost.) Then the fireman flings wide the door of the furnace to be cleaned, plunges his tools into the heart of the fire, and thrusts, rakes, and slices until he presently, half roasted, drags out to the stokehold floor a mass of clinker. This sends out such a fierce upward heat that it must needs be damped down, the process being accompanied by clouds of suffocating smoke. But there is no time to be lost. Again and again he dives into the heart of the furnace, each time purging it of some of the deadening clinker, until at last with smarting eyeballs, half choked, half roasted, and wholly exhausted for the time, he flings a shovelful or so of coal upon the now comparatively feeble fire, and returns to call up his reserve of strength.

The providing of coal for the use of the fireman is the duty of the 'trimmer', the nature of whose work is so terrible that he should receive the sympathy of every kindly man and women who he serves. The coal is kept in vast magazines called bunkers, giving on to the stokeholds by means of watertight doors. In merchant ships, these bunkers are placed so as to be most convenient for the transmission of coal to the stokehold, and are as little subdivided as possible. What their capacity is may be imagined from the fact that some ships require 3,000 tons of coal for a single passage, it being consumed at the rate of between 20 to 30 tons per hour! At the commencement of the passage, the trimmer's work is comparatively easy. The coal lies near the outlet, and by a little skilful manipulation, it is made to run out upon the stokehold floor, handy for the fireman's shovelling. But as the consumption goes on, and the 'face' of the coal recedes from the bulkhead, the trimmer's work grows rapidly more heavy. His labour knows no respite as he struggles to meet the fireman's needs. In addition, there is no ventilator pouring down fresh air into the bunker. In darkness, only punctuated by the dim light of a safety

Between the decks on an emigrant ship. *Illustrated London News,* 17 August 1850.

lamp, in an atmosphere composed of the exhalations from the coal and a modicum of dust-laden air, liable any moment to be overwhelmed by the down-rushing masses of coal as the ship's motion displaces it, the grimy, sweat-soaked man works on.

By 1874, it was such work that had become the forte of the Arab seamen in other ports. Richard Lawless tells us their recruitment 'was certainly well-established', probably because it was thought that they were more adept at handling the extremes of heat, though more likely because of their sobriety, they were less likely to staunch their desperate thirsts with mass quantities of beer and jump ship, or not turn up for sailing.

On 17 May, many of the shipowners, rather than give way to the Seamen's Protective Society, ceased running their vessels. The truth was that the shipowners could not get enough men to man the ships, and the non-society men who had volunteered to work at the lower wage were simply being paid to do nothing, as the owners vainly waited for a sufficient crew of regular seamen to materialise. Mass meetings for business and agitation were being conducted everywhere, most of time by the seamen. One such meeting on 16 May was called with the sole intention of refuting some of the 'foul attacks' made in the press against the strike leaders and the society. Mr Kavanagh pointed out that the strike in London in 1851 (and in Liverpool) was not for wages as had been stated, but was against the Mercantile Marine Act. Mr Kavanagh was one of the deputation who went to see the president of the Board of Trade, who had then withdrawn the harmful clauses, giving the seamen a complete victory. He also went on to defend the boarding house masters; the real crimps, he stated, were the missionaries sent on board ships, the river police, and the dock gatemen, all of whom recruited for the sailors' home. It had also come to light that the sailors' home had runners recruited for them, and men who went in for haircuts were being charged 1s for washing their hair with a drop of dirty water, and on top of that sold such things as watches and chains for £2 10s when their actual cost was 15s or so. The meeting was also to hear reports that in a few districts, fighting had broken out between union and non-union seamen who were trying to obtain work below the union rates. The chairman called upon all members to restrain from violence and to conduct themselves peaceably. Another crowded seamen's meeting took place on the 19 May at the Albion Hall, School Lane, the use of which was permitted by the sympathetic owner without charge. The largest employer of the men still refused to concede to the men's demands. In order to get his vessels to sea, Liverpool being solidly out, he had sent for men from London to crew the ships. A crew had been in fact obtained, but on arriving in Liverpool and discovering that the men were out on strike, they all refused to man the vessels. On hearing this, loud cheers echoed again and again around the room. It was proposed that in view of this great action of solidarity, these London seamen would be well treated and taken in while they remained in Liverpool, and that their passage back home be paid for. This was unanimously agreed to.

The sectional build-up of the strike movement continued to grow. The coal heavers from Birkenhead, now following the example of their Lancashire brethren, put an ultimatum to their employers, demanding a rate of 5s per day and 8s per night. Then came the provision porters. 21 May saw a huge meeting of provision porters of Liverpool. It was held in the Norfolk Arms, Vernan Street, with a Mr Patrick Devlin in the chair.

After some discussion, it was agreed that a society be formed under the name 'Liverpool Provision Porters Association', and that the body would function on behalf of mutual protection. One of the basic objects was to achieve 'a closed shop' as it came to be called, and to this end, it was decided that all union members receive a card and would not work alongside any man who did not also possess one. Mr Devlin was elected chairman and Mr T. Deece the secretary.

West Salthouse with Wapping Basin beyond.

The very same day as the provision porters were meeting, another meeting was in progress at the North Shore Vaults, Boundary Street, namely the Liverpool Marine Stokers Friendly Society. The meeting was told that due to militant action, 400 of the Society's members were now working at the union rate. It was proposed that recognising this, all Society members who were working should contribute 3s per week to those on strike. The resolution was accepted without a single hand raised in protest. The meeting was then addressed by the secretary Mr M. Clare, who once more pointed out that it was only the biggest employer, a Mr MacIver, who was holding out against the men. Mr MacIver hated unionism with a passion. The stokers had told him that even if they did not get another ship for years, or that their hands never touched another stoker's shovel, they would not be broken by him. The society had 820 members, with more joining. It could raise more than £1,000 any time it wished. Apart from this, the coal heavers' and lumpers' societies were offering support in their struggle.

By the end of May and beginning of June, many workers, seamen especially, had been out for some time. Blacklegs were being introduced and the strikers could see little sign of surrender on the owners' part at that stage. Tempers were becoming frayed, as many dissident forces, which would have included all the Albert Dock workers who had been locked out, drifted about in close proximity to the owners, the blacklegs, and their jobs. Not surprisingly, we get the first cases of violence being reported in the press. At the sailors' home, a scab crew was signed on to sail the *Spirit of the Age*, which was ready to sail to South America. The wages of the port had been £2 15s, at which price the scabs signed on. One of them, on setting foot into the street, was set upon by union men. John Connor, a union man, 'knocked him down and kicked him, pulled a considerable quantity of hair from his head, and kicked him upon his nose, and knocked skin off it'.

At the same time, the lumpers and stevedores were far from happy with the similar introduction of blacklegs to do their work. A union man named William Connell was working at the union rate at the Princes Dock on board a vessel called *Sarah Ann*. Working in the next ship to him was a non-unionist, who seems to have been working below the union rate. All day, the union man insulted the scab, until in the afternoon, a group of men on strike came along the dock and joined the abuse. Connell threatened to pitch the hapless blackleg into the dock, and for this he was charged with intimidation and bound over in order to keep the peace.

The entrance to Princes Dock at half-tide, with the Dock offices and dockmaster's residence.

A day later, another case appeared before the eyes of the Liverpool public. A lumper called John Dunn for assault on Myles and John Murphy, who had been trying to get work at the old, non-union rate. They had been met by a force of about fifty pickets. Mr Dunn had tried to dissuade them by trying to throw one in the dock and hitting the other. He was sentenced to two years hard labour.

Set against this sort of background, and with similar cases being reported from elsewhere, the strange occurrence of a big fire in the town was the excuse for much speculation. At 11 p.m. on Wednesday 30 May, a big fire broke out in the large range of warehouses in Fulton Street. The fire was very severe, with flames bursting through the roof and windows, demolishing the roof in a matter of minutes. An army of police and firemen fought the blaze, but it was not extinguished until 770 bales of cotton in two rooms had been destroyed. Large stores of flour and grain also went merrily up in smoke. The great frequency of these warehouse fires, and their suddenness and intensity, strongly suggested the work of arsonists. The press in turn blamed the Fenians, the strikers, then all the strikes *and* all the fires on the Fenians, or if not, at least some of the strikes and some of the fires.

The strike of 1866 more or less secured a bench mark of 4s per day for quay porters with the added 6d per day for stevedores. However by 1870, the labourers had added 6d to their day wage too. This was illustrated in the action on the Nelson Dock in November of that year. That action was led by the previously unreported Steamboat Labourers Friendly Burial Society; a body that clearly acted in the role of a union choose what its name suggested. This union had been the principle body in negotiating the extra 6d per day in October, apparently along the entire length of docks. The union was in action in November because of the 'dishonest and untrustworthy nature' of new hands on the Nelson dock. This is usually code for 'non-union dockers', and would suggest the strike was to enforce the close shop and maintain their bargaining position. Taplin comments, 'The increase was, nevertheless, confined to dock labourers employed by master stevedore porters and the shipping firms. Other waterfront workers, such as cotton porters, surprisingly remained at the old rate until 1872.'

The Nine Hours Movement, which reached its crescendo in Newcastle-upon-Tyne with the strike of the engineers, became a fast-spreading, nationwide cause, rapidly spreading through cities and towns. The Nine Hours Movement ended on Tyneside in October 1871. Weeks later, the railway men of Liverpool were holding mass rallies to secure the 'nine hours day'. The engineering masters in both Liverpool and Birkenhead more or less conceded to the demand by the end of that year or the beginning of the next.

Unloading a cargo of meat.

1872: The Spirit of the Union

The events occurring on the Liverpool waterfront can be seen as part of the continuing collective struggle of the Port's labour and also as a part of a general movement that spread across the country. Large sections of the working class, particularly those with unions, but also those without them, felt themselves to be in a period of advance, when it would be possible to push forward their living standards. In many ways, the period was of equal importance to the great period of working class advance that was to occur later in 1911; an advance that gave victories to dozens of different trades. A successful strike by dockers in Southampton or Hull for example, will strike sparks of militancy in dockers all over the country, and this will be readily seen. What is perhaps less easy to grasp is the fact that a victorious strike by fruit pickers in Somerset or agricultural workers in Warwick would lead totally unconnected workers in far distant regions to strike also. There was a growth of a common *class* identity that transcended *trade*. The Liverpool strikes of 1872 were but a microcosm of the developing national situation. *The Beehive,* a trade union paper of the period, reported:

> The spirit of the unionism is taking possession of all sorts of employed persons; carters, man-servants, and maid-servants among the rest. The 'domestics' of Dundee have set an example that is sure to spread southwards. In many respects no doubt, a service in families is very comfortable, and it is paid ... wages. But a large portion of man-servants are subjected to an endless drudgery little removed from slavery. The man-servants who met at Leamington to discuss their grievances were told by their chairman that their condition is 'even worse than that of slaves'. 'They have formed a union to comprise of butlers and footmen, coachmen and grooms, gardeners and porters. The carters of Liverpool are on strike to the number of 2,000 for increased wages, shorter hours, and extra pay for overtime. It is calculated that the strike has put a stop to the work of 5,000 dock labourers. Many of the masters are described as driving their own teams in their silk hats and kid gloves. A collision has occurred between the men on strike and those at work. A scheme to fill the vacant places by means of men from Warwickshire seems to have utterly failed.

General unrest on the British waterfront and seaways was rife that year. In March, the Hull Dock Labourers Association was the catalyst of a general strike in that port following a resolution put to the Hull steamship owners demanding an increase in wages to 5s per day. They demanded that their labours be from 6 a.m. to 6 p.m. with two hours for meal breaks. The hours after 6 p.m. until midnight were to be counted as a full day's work. A short time later, the seamen at the port of Southampton struck for various increases, particularly the men employed by the famous P&O line. In May, Liverpool saw the simultaneous strikes of many port workers. A very unusual and colourful strike took place on 4 May. The strike was that of the Wallasey steam ferry men, who were, it appears, subcontractors to the port's ferry manager. They claimed that they were overworked and needed shorter hours, that their boats were in bad shape, and they required greater assistance in maintaining them. To reinforce their point, they held a highly colourful demonstration. Early in the morning, the entire steam service of Wallasey sailed off in procession to meet the manager. They wound their way to the pier head at Egrement, passing slowly down the river from the Birkenhead Graving Docks. It took up the following order: *The Heather Bell, Wild Rose, Water Lily, James Atherton, May Flower, Thomas Wilson,* and *The Gem.* After the manager had promised to try and shift his fellow board members into action to get the men an additional boat, the procession made off in a great stream of smoke.

That same day, news came that the carters had won a great victory. Some 3,000 of them had struck work in support of a claim for 29s per week with 6d overtime after 13 hours work per day. The strike had lasted for some time. Mr Simpson had acted in the role of men's adviser and representative. He had called on them to accept the master's terms. They point blank refused this, but agreed to stand by the result of an arbitration, which as it turned out declared in their favour.

The bus workers, drivers of the horse-drawn omnibus and tramway system, next joined the action. These were in the hands of two firms, The Liverpool Road & Railway Omnibus Company and the Liverpool Tramways Company. Both were described as 'tyrannical employers'. Men worked seven days per week with hours of up to seventeen per day. They suffered low pay and were subject to stringent company rules and a system of fines together with rapid dismissals, as well as prosecution before the courts. More than 1,000 men were employed over the two companies. In April, a petition was presented to the employers for a reduction of hours and an increase in wages. It was ignored, and a mass meeting of the men was presided over by Mr William Simpson. The Tramways Company, seeing the sound argument of Mr Simpson together with the threat of strike action, conceded to the demands. The Omnibus Company was more stubborn, and on 22 July, the workers struck. The company responded with blackleg labour. With Simpson's renewed efforts, they agreed a compromise to call off the strike. Drivers' wages were increased from 28s per week to 32s per week, with either one day off per month or two half days instead of the 35s per week. Stablemen were to receive 2s a horse per day, but a ten-stall stableman's pay of one guinea per week was to remain unchanged, but with improved promotion opportunities. The poor, old guards however were to receive no increase and to remain on 17s to 24s per week according to grades. When put to a mass meeting of the men, the workers accepted, and even the guard's representative urged acceptance of their standstill, for it marked an improvement for all the others and therefore should not be jeopardised.

Mr Simpson was in fact a man of great stature among the labouring class of the port. He was often called upon to act as go-between in industrial disputes. Despite his earlier advice to the carters, his aura swelled with their victory. So it is that in the early stages of the cotton porters' renewed agitation, he features yet again in a mediating role.

In May, a union under the name of the Cotton Porters Association was formed with the guidance of Mr Simpson. 6,000 porters rapidly registered as members of the Union. On 20 June, a mass meeting of cotton porters was held in Footit's Circus, William Brown Street. With Simpson in the chair, they demanded an advance of 6d a day. Simpson told the porters of the evils entailed by strikes, and said that even if they considered strike just now, they were in no position themselves to use it. After receiving an indication that the men had no intention of going on strike, he agreed to represent them. It was agreed that copies of their demands be issued to the provision merchants and brokers, and to give the masters a further week's consideration of their demands. Strike action it seemed, was still on the agenda.

The next day, a meeting of porters packed the hall to some 4,000 capacity. Simpson told workers that because the merchants were in an association and their chairman was away, they could not give a straight answer as to the wage claim at that time. He had been told by many individual merchants that they were prepared to concede, and the general view was the same. In the light of these facts, he asked what they were going to do? Cries of 'strike! Strike!' and 'No, no, no!' answered. His suggestion of giving the masters one week before a strike was accepted.

The Liverpool Seamen's Union, based mainly at the south end, were agitating about wages, the sailors' home, and non-sailors shipping on vessels. Taplin suggests that seamen's terms and conditions were improving to the point that they were not heavily involved with the general unrest:

Board of Trade statistics on seamen's wages show that wage rates rose throughout the country in June 1872 for men in both sailing and Steamships. Seamen in sailing ships enjoyed increases of about 10s a month (their income varying from £3 to £4 10s per month according to destination, while seamen on Steamships secured smaller increases of about 5s per month (their incomes remained marginally above those in sailing ships.

Carters on a quiet day near the exchange and Customs House.

Liverpool dock gatemen were also up in arms for an increase in wages, again under the guidance of none other than Mr Simpson, who was clearly something of a one man arbitration service. Again no strike was to be engendered, and their first meeting duly ended with three cheers for the Queen. A petition was presented on their behalf to the dock board.

Meanwhile, a brief and confusing strike took place among the dock porters and stevedores employed by MacIver. The men stated that the wages they received were 4s 6d per day, while other firms paid their men 5s per day; they wished for the same. The Cunard Line had never paid its men on a daily basis, but always at a weekly rate. Most of the men, so it was stated, received 27s per week with overtime, but had the benefit of permanent employment rather than the casual, daily basis operated elsewhere. Basically, the men seemed to be asking for the abolition of the permanent system and a return to a casual daily system of employment. A compromise was reached, which resulted in the retention of the permanent weekly employment, but with a rise to 7s per day – the men having benefited from the best of both worlds. Despite the strangeness of the demands to modern eyes, workers during this period felt well satisfied that they had returned to work victorious.

On 20 June, the commercial saleroom on Victoria Street saw a mass meeting of the provisional porters convened in order to formulate rates for a new wage demand. 4s 6d per day for ordinary porters and 5s for weighers, 'bottom room men, and those on various duties'.

By 25 June, the dock gatemen had accepted an offer made to them by the board. Terms of the offer were a bit vague, but clearly the men themselves felt well satisfied, leaving only smaller points of superannuation yet to be worked out.

The grain porters, workers of the Waterloo Dock warehouses, struck in support of their claim despite their earlier resolve not to. They presented themselves for work, demanding the increased rate. Upon being refused, they struck, but then called upon the hard-pressed town philanthropist Mr Simpson to mediate on their behalf. He met them at the Waterloo Quay, and after some discussion, they agreed to abide by his advice whatever it might be, and to return to work at the old rates while he went into negotiations. All hands agreed to this procedure, but in fact nobody went back to work. Instead, they held another meeting in Oil Street and passed a different resolution that they would not return to work until their demands had been complied with. A notice was posted at places of employment:

> To the working men of the port of Liverpool: we the porters, shipmen, and others connected with and following the employment of the Waterloo Grain Dock, beg most respectfully to inform you that we are now on strike for an increase of 6d per day on our daily pay, from 4s per day to 4/6d, and from 6d per hour to 7d per hour for overtime. We trust you will give us your support and comply with our wishes by not working for less wages than the above named, and oblige.
>
> Yours respectfully,
> the working men of the Waterloo Grain Dock.

A joint meeting of the provision merchants and brokers sat to decide upon the demands of their men. After long discussions, they passed a resolution to the effect that 25s be paid to ordinary porters for six days work, they were to work from 7 a.m. Until 12 p.m., and 1 p.m. until 6 p.m., except Saturdays when they were to knock off at 5 p.m. The men's delegates, on being made the offer, declined to accept anything less than 4s 6d per day for ordinary labour and 5s for weight-takers, adding that the general feeling amongst them was for daily instead of weekly employment. At first sight this again may appear strange, since it seems to reject regular weekly employment. However, at key months in the year, labour was at a premium, as ships were coming in on every tide, demanding unloading and a fast turnaround. Thus, various docks often upped the price of labour to draw away dockers from other docks, and the men wanted to leave that option open for themselves while increasing the overall price of their trade. The men held a mass open air meeting in Victoria Street and agreed to strike against all but Davies and Gee Warren & Co. who had conceded.

Meanwhile, unrest on the Birkenhead side was building with a mass meeting of unskilled labourers from the engineering works, the sawmills, the shipwright yards, boilermakers, dock labourers, and gas workers. These were meeting at Queens Hall, Claughton Road. We often see trade unions criticised from the left for their traditional advancement of purely sectional interests. However, we see in this example from the early years of the mass unions of labouring men a universal identification, one with the other. A clear class identity that transcends trade or skill identity. It is clear to me that in this period and almost certainly in the preceding century, workers saw themselves as organised in sections of the same general movement. Simpson, striking up a more militant stance at this meeting, had urged the men to strike together rather than one group at a time. He went on to urge each branch to form a committee, and from each committee a delegate be elected to form a centre.

'He hoped that they would not strike until every honest and fair means had been tried, but if reason failed, rather than submit the neck to be trod upon, he would be the first to say that every man, skilled and unskilled, should go on strike. (Immense cheering).' A delegation would go forward to meet the employers. On 28 June, it was reported that eighteen of the provision porters employers had conceded to the men's terms. On 4 July, a strike meeting of the warehouse porters of the Mersey Docks and Harbour Board were held on the west side of the Georges Dock. Mr Simpson addressed them. He advised them to go to work while he negotiated for them. This they refused, and by and by, a large majority decided to hold out and not work for less than 4s 6d per day.

Liverpool seamen had also been in action. Early in May, they had got wind of the increased wages being paid to the seamen of London, Hull, Glasgow, and Greenock, and as such refused to ship below the rate paid to their brothers in other ports. Some of the larger companies give way, but the smaller companies refused. In one largely attended seamen's meeting, the committee convened to hear the recommendations of the men as to what rates were to be demanded. After discussion, these were to be set as follows:

To the west as far south as Orleans, considering yellow fever, £5 per month.
To Cape Horn, £3 10s.
The Pacific (a healthy voyage), £3 5s.
The Mediterranean (a short voyage), £3 10s.
Coast of Africa, £4.
East Indies, China, and Japan, £3 5s.
A months advance in all cases.

STOWING LOGS THROUGH THE BOW-PORT
'Wuz ye ever in Quebec?' (Capstan Shanty)

Timber dockers and sailors slinging giant timbers through the timber ports of the vessels such as those which frequented the Canada dock.

The present rates with the respective voyages (with no advance) being £4, £3, £3 10s for firemen and £3 for sailors, to the West Indies etc., from £2. 15s. to £3 a general rise having recently taken place on account of the scarcity of seamen.

As in the 1854 collective actions, the rail porters moved in conjunction with the men on the waterfront. It was reported in *The Beehive* of 27 July that the goods porters in the employment of the Lancashire and Yorkshire Railway Company had been agitating for an advancement of 6d per day. The men had been waiting for an answer from the company's directors. As soon as news got through to them that their request had been turned down, they answered with an immediate wildcat. The result, we are told, was a complete stoppage in the receiving and delivering of goods. The company
could do nothing else except close its gates. The action of these men at once spread to the porters further down the line. A few hours later, the men employed by the London and North Western Railway Company at the Waterloo and Canada docks struck for an increase in wages. All traffic to and from the town to the city via rail was halted.

The aftermath of these movements showed the men of the waterfront once again riding high, and as on previous occasions, trying to ensure the advantage of the moment by trying to enforce what in later years would be called 'the closed shop'. In October for example, we find a mass meeting of several thousand dock labourers, including non-unionists and Birkenhead men, assembled in a large field off Victoria Road; despite the streaming rain, the men stood listening to the speeches. The real issue, it was stated, related to the foremen who were not members of their trade union society, while the masters did not recognise their right to enforce that rule. Some of the employers refused to recognise them at all. On 16 October, the men met and decided to hold out and never work with non-union men. The last report on this issue was given in the *Liverpool Telegraph* on 21 October, and from this we might glean that all but a few of the employers were determined that the men should amend their rule relating to foremen. The men, having refused, were then locked out.

The sequel followed that the men who were taken on in their places were described in other papers as 'the refuse of the town, loafers, land sharks, rowdies and jail birds'. It seemed these men came drunk to work, fell down holds, split their heads open, fell asleep, and generally messed up the cargoes.

This had been the action of the North End Dock Labourers, a body that, as we have seen, had been around more or less intact since the 1854. The *Liverpool Mercury* reported in relation to the dispute that The Liverpool North End Steamship Dock Labourers Friendly Burial Society had been founded in the summer of 1872. As we have seen, these bodies change, swell,

George's Dock Basin, 1871.

and take on complexions as events dictate. The north end dock labourers had been in action in 1866. It is doubtful if this is a different body, though its friendly society aspect may have been added in summer of 1872. Likewise, Taplin concludes that the society probably collapsed with the failure to enforce their closed shop rule on the employers. I think that unlikely, as the North End Dock Labourers' body emerges again in 1876. In April, the journeymen tailors resolved:

> That in the opinion of the Journeymen tailors of Liverpool, the time has arrived when an advance of one half penny per hour on the rate of wages is essentially necessary to meet the legitimate demands of our position; and although we are convinced that the 'log' or 'time' list under which we at present work is unfair in its construction and unsatisfactory in its working, yet we trust that at some future time it will be revised by the masters and men duly appointed for that purpose.

The Liverpool coopers, at their meeting the in the Operative Trades Hall, Duke Street, were also talking of strike action if their demands for an increase in piece rates were not met.

False Dawn of New Unionism?
Labour Unrest in Liverpool 1871–1873

Under this chapter heading, Eric Taplin adds his contribution to the collection of essays, *Liverpool's Popular Politics Riot and Labour*. My first point of many departures with Eric is his borderline preoccupation with the theory of so-called 'new unionism'. As I discussed in my introduction, I consider the concept not so much a 'false dawn' as a false premise. 'Unskilled labour' is only relatively so, indeed some so-called 'unskilled' sections were highly skilled; coal face workers, shaft sinkers, seamen, firemen, and many branches of dock work and labour. Manual workers did not require the kindly intervention or accidental inspiration of artisans or skilled workers to organise, strike, set up organisations or handle *ad hoc* mass assemblies and movements. This new unionism was supposed to evolve in the 1890s. Clearly, Eric came across evidence of 'unskilled' workers' actions and organisations twenty years earlier. Instead of drawing the conclusion that the concept was at fault, he poses the idea that it was actually a premature attempt, or 'a false dawn' as he puts it. With this conceptual baggage, I feel he damaged any clear insight into what he was looking at.

> As might be expected, organisation was largely confined to craftsmen, and in the first half of nineteenth century, unions of shipwrights, iron founders, and coach makers among others enjoyed considerable power. It is not surprising that collective action by work groups among the unskilled was rare and spasmodic.

Eric then goes on to mention sailors' strikes of 1775 and 1791, and dockers' action in 1853 and 1866, which had been successful. He also mentions the presence of trade organisations (he does not call them unions), which he wrongly regards as simply savings and burial clubs. He mentions efforts to form a dockers' union in 1830, goes on to identify the South End Dock Labourers Association that formed in 1849, but again wrongly concludes, 'Its primary function was probably as a sick and benefit club.' Readers will have readily seen through the pages of this history, the combativity, the confidence, the dynamism of life and labour on the waterfront of this period. How does Eric see it?

> As the casual system of employment expanded so a rising proportion of the workforce was condemned to live in the margins of poverty. Casualism limited the horizons to the daily struggle for work; fickleness and brutality were encouraged and corruption and indiscipline endemic. Motivated by short term and narrow considerations, casual workers were poor material for sustained protest or trade union organisation.

I disagree; there is ample evidence of sustained protest throughout the period, this book chronicles it, as it does many examples of trade union organisation both of the temporary 'guerrilla' form and the permanent variety. Eric does not understand that, surprising though it may seem, they actually liked the casual system of work, poverty or no. They did not actually like to work every day any more than colliers of the period did. Whereas the miners were expected to come and did not, the dockers did not have to turn up to the stand. R. Williams, talking of the first year of the docks scheme, says 'The doctrine of permanent men stinks in the nostrils of the docker.' While this obviously lowered the weekly wage, wages themselves were not the only consideration. A famous area production manager for the NCB in Doncaster, incensed at the ever-worsening absentee figures, asked a mass meeting of Bentley miners in their welfare hall why they only worked four days in the week. Back came the chorus, ''cause we can't live on three!' In 1912, a new dock labour scheme was introduced with the backing of the employers, union officials and the Board of Trade.

> Employees were now to be registered as a first step towards control over numbers applying for work. Clearing houses were set up for the centralised payment of wages, while a system of surplus stands connected by telephone was intended to prevent local shortages of labour in particular parts of the port.

What was the response of the dockers? It met with considerable resistance and opposition. We are told, 'Syndicalists played a significant part in organising opposition to the scheme.' It strengthened the hold of the employers over the dock labour force. It allowed them to keep a check on individuals. In addition, this was not a demand that had come from the dockers themselves. It had been thrust upon them with the aid of the NUDL officials, but without consultation, never mind agreement from the rank and file. Several thousand copies of a pamphlet entitled 'What's This. It Is Important To The Mersey Dockside Workers' circulated the docks and the port with the assistance of Larkin's local associate. Peter Larkin, a 'local syndicalist', was calling for strike action against the scheme, and this did take place as a disparate wildcat. Birkenhead stayed out for a month against the scheme. The casual system gave workers licence, and can be viewed as a strength not a weakness. It sat well with their sense of independence and workers' self-management. Likewise, what are we to make of the charge of 'indiscipline'? Whose discipline are the dockers expected to accede to? Despite the evidence of his own research, Eric considers, 'By 1870, Liverpool labour had achieved very little.' Even more incredible given the evidence of this work, 'The increasing numbers of unskilled workers remained *largely un-organised and passive.*' (My emphasis.) He later tells us, 'Liverpool workers had struck work well before the explosion of the early 1870s, but

Princes Dock *c.* 1880.

activity had been *confined largely to skilled artisans.*' (My emphasis.) 'Thus, the influence of unions among the less skilled can virtually be discounted. It was a false dawn for workers organisations in Liverpool, and indeed for most, the objective was not to organise at all on a permanent basis.'

> In the early 1870s, Liverpool's unskilled workers accepted their lowly position in the economic and social order. They sought limited gains in wages, rates, and conditions, but had no pretensions to radical change in work practices or job control ... Indeed, by turning to Simpson and Samuelson for advice and leadership they emphasised their servility and acceptance of their position in society ... Other factors contributed to the narrow base of trade union organisation. The tidal wave of immigrants from neighbouring agricultural districts North Wales and Ireland, especially from the 1840s, ensured an over-stocked labour market, particularly in unskilled sectors. Thus, there was normally a plentiful supply of potential blacklegs to take the place of those who might be tempted to organise into trade unions and/or take militant action.

Well the proof is in the pudding they say. This story shows that despite problems of over full labour markets and the potential of real blacklegging, strikes and organisation persisted throughout, often successfully. The Irish were frequently a boon to labour organisation; they did not come as 'country bumpkins' innocent of the class struggle or bereft of class solidarity sympathies or culture. Quite the reverse, and in every trade they entered it was the Irish who could be expected to take the lead in organising and agitating. In any case, as I have said, the work was not totally unskilled; tens of thousands of skilled dockers could not be easily replaced. As will be seen, attempts from the masters and shipowners to do so often led to expensive failures.

Eric goes on to tell us:

It was events outside Liverpool that led to the unexpected explosion of militancy in 1872. At national and regional level, there was an outburst of labour militancy in the boom of the early 1870s among semi-skilled workers and the labouring poor ... Nevertheless, the most important development in so far as Liverpool was concerned was initiated by the skilled engineers of the north-east who had been seeking a 9 hour day since 1866. By 1871, the Nine Hours League had been formed ... Of the 7,000 men who struck work in support of the demand, only about 800 were members of a trade union, and of those, only 500 belonged to the ASE. In effect, the league was a general union embracing engine makers and unskilled and non-unionised labourers in the engineering workshops and shipyards of the north-east. This resounding victory reverberated across the country and led to the adoption of the 9 hour day in many occupations.

Well these events fed each other, but why specifically was Liverpool influenced from outside any more than anywhere else? I doubt that the assertion holds water; the events of 1872 were of no more substantial than those of 1866. Eric identifies the growing unrest between 1871 and 1873 in the port, town, and spreading to Birkenhead, but far from being the tidal wave from the Tyneside engineers' victory, it had been part of a steady local agitation and class war evident since the turn of the century, and itself part of a national process. The impact of Tyneside was felt in Liverpool certainly, but no more than anywhere else. Eric is in my view looking for exceptions to prove his rule, but finding too many exceptions.

Eric concluded on the whole period:

It was perhaps inevitable that sectionalism was a characteristic of the unrest. Each work group acted independently, no effort being made to coordinate activity even among cognate workers. This is best illustrated

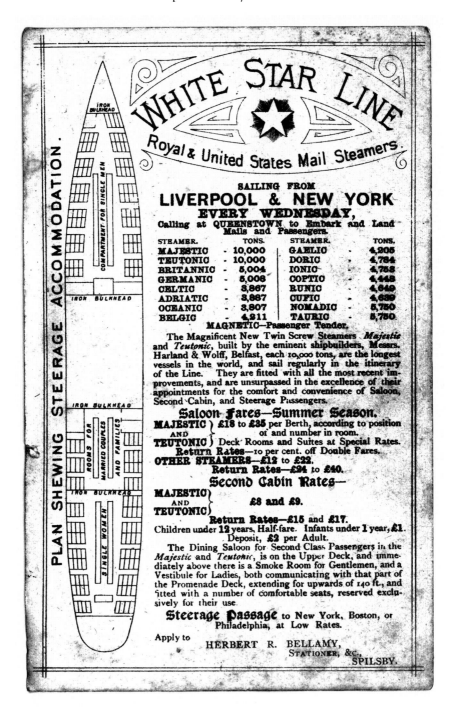

White Star 1890's advertisement.

by reference to events at the waterfront. Dock gatemen, cotton porters, provision porters, grain warehouse men, carters, and some north end dock labourers were all involved in separate disputes *without any perception of a common cause.* There must have been over 20,000 dockers seeking work at the waterfront, yet only a few thousand were involved in any show of militancy. The explanation is to be found partly in sectionalism. Men were divided by status and spatial factors into a 'caste system quite as powerful as India's, as James Sexton later commented'.

Readers will form their own view from the evidence presented here. I do not recognise the picture as Eric paints it; quite the contrary. I likewise believe Sexton's comments, although illustrative of the respective skills and areas of job controls, do not weigh when the chips are down in strike situations. In such cases, each section actually closes ranks.

The spirit of 1872 roared on into 1879. In that year, we see a strike of the Liverpool marble masons. The journeymen marble masons had presented a memorial to their employers asking for wage increases. In the previous year they had received a reduction in their hours, but were complaining of the lack of a wage rise in eight years. Their wages at this time stood at masons 30s, polishers 24s, and sanders 20s. They were demanding an increase of 3s and 2s per week respectively.

In 1871, a movement of trade union shop assistants had started in Birmingham. A few weeks later, an organiser visited Liverpool and met with the shop assistants shortly afterwards. The Liverpool Shop Assistants Association was formed. The union recruited hundreds of members within weeks, and succeeded in gaining a reduction in working hours in the drapery trade. The support for the union in Liverpool became so great that the National Union HQ was established there.

Four years after the upsurge of 1872, some sections of the press expressed their astonishment that workers were still going on strike. In April 1876, the *Journal of Commerce* reported:

Yesterday morning a strike of the most unexpected character occurred in Liverpool, and unless measures of a conciliatory kind are speedily taken, it is feared that a great deal of inconvenience and annoyance will be experienced by several of the Atlantic Steamship companies, whose vessels are advertised to leave Liverpool this week for New York and other ports.

Actually, dockers had struck in a wildcat, hence 'the unexpected character'. Dockers' strikes on Liverpool waterfront had not been, nor were they, unusual features of the port's life. This strike was of a different nature than previous ones however, in that it was defensive. The owners and masters were trying to pass, as they have done before and since, the losses of a national recession in trade upon the backs of their workers. As such, they had instructed the dockers that they were to receive a reduction in wages. On 1 April, a placard was posted very prominently along the docks to the effect that on and after Monday 3 April, the hours worked for stevedores, dock porters, and quay men would be from 7 a.m. until 6 p.m., and on Saturdays from 7 a.m. until 5 p.m., instead of hitherto from 7 a.m. until 5 p.m. and on Saturdays from 7 a.m. until 4 p.m.

This was in essence an attempt by the masters to take the workers back to the pre-1866 conditions of labour. Readers will remember that a 4 p.m. finish on a Saturday had been a crucial part of the demands of 1866. The men for their part were not prepared to return to the conditions of the past, and the day the masters' placards went up, so did the notices for several meetings to take place that night. The dockers unanimously decided to strike on Monday unless the notices had been taken down by the people who had put them up. The work was entirely suspended at the vessels belonging to the White Star Company, the National Company, Guion Company, the Cunard Company, Burns and MacIver, the Dominion Company, Richardson Spence & Co., Allen Bros. & Co., The Inman Company, and several of the Mediterranean lines including Messrs F. Leyland & Co., and the South American Steamship companies. The whole of the men who were employed by Messrs Durant and Mack, master porters and stevedores, numbering 1,300 men, struck right away. Many of the placards had been torn down in anger, and as such, quite a few of the men turned up in ignorance of the reduction. However, as soon as they got to know the situation, they struck immediately. In the neighbourhood of the Wellington Dock, something like 1,400 men congregated, refusing to go in on the new terms. It was rumoured that the move had been initiated by the arch 'militants' among the masters Messrs Durant and Mack, although they denied it and issued a £20 reward to whoever could track down the people who first started blaming them for it.

The day after, a fire broke out on the steamship the *Andean*, a vessel belonging to the West India and Pacific Steamship Company. She had been inward bound from Port-au-Prince laden with cotton. The *Liverpool Mail* reported, 'No clue has been discovered as to the origins of the fire. The hold of the steamer had been closed since Saturday last and none of the cargo has been disturbed.' Meetings were held on the Saturday, at which it was decided unanimously by stevedores, porters, and quay porters not to work at the proposed hours. The local press were confident, and said
that the depressed state of shipping and employment must render the masters victorious. However, the press was meekly to announce on 5 April that Messrs Burns and MacIver returned to the old conditions and the men accordingly returned to work.

Horse drawn buses approaching the Exchange and Custom House.

As soon as the strike had started, Mr Harver, the proprietor of a public house right opposite the gates of the Bramley Moor Dock, posted the following notice in his window:

Men that are on strike and that have used this establishment during the last six months as customers can have their pint of ale and bread and cheese free every day from twelve to one.

G. Harver

On the Monday and Tuesday, hundreds of his customers were served, as promised free of cost. Posters containing the new hours had been posted on all docks; by 6 April, all of these bills had been removed, much to the blushes

The Eastern Monarch, emigrant ship for New Zealand. *Illustrated London News*, 9 May 1874.

of the press. The men subsequently resumed work at the previous hours, all increases in workload having been withdrawn. Finally, when further placards went up withdrawing the earlier changes, the men could claim a total victory to their action.

The victory of the dockers of 1876 is a clear demonstration of the way in which large groups of workers are capable of moving in a common direction even without the benefit of formal coordination. The reduction notices had been served at the north end only, where no union organisation existed. The employers thus thought they were hitting the weakest link and starting a chain of reduction right through the docks. The men were certainly without the benefit of a union no matter how loosely one uses the term. They were not however disunited, their labour and society was their 'union'. The common assault served to weld the men into a close knit 'association' of common interest. When they struck, they did so in an 'affinitive' manner rather than an organised way. This affinitive bond however was equal to the strength of the employers, coupled as it had been with the immediacy of the wildcat. The employers may have gambled that the impact of the changes would take time to sink in, that the lack of organisation etc. would give them time to get their ships away before unrest manifested itself. However, the swiftness and directness of the men's response caught the masters and owners off guard and all shipping in the port became at once stranded.

1879: Reductions, Depression, Shipping Wars, and Lock Outs

1879 was a year in which all commercial activity reached a very low level. All over the country, workers of all descriptions were facing reductions in wages as the capitalists tried to offload more of their losses onto the workers. The Liverpool employers had been faced with not unconnected, but specifically different problems of commerce. These problems in turn shaped the whole cycle of labour unrest.

The first fundamental change that greatly affected the labour of dock work and seafaring was undoubtedly the simultaneous rise in steam shipping and decline of sail. The great sailing lines, particularly in the 1870s and 1880s were hard pressed in competition with one another and with the ever threatening expansion of steam companies. Sailing ships strained to build up records of fast crossings and cheap transportation. It was within this struggle that the seaman was reduced to an all-time low of working conditions as the level of exploitation increased. Companies had to depend more and more upon illegal activities to procure crews such as criminal crimping and shanghaiing. Simultaneously, the steamship companies, apart from their task of outstripping the sailing ships, were also in competition with one another for cargoes and routes. Once more it was the seamen and dock labourers who suffered in terms of wages and conditions from these battles for survival among the maritime capitalist class. Shipowners of the 1880s faced an ever-mounting problem with freights, which were priced so low, many deemed them not worth accepting and laid up their vessels. The development of fleets had been marked in Liverpool, but now this only aggravated the condition of poverty that many were found in in the wake of the shipping wars. Previously, some sort of decorum had been maintained as to which company sailed where. However, after the Americas became unsure, pressure to find markets and drive competitors off the sea became vital. There were two main reasons for the causes of the depression. One was the competition already spoken of; the other was the unsettled nature of the American trade and finance, bank failures, and mountains of speculation by industrial adventurers. All of this made cargoes highly uncertain. A company might have established a trade route in collecting some speculator's produce, but suddenly the bubble would burst and that cargo would be no more. The knock on was then a rush to find alternative freights. The 1880s saw a decline in what was once the staple backbone of trade. Grain, provisions, and cotton gradually became pushed out of international trade.

By the end of August 1884, no less than fourteen large steam vessels and thirteen sailing vessels were lying redundant at the Great Float, while at the Alexandra Dock, sixteen large steamers also lay out of work.

It is true to say that the Liverpool employers were somewhat slow to turn on their labour force as a means of mitigating their losses. They had made a spirited attempt in 1876, expecting the workers to be unable to sustain a strike. However, they had underestimated the degree of class solidarity that was to manifest itself and ensure the defeat of that particular employer's offensive. The renewed offensive of 1879 was a sort of corollary of the workers offensive of 1866. The massive, broad nature of the struggle was virtually unprecedented. The Merseyside capitalists, entrepreneurs, and contractors bound together to announce wholesale reductions in dockers' wages on both sides of the Mersey from 1 February. Along with the casual workers, those with skills and long-standing traditions of organisation were also to be targeted.

The wages of engineers, boiler makers, and ships painters, both at Liverpool and Birkenhead, were to be slashed. Groups previously regarded as 'privileged' and protected, cotton porters, provision porters, timber workers etc., would be hit along with the casual dock labourer.

The Great Lock Out started in the iron trade, with attacks upon the wages of engineers, fitters, pattern makers etc. All of these workers had struck against a proposed reduction of 7.5 per cent. In one of the iron firms on the Liverpool side, some 500 operatives stopped work and left the factory to the foremen and employers. On Saturday, the numbers of those refusing to work at the reduction had swelled, as iron founders, brass finishers, and shipwrights joined the engineers.

The iron trade workers were split in many small craft groupings, but meeting the common offensive, their societies pledged to fight together. Their numbers had been quoted as:

The Iron Founders Society of Liverpool: 498.
The steam engine makers of Liverpool and Birkenhead: 170
The amalgamated engineers of Liverpool and Birkenhead: 1,320

The biggest group were, however, the boiler makers and iron shipbuilders whose numbers I was unable to accurately record, but must be estimated at 2,000.

By the Saturday evening, the turn-out was being described as 'general', with some 10,000 workers on strike. The docks were seething with discontent over news of impending reductions in their wages. Saturday was to be the day designated by the shipowners for the dockers' wages to be reduced by 6d per day and 1d per hour overtime. Up until the Friday there had been considerable speculation as to whether the dockers would submit peaceably to the reduction. Saturday dispelled all doubts. The whole of the dock labour force struck, with the exception of the permanent hands at the Cunard Line. We are told the strike was marked by deathly silence, which descended upon the waterfront as all of the men cleared the streets. Here and there along the dock walls, militant dockers had chalked slogans in support of the strike '... And of a half threatening nature.'

Along the Huskisson Dock were the words, 'Hold out like men. Beware. Bucky of Rory,' and '"No surrender" says Rory.'

Meanwhile in the corn trade, the masters determined upon a reduction of 6*d* per day for porters and 2*d* per 100 sacks for bushellers, scalers, and carriers.

The men at Messrs John Bingham & Company, corn merchants, were at work on Saturday, but only twelve turned in on the Monday. At about 8 a.m., one of the men was sent from the warehouse in the Old Roppery to a vessel in the Victoria Dock. However, while crossing the back Goree, a set of men jumped on him, and calling him a blackleg, knocked him down. He got up and made off as fast as he could.

The movement of the dock workers appears to have been spontaneous, and no clear leadership from their own ranks was apparent. Collective decisions were being made, but in different places, attempts at a single, unifying meeting were attempted and failed. Three attempts were made, but came to nought. Thousands of men marched to Sandhills and gathered on the waste ground, but the meeting never started. A similar scene was enacted with the other two. This lack of an organising centre and leadership was to be fatal for their movement, for it left the way open to philanthropists and liberals to intervene with the dockers' movement and 'guide' them.

By Monday, the action was starting to bite as all loading and discharging of vessels was at a standstill. The owners started looking around for blacklegs to load their vessels. If the men had been slow and disorganised getting their meetings together, the employers were just the opposite. Calling together all employers in the shipping and steamship trade, they resolved to do without the strikers no matter the cost or the sacrifice.

It was around this time that the blacklegs started to trickle into the port; a little later, it became a flood. Dock labourers arrived from Bristol and were set straight to work loading for the Mediterranean fleet. At the same time, a body of men arrived from Newcastle-upon-Tyne to work on another line. The owners felt confident they could replace the strikers.

It was on the Tuesday that John Fuller, a docker from Hopwood Street, emerged as a leader of the north end labourers. He was to be latterly overshadowed as the strike progressed. Twenty-six of the men from Bristol arrived by train, but on finding a strike in progress, sixteen of the men refused to work. The other ten confessed to doing so, only because they had no money with which to return home. Meanwhile, the Waterloo Dock and its approaches were crowded by strikers. One of the Bristol men said they had been engaged by an agent who had told them the work would be for one week and that there was no strike going on. On arriving and realising the actual situation, they all demanded to be sent home, but the employers refused.

On Tuesday, a mass assembly took place at the pier head, with some 8,000 men assembled. They were addressed from a cart by Mr Simpson, and five

George's Dock.

from their own ranks: John Fuller, John Maitland, James Skelly, J. Hawkins, and a Mr Jardine. All seem to have been dockers of long standing.

A day later, two contingents of labourers arrived from Glasgow to take the place of the strikers. One of these groups numbered 100 men and was destined for the western ocean companies. Meanwhile, a large number of posters had been stuck up all over the port of Bristol warning dockers not to go to Liverpool since a strike was in progress. A group of the Bristol recruits were escorted by police through their own city as they made for the train, while Bristol trade unionists hissed and hooted at them.

Early in 1879, a large meeting of seamen assembled at the Malakoff Music Hall, Cleveland Square, having been loaned by the proprietor, a Mr Dan Lowery. Mr Simpson had the chair. His main goal to maintain order in any dispute between the men and the masters. He supposed the meeting was called to give vent to the grievances of the men, but felt he himself could not pronounce upon these as he did not know what they were yet. He applauded their course of action so far and urged that their conduct would be worthy of British sailors, although he had heard something that was scarcely credible. He had been told that groups of seamen had been down to the south end and interfered with work there. He warned them that they would never redress for their grievances by use of violence. 'They had their labour in own hands, and they had no occasion to lay violent hands either upon anybody or any property (cheers).'

Mr Spalding took to the platform, saying that a wage of £2 5s per month for a southward voyage was utter madness, and he proposed £3 as a wage. A voice shouted out, '£3 10s and £4 westward'. Mr Spalding then responded that no man should sail the western ocean without £4 10s per month wages. 'Mr Spalding addressed the meeting and said the seamen wished to get living wages for their work. As the case at present stood, a coolie was proportionately better paid than an English sailor.' The question he put forward was, 'Were they going to be men?' Cries of, 'Yes we are!' answered. The wages now being paid were quite absurd. They received £2 5s. per month going southward, and had come to the conclusion none ought ever to go across the western ocean without £4 10s.

Mr Farricker was loudly cheered when he said that twenty-two years ago, he shipped out of Liverpool for Calcutta for £2 5s per month. He had never known wages so low as at present. During last winter, standing wages had been £3 per month 'Heavens knew this was little enough for any man to keep a family on.' He knew times were bad, but now they had reduced seamen's wages from £3 to £2 or £2 5s a reduction from 15s to the southward. He dared say that thirty of the finest ships that ever floated on water were waiting for cargoes, but they could not get them because the dockers had struck, the same as the sailors were now doing. The difference was that they were striking against a reduction of 15 per cent of their income, enough to pay a poor man's house rent. The large amount of distress among seamen in Liverpool was entirely their own fault, and this was especially the case of the single men, who if they saved their money, would be able to stand out against the employers reduction in wages. The Mersey Mission had been feeding 100 men daily, and now they had nowhere else to go. The sailors' home, thought by some as a sort of charitable institution, threw them out if they could not pay, or if they were two or three days in arrears. It was this fear of being without accommodation and work that forced sailors to accept reduced wages, and so visited the same reduction upon them all.

The meeting also heard complaints about the charging of fees for advances on wages. Mr Bentley said that he believed there was a Seamen's Protective Society in Liverpool, and they ought to be made aware of the stoppage here and in other ports, as it would benefit the society to have advanced the cause of the seamen.

It is clear from this statement that the strike was one of the spontaneous ones and organised outside the formal union, which was yet to be informed of the action.

Mr Fairchild said he had looked after the interests of the seamen for years and been driven from one employ to another and from town to town for doing so. He said he had heard some men complain of foreigners. He was sorry to say he had heard on many occasions that foreigners were refusing to work for the wages that English sailors had accepted.

The men resolved to keep the peace, but a borough magistrates' meeting in the police building of Dale Street, 'considering the present unstable state of the labour disputes', thought it desirable to retain troops with a view to preventing riot. By Thursday, all the approaches to the river were crowded with teams and wagons waiting for work, but the docks were almost deserted despite the efforts of the employers to introduce strike breakers. A mass meeting on the George pier head unanimously rejected any notion of arbitration. They further rejected any idea of forming a deputation to meet the masters until the latter removed their notices of reduction. Meanwhile, the remainder of the port's labour force was starting to engage in the movement. There were rumours of solidarity action by coal heavers, and sailors pledged not to offer themselves for employment until the dispute was over. Ship painters were meeting to draft a policy on the current events. At Birkenhead, one of the Guion Line boats entering the docks with a large quantity of meat had to bring the town butchers themselves down to unload the cargo after finding no dockers willing to unload it at the reduced rates.

A number of coal heavers then struck when they discovered that they were to be used to load cargoes of coal and not coal for the ships' bunkers. Soon, between 3,000 and 4,000 coal heavers were reported to be on solidarity strike, and a pledge of similar action came from the skilled artisan sail makers of the port.

Now for the first time, the South End Dock Labourers Association (the Old Dockers Club, highly organised and operating virtually closed shop,) issued a notice that unless their north end brothers were victorious, they too would be turning out although did not itself seem to have been issued with reduction notices. Despite this and the fact that true to their word, the south end docks turned out, Taplin states, 'Although the courier mentioned the South End Dock Labourers Association, the latter played no part in the strike.' I can find no justification for such a conclusion in the footnote that he cites, which is from the same source as mine. The union issued the notice, carried it through, and struck work in solidarity with the north end. This *is* playing a part in the strike.

Against this support, the influx of blacklegs continued with a further 120 Glasgow men arriving, along with news that tradesmen were volunteering to take up the struck labourers' work. Meanwhile, the sailors were now parading onto the docks to call out their fellow seamen in solidarity, and also in an effort to regain advances in wages previously cut. They further gathered around the sailors' home, English and foreign seamen side by side in determination to gain an increase. They had taken to wearing pieces of blue ribbon in their caps and jackets as a badge of militancy.

For most of the nineteenth century and maybe earlier, Irish workers had formed secret 'ribbon societies' to fight for their industrial and political demands. This could represent such a caucus, or simply the wider workforce adopting their method of identification. Simpson was horrified by such a scene and scolded the seamen:

> I see in the crowd sundry pieces of blue ribbon. Personally, I am exceedingly fond of a little blue. But I must tell you that if you go through the streets with a bit of blue in your hats or coats, you are bringing yourself under a by-law that enables a police officer to make you take it out.

This brought cries from the crowd of, 'Never mind that!' Simpson persisted, 'You are breaking the law by wearing such emblems, and I hope you will take them out ...'

That day, only three vessels had been waiting for men to voyage outward to Calcutta, Bombay, and Shelburne, Nova Scotia. All of the seamen presented themselves and demanded the increased rates, and on being refused, the would-be crews left the ships unmanned. Soon afterwards, groups of men mustered by the east side of the customs house, where they were addressed by speakers from a pedestal. One of these, a youth, called attention to the leaflets circulating the docks, calling all seamen to the meeting on the pier head. While the authorities were arming police with sticks and staves, the labourers of the coastal trade joined the action. The Central Dock Labourers Club announced a cessation of work.

Next, we see the first real outbreak of violence and the introduction of troops. A troop of Dragoons from Rupert Lane barracks begin patrolling the line of docks from the north end southward as far as the   Canning Dock and back. 35,000 men were now reportedly on strike. At about 2.30 p.m. on Friday 7 February, several hundred men armed with sticks made a charge against the blacklegs working on the Waterloo Dock warehouse and succeeded in driving them out. Yelling and hooting they tore down sacks of wheat and threw them into disorder. Work was stopped in the sheds. On the other side of the sheds, strike breakers from Bristol were unloading the steamer *Victoria*. The crowd made a dive toward them, charging over barriers and piles of cargo. The Bristol men made off on board the steamer and fastened themselves in. The crowd also attempted to get on board, but were unable to. They next made toward the *Eulanene* to clear it of scabs. Meanwhile, the police made no move against the pickets until reinforcements built up and the men were forced to

Canning Dock Basin.

disperse. Later that day, about 1,000 men boarded the three-masted schooner *Cora*, which was lying in the north side of the Georges Dock, and drove the blacklegs off. They tore up hatches and put out the donkey engine, and the strike breakers were warned that if they recommenced work they would be hurled into the holds.

Major Greig, the chief constable, had approached Simpson, the liberal gentleman who was trying to act as arbitrator in the dispute, and asked him to stop the men parading. He did not object to the mass meetings, but the parades obviously worried him. The men had taken to parading to their meetings in great numbers, usually carrying the men who were acting as spokesmen on their shoulders. They would route the major streets and past the Exchange, groaning, hooting, or cheering depending on the part of the town they were in and its hostility or loyalty to their cause. On that very day, we are told that another parade was taking place; the seamen and coal heavers marched across the Exchange with flags, 'Singing doggerel songs and indulging in threatening attitudes.' Captain Greig, as he had been when he was appointed, was considered 'a moderate' man. There had been too much use of violence previously.

In August, at Greig's recommendation, the heavy bludgeon used by police was replaced by a lighter stick. In December, he again addressed the men about unnecessary force by threatening dismissal. During his first year, there were 161 dismissals out of a force numbering 806 ... From 1853 onwards, discipline improved, but police violence was not eliminated.

On the pier head, another liberal gentleman made his appearance. It was Mr Samuelson, who was offering his services in helping direct the movement. Despite the help of middle class mediators, the massed crowds determinedly rejected any talk of arbitration as such. Samuelson, a Hull-born man, was chairman of the Working Men's Liberal Association, and he patronised all causes of the Irish and the trade unions. The cause of the association was 'to secure all just political and social privileges for the working classes, and to promote civil and religious equality.'

Meanwhile, the strike was spreading to the few remaining docks that were working at non-reduced rates of pay. The Queens Dock, the Nelson, the Bramley Moor, and the Salthouse Dock all stopped work when they heard

Canning Dock in the late Nineteenth Century.

the south end was out with the north. Mass meetings at Birkenhead voted to
stand out against reductions in solidarity with the Liverpool men. Sympathy
strikes spread to permanent staff at the Waterloo and Stanley docks, and the
carters were rumoured to be joining the action.

In the meantime, the authorities' efforts to impose their mark on events
somewhat backfired. The men at the south end congregating in large numbers
were surprised to see a patrol of cavalry coming down the street, headed by a
van in which sat Major Greig, the chief inspector. Instead of being intimidated
by this display, they greeted the column as if it were some procession laid on
for their entertainment, as indeed all other such parades probably had been.
They trooped along beside the column cheering and waving. Greig, realising
any plan to coerce these men with such a demonstration had failed, entered
into the swing of things, sticking his head out of the window and waving his
hat to the delight of the crowd. Attempts to mobilise greater forces however
continued apace with an emergency meeting of the magistrates, presided over
by the mayor. They authorised a call out of more troops, and another troop of
Dragoons prepared to leave Manchester. Ninety horse boxes were got ready
at Ordsall Lane Station.

At the Huskisson Dock on 9 February, a force of 500 'strangers' had been
introduced by MacIver. The pickets had been awaiting their arrival at the

Clarence Dock at half tide.

Clarence Dock and were secretly outflanked. These 'strangers' were to be housed on ships in the river, and with the dock gates tightly patrolled, no opportunity was to be afforded either to dissuade the blacklegs or give them room for second thoughts.

At a preliminary meeting of the seamen's leaders the next day, it was decided to form another seamen's union. After discussing basic causes and the need for such a society, it was decided to form the Seamen and Firemen's Union of the Bowl. Virtually at the same time, the AGM of the Liverpool Seamen's Protective Society was meeting at Milburns Rooms, St Anne Street, with R. H. Hughes in the chair. Mr J. Callaghan, the treasurer, stated that the society had a decent balance in hand, commenting that their society had nothing to do with the current strike movement.

The second week saw striking numbers maintained, with slight increases here and there. 2,000 carters were now not working, although how many were actually on strike and how many were laid off as a consequence was not too clear. Reports would suggest a large section of carters on strike. Meetings on the pier head saw crowds swelled to 40,000 and more. This was probably the height of the strike, in which meetings were taking place two or three times a day on both sides of the river. The pier head and the Malakoff Music Hall were the main centres of the seamen and dock labourers' rallies. The *Liverpool Albion* reported some 60,000 of various trades were out on strike. The *Daily Courier* of 11 February reported that the strike was spreading; 2,000 more carters joined the movement, followed by boiler cleaners. The firemen on steamships were refusing to work, as were the coal heavers and salt heavers on the Birkenhead side, as well as all workers engaged in the grain warehouses; in all, 60,000 workers were estimated to be out. The *Liverpool Mercury* reported this as 'the largest strike that has ever occurred in any one town'.

It was around this time that those who had intervened as mediators tried to move toward arbitration, despite the fact that both parties had shown no time for it. While the mediators looked for possible forms of compromise, the owners seemed to want nothing but complete surrender. That at least was the broad front being presented behind the scenes, although a few employers were on the brink of compromise. Gradually, the men were being won over to the idea of arbitration, but showed no signs of surrender on the actual terms. Mass meetings of the men were stormy. Violent exchanges were to break out between Mr Fuller and James Samuelson, and Mr Fuller and Mr Simpson before the mass assemblies of men frequently yelling their own views from the floor. There is no way that the rank and file were obediently rolling over and taking orders or even mild suggestions from Samuelson or Simpson, and noisy disagreement and rebellion accompanied many of the meetings. Fuller seems to have reflected the most militant views of the men.

George's Dock.

At Bootle, the women and girls attached to the manufacture of soap and sackings struck work against an extension of hours without payment. The women then actually applied for membership of the dock labourers' societies. Both the north end and south end societies were functioning at this time. The whole nature of these organisations is that they expand and contract in accordance with the movement of the struggle. However, I was unable to ascertain whether the women were admitted into membership. The dockers themselves seemed not to be taking action through the existing dock labourers' unions, not at the north end anyway. Clearly, the 'disorganised' dockers' action and the redrafting of a new seamen's union would indicated discontentment with existing structures and direction.

Thomas Cann, a fitter, was charged with threatening and abusing Joseph Wilson. He referred to him as black sheep, adding that he and all the other scabs should be done in. He was remanded to appear before a higher court. Incidentally, about twenty soldiers were in the court all that day. Mr Raffles, the judge, asked an official of the court what the meaning of their presence was. He was informed that they were in reserve down that end of the town. When he asked if they had nothing better to do but sit in court, the soldiers replied 'no' and stated they did not like police duty.

Wednesday 12 February saw the biggest dock labourers' meeting yet at the Georges Dock pier head, with some 60,000 in attendance. Mr Maitland was in the chair, or actually on the cart that had been adapted by seamen and dockers as a platform. He said that he was proud to see how the men had stuck it out for twelve days with such determination and quietness. A voice in the crowd replied, 'Far too quietly,' and in doing so, gave expression to the mounting unrest at the management of the dispute.

The crowd extended from the west wall of the pier, by-passing the landing stage and reaching the boundary wall of St Nicholas Parish Church, standing in silence as the employers terms were revealed. The 'terms' took the form of an ultimatum:

> As an alternative for the proposed reduced rate of wages, the following are now offered: 5s per day for the lumpers, and 4s 6d for porters, the men in each case to work 1 hour extra per day. The overtime for the time worked to be at the following rate: 7d per hour for lumpers, 6d per hour for porters.

The terms had barely concluded when the crowd let loose a great cry of disapproval, and when put to the vote, a forest of hands rejected the terms.

Then, the proposal of arbitration itself was rejected with such force that the mediators seemed thrown into confusion and retired to consult. Two proposals were then offered to the men, one from Simpson the other from Samuelson. The latter proposed the men accept a reduction of 3d per day. We are told that idea was 'received with great disfavour' and rapidly outvoted. The next offer came from Simpson, who removed both his coat and cigar to speak. He warned against 'taking up a position injurious both to the interests of themselves and the trade of the port, and obstinately refusing to move from that position'. He expressed regret that the men had rejected arbitration. When it came, his proposal also offered a reduction, although couched in complicated language; not so complicated however that the men did not see its meaning and loudly condemn it. Instead, they voted to stand out against all reductions and to seek no arbitration. It is clear from this point that the movement was too explosive, and those who had set themselves at its head were not sure how to get out of it and bring matters to a close without losing too much face.

Into this, 350 Scottish dock labourers started work that morning, together with 37 shipwrights and eleven foremen stevedores. Coal heavers were said to be being introduced also, while at the Stanley Dock, 250 men had taken employment and 50 who had struck at the Waterloo warehouse returned.

Numbers of blacklegs being introduced to the port vary in different newspapers, but it is clear overall that large numbers were arriving and the strike was losing ground. However on 13 February at the Home Rule Hall, Great Howard Street, a mass meeting of shop keepers resolved to support the strikers. In the chair was Mr J. M'Cabe. One of the speakers, a local councillor named Connally, said he was proud of the way the men had stood out and conducted themselves. He was quite prepared, he said, to support this cause with money. A committee of sixteen shopkeepers was appointed to raise subscriptions, and a donation list was started. The three town councillors present each contributed £10 each. Mr Connally promised to subscribe £50 more if the strike continued a further week.

At the labourers' pier head meeting, Mr Fuller was giving an optimistic view of events, stating that if they continued to stand firm, they would win that very day. Both Maitland and Fuller stood four-square against the recommendations of Simpson and Samuelson. Fuller shouted, '... What I want to know is whether any of them were going to give way at all?' He was sure they would not. There were two gentlemen waiting on the landing stage, and they had put their services at the disposal of the meeting if they could do any good. The gentlemen were Mr Samuelson and Mr Simpson. If the meeting thought their propositions were good, why not take them? Cries of, 'No!' resounded. The gentlemen were ready to do the same that day as they did on the previous day. A voice called out, 'We don't want them!' Would he then tell them that he had offered their services to the meeting and the meeting had rejected the offer. Both, 'Yes!' and 'No!' were shouted, along with a voice that claimed, 'We don't reject them if they can get us 5s per day and 8d per hour.' Did the meeting reject the offer of these gentlemen? 'Yes!' Then why did someone say no? Fuller went on to put the full claim to the men once more, which was passed.

In drenching rain, the corn porters held a large meeting at the Georges pier head, with Mr John Baillie elected as chairman. They stated that it was not their intention to separate themselves from the other dockers, but they would constitute a distinct deputation to meet the Master Corn Traders Association. They proposed that wages for sack holdings, lowerings, and takings in should be 5s per day and for ordinary days work, and 4s 6d and 6d per hour overtime. They demanded 5.30 p.m. for finishing, as maintaining the 6 p.m. finish was too long a day. They resolved to stick out for those wages and just demands.

That week came further cases of intimidation. Mr James M'Nally and Mr M'Creary were charged with assaulting and intimidating Robert M'Lagan, who was a labourer and one of the men brought down from Glasgow to break the strike. The two local workers asked the strike breaker what he thought he was doing there and what he was doing on the ship. Anticipating his answer, one of them hit him in the face. M'Creary struck him again and knocked him down, and they kicked him on the ground. The police intervened and they were arrested. One received a fine and the other hard labour.

Cunards' *Britannia*.

Another docker called M'Corniel was sentenced to two weeks hard labour for begging; the judge ruled that if he wished to eat, he should not strike.

Another sailors' meeting was held at the Malakoff Music Hall on 14 February. This had been convened to encourage the Liverpool mariners, and the whole body of fireman and sailors who had been brought from Hull, to break the strike. These men had refused point blank to go to sea. It was also reported that the crew destined for a ship called the *Sarmation*, which had also been recruited from Hull, had been sincerely promised that there was no strike in Liverpool and that they would be paid £5 per month. On arriving however, they discovered that there was a strike and that they would only be paid £4 10s. The men outright refused and struck themselves. All of these men were to be put in the care of sympathetic boarding house keepers, either until the end of the strike or until money was secured to send them home.

On Friday 15 February, bright sunshine encouraged a mass attendance of dock labourers at their meeting, filling the pier head, crowding the landing stage, and all approaching roads and adjoining streets. One of the local papers described the workers as 'a fine body of men, of excellent physique and bearing few visible signs of suffering that the fortnight's enforced idleness has thrown upon them'. The meeting was informed of the Liverpool Trades People Collection and how they would be supported (of how at least they would not starve). Mr Grannel of the Rotunda Theatre had subscribed £20 to the funds.

At 2 p.m. that day, the men started congregating at the Georges pier head. 20,000 were soon assembled, and Maitland and Simpson arrived to address the meeting, despite the earlier resolve that Simpson at least was not needed. Maitland said he had hoped there would be news from the employers, but none had so far materialised. Councillor Connally seems to have jump-started the meeting by proposing that the entire fate of the movement be handed over to Maitland, Fuller, and Simpson in order to achieve the best terms of settlement possible. Despite the unchecked scope of this proposal, little opposition was expressed. Mr Simpson advanced and stated that he was ready to accept responsibility if it was the wish of the men. Mr Fuller stated that he was prepared to give up his duty in representing the men, but let no one say he had not done all he could for them. Something afoot must have dawned on the crowd now, as some men started shouting, 'You've sold us,' followed by cheering and shouts of 'no!' Despite the opposition, the councillors' proposition was accepted when put to the vote. From now on in, full control of the settlement rested in the hands of 'leaders', and not their own ranks. The tens of thousands still on strike were however still confident of a victory, and now confident that their middle class friends could get it for them. The blockade of the quayside continued, the sheds lay idle and packed with goods, and the vessels wallowed deep in the water with their cargoes still unloaded. Despite the best efforts of the masters scouring the country far and wide for crews, the effort had not yet had its desired impact. Yet still they persisted, almost in spite of that fact.

Certain of the masters on the south end had taken on their old hands at the old rates of pay, with the men breaking their own rules (of the South End Association) and returning before the north end. Unrest meanwhile was growing among the imported men, who since their introduction had been virtually imprisoned 'in the safety' of the vessels, constantly watched over by the dock's police.

That very day at 4.30 p.m., a train arrived at Tithebarn Station bringing a group of dock labourers from Hull. A large body of striking workers assembled to greet them. Three buses arrived to carry the blacklegs away, and on their arrival, the bus drivers were pelted with wet mud and their passengers greeted with loud choruses of boos and hisses. A similar picture was unfolding in Birkenhead. Blacklegs had been pouring into the city from all over the country, most completely ignorant of the strike.

About forty labourers were brought from Glasgow to load the steamship the *City of Canterbury,* which was lying off the Morpeth Branch Dock. These men got to work early in the morning and should have been joined by another

Riverside Station.

group of Glasgow men who had been engaged for one of the ocean-bound steamers.

The arrival of this second group was awaited by several hundred of dock labourers, who hung about on the bridges and massed on the quay waiting for the expected tug. Shortly after 2 p.m., the tug *Gypsy King* came into the Morpeth entrance and made its way in the direction of the Morpeth Branch Dock, finally drawing up at the pier for the purpose of disembarking. The strikers quickly ran to the spot, converging on it from all quarters and catching sight of about forty to fifty men, described as dark in aspect, strange in attire, and dubious in demeanour, who by this time had come onto the deck heralded by the moaning, shouting, and hooting of the strikers. It is probable that up until this point, the Glasgow men had known nothing of the strike, and at once recognising the situation, refused to step upon the quay.

After a stay of nearly 45 minutes, the *Gypsy King* finally made a detour and came around into the Morpeth Dock alongside the *City of Canterbury*. Before this change could be made however, it was necessary to open a bridge, which also had the effect of massing all the strikers away from the ship. After the tug drew up alongside the ship and the gangway was put in position, the strangers still refused to move. The master was screaming at them, who in turn was being barracked and booed by the hundreds of watching strikers. He wore a broadcloth and a monocle, which provided the jeering crowds with ample ammunition with which to mock him. The strangers could be heard moaning and shouting, 'No' and 'Never!' But due to the effects of the threats, the lure of the money, poverty at home perhaps (whatever it is that makes good men scab), the first six men gave way and mounted the gangplank to moans from the strikers. The total rose to fifteen, but the remainder refused to move and were heard threatening the tug captain, which was greeted with a great storm of cheers. After more than an hour, during which time the men all positioned themselves in a group aft, the *Gypsy King* moved out of the dock and cut a clear course through the Morpeth Dock entrance, passing lines upon lines of cheering dockers as she did so; she was quite clearly heading back to Scotland with her defiant cargo. Sadly though, we read a further fifty or sixty men were introduced after the strikers had withdrawn pleased with their victory. The strike was starting to fragment at the edges and among related sections. Although the central core stood fast, there was a certain weakening of resolve over the direction the movement should be taken in.

The employers were still working on the central strategy of displacing the men with strangers and restarting the port. To this end, they introduced 200 paupers from Wolverhampton. Poor down-and-outs had jumped at the chance of the jobs on offer, and more than the 200 required crammed into the railway carriages that the masters had provided for transportation to Liverpool. When they arrived, it was the familiar story; they had not been informed of the situation, and as such demanded to be sent back home. They refused, poor though they were, to do any work. The masters declined the demand to send them home. To this they marched in determined fashion to the town hall to demand justice of the town mayor. The mayor helpfully suggested that they do the work on offer to raise enough funds and then go home, but still the men refused to do so. Being unable to get help, they desperately hung around the town; about 150 of them went to the workhouse to be accommodated.

Later, we learn that the Wolverhampton men had started the long tramp back to Wolverhampton via Manchester in a magnificent act of working class solidarity, determined not to become blacklegs.

On Wednesday 18 February, the north end docks were impassible with barrels, boxes, and bales. There was a crush of wagons at all entrances. Men working the north docks were receiving full rates. From the south side of the Samson Dock to the Carriers Dock there were 260 men working; had there not been a strike, twelve times that number would be at work. The coal heavers went back to work on the understanding that they were to receive the old, non-reduced rate. On arriving however, they discovered that they would not receive that rate, so simply turned on their heels and walked out again.

The corn porters, as we know, had already returned in the face of armies of blacklegs introduced from Scotland and Ireland. The mass rallies of the men were the major thread holding the strikers together in the absence of any strike committee or elected leadership. It was therefore unsurprising that the police then targeted the rallies assembling in force before the start of the planned mass meeting at the Huskisson Dock. Patrols were being performed inside and outside the dock gates. They were backed up by a detachment of the 5th Dragoons from the Rupert Lane barracks.

Mr Fuller arrived 45 minutes before the start of the meeting, and was seen engaged in a long argument with the chief superintendent. Soon after, Maitland arrived. Afterwards, both mediators ascended a pile of logs that was to be used as a platform. The crowd, which by now was thronging around them, was forced to divide into two groups as Major Greig theatrically rode through the crowd to the foot of the 'platform'. He shouted out in a clear voice that public gatherings such as these, from which it was apprehended that disturbances might arise, were illegal, and that if any breach of the peace did occur after that morning, the leaders of the labourers would be held responsible. Mr Fuller then pledged his word that no more public meetings would be held at the docks after that day, and Maitland added his pledge. The authorities had in fact already banned all meetings of the men in either public thoroughfares or on land that was public property anywhere along the whole line of docks. Greig, on receiving these pledges, withdrew his men.

Fuller announced to the crowd that late the preceding night, a group of labourers had made a charge on the dock gates and tried to force their way in. Maitland for himself stated that he had made the pledge because he had no wish to see himself in Walton Goal or any similar place.

The closing down of the public meetings was a body blow. These had been the lifeline of the strike, and had broken any feelings of isolation or stagnation in the action. They had communicated strength and solidarity, and doubtless given the culture of the port a great deal of good humour and high spirits.

From now on Maitland informed them, they would communicate in the form of wall posters on the dock walls. A vote was taken that the strike would continue and they would stand out until their just demands were met. Maitland told the crowd there were few employers not feeling the pinch. The imported men that were not deserting and going off home were being sacked for drunkenness, laziness, and plain uselessness. For the first time, 8,000 hands were at work, and of them, 6,000 were boys.

The Final Phrase of the Strike

The strike entered its final phase on Monday 24 February. Maitland became the main author of a move to end the strike, hosting small meetings of individuals at the north end. He informed all who would listen that he was deeply affected by the sickness and destitution brought about by the strike, and it should be ended as soon as possible. He resolved to approach the chairman of the Steamship Owners Association and offer them a scale of 4s 6d per day and 8d per hour overtime, or 5s per day and 7d an hour overtime. The response was that the reductions were final. At this response Maitland surrendered, posting placards throughout the docklands that read, 'Under existing circumstances, I advise you to return to work at 5 o'clock this day, accepting for your labour the reduced rate of 4s 6d per day and 7d per hour overtime.

Signed John Maitland, 24 February 1879.'

Tellingly, the placard notice was not signed by Fuller, who refused to do so. At Birkenhead, a mass meeting of labourers had been convened to promote the same surrender there. It was held as usual in the Craven Rooms, Chester Street. Calvert Varty presided. He started the meeting by announcing that Mr Maitland, who had always had their interests close to his heart, did not think it right to stand out any longer. It was suicide to endure the fight now that the Liverpool men were returning. He could do no better than urge them to return at the former rates, although he admitted that he did not have the opinion of Mr Fuller on this matter. He requested permission to post the surrender bills around Birkenhead too. A voice cried, 'We'll let the Liverpool men have it, I always thought that they were a bunch of rotten sheep in Liverpool!' 'I'm only trying to give you my advice,' said Maitland. 'Keep your advice to yourself,' came the response. 'Are you willing to have these posted?' he asked. 'No, let them stop in Liverpool!'

Shouts ran around the hall from the crowd. 'They will give in tomorrow if we will only stick it out.' Maitland then left the platform, realising that he had done all he could to end the strike. The chairman continued that Birkenhead had been sticking out for the Liverpool men, what was the point now? The answer from the floor was loud and clear. 'We'll stick out for *our* rights!' The Liverpool men said that Calvert had forsaken them at Birkenhead. 'They always did,' shouted a worker. 'We fought our battle twenty years ago and won it then when the Liverpool men didn't.' Calvert again suggested they return, but they should form a union and bide their time until they could win further wage advances. A vote was taken and a majority declared in favour of posting the bill, at which point someone shouted, 'I should have liked to have seen his mate.' Maitland remounted the platform and exclaimed that he did not have Mr Fuller's approval, although he had waited some time to get it.

At that precise moment, Mr Fuller burst into the room flushed with anger and strode toward the platform in what must have been a drama-filled atmosphere, heavy with spirit and emotion. He began, 'I am agitated, but well I might be.' Their brother Maitland, he continued, had signed a paper for the men to go to work at 4s 6d per day and 7d per hour overtime. Now all he had to say about what Mr Maitland had done was that if they wanted to

The Rembrandt, a classic 'tramp' entering Bristol docks, 1886.

go to work, he would not hinder them, but if they went, they would go not because bills had been signed by John Fuller. People had gone behind his back. He could only conclude that all the dockers of Liverpool believed that he too agreed with these bills. Maitland stated that this was not true. Mr Fuller retorted, 'Well you have signed it, and what business had you to sign anything of that sort without my sanction?' Evidently, Fuller was terribly hurt.

He promised to meet Maitland at 1.40 p.m., but instead met a man going to the printers' office with the bill. A voice declared, 'Our names won't go to it!' This might have been done three weeks ago easily. 'In conclusion,' ended Fuller, 'I thank you for the manly way you have stood together, but henceforth, you shall have Mr Maitland and not John Fuller as your representative.' Maitland then asserted that he had taken a consensus of 100 north end labourers and he thought this was typical. Fuller pointed out that in Birkenhead, they had never consented to 4s 6d per day and 7d per hour overtime. He left the platform and forced his way to the door amid cries of, 'Don't let him go!'

Prior to the contentious surrender of the strike, the shipowners had been making conciliatory offers to the seamen, although the terms are unclear. Solidarity strikers like those of the Docks and Harbour Board who had not been given a reduction had returned on the old, non-reduced terms. The spirit of combativity was anything but quashed. On 26 March, a new Birkenhead waterfront union, the Birkenhead Amalgamated Dock Labourers Union and Benefit Society, was formed, uniting lumpers, coal heavers, quay porters, and coal and salt heavers; a formidable alliance. A union on the opposite side of the Mersey, the Liverpool Union of Stevedores, Labourers and Quay Porters, was also being created. Some sections, such as the Operative Ships Painters Society, sustained reductions, but maintained the normal hours of work. It seems clear that some compromises or preservation of the status quo were being ensured.

Overall however, at least so far as the mass of the Liverpool dock labourers was concerned, the defiance of the men was defeated and the reductions imposed. This is not to say the action had been futile. The masters and shipowners had paid dearly for the reductions, and the men had learned lessons of solidarity, as well as treachery and misplaced trust in the 'gentlemen' who sought to lead them from outside of their own
ranks. The building of unions on a more formal structure seems to have been undertaken, and the issue of the reductions was far from forgotten.

Twelve months later on 28 April 1880, we see the exchange of views via the local press:

Sir,

More than a year has passed since the wages of the men employed as stevedores, quay porters, and dock labourers were considerably reduced owing to the depression of trade, and the reduction, as well as the mode in which it was enforced, engendered a very bitter feeling amongst the labouring classes connected to shipping. With a view to recovering the old wages, a strike was contemplated in January, which was with difficulty averted by the efforts of our association, supported by well known friends of the working class. Another such movement is threatened, and we are again using our influence to prevent a proceeding that we judge would be very injurious to all parties concerned. We feel however that the time has arrived when on behalf of our fellow labourers we may fairly ask for a restoration of the old wages current before the last strike.

If you will consult with those who act for you in the engagement of labourers, you will find that the wages of casual porters average about 15s per week, which with the enhanced price of the necessities of life, is totally inadequate. It has been stated that this is due to surplus labour, but you will find that the demand already exceeds the supply, and that it is always necessary that there should be a reserve of labourers in this port to meet emergencies. You will find that several leading railway companies have just raised their porters' wages to the old rate, owing to the increased traffic; and that the lines of steamers in every part of the world are actively employed. These circumstances will, we hope, have your earnest consideration, and we respectfully suggest that you allow the old rate of wages to come into operation on Monday 10 May.

For the association committee of the Liverpool and Birkenhead Stevedores and Quay Porters Union, James Clark, chairman, Thomas Crimes, vice chairman, J. J. Baillie, secretary

On the face of it, the reply was conciliatory:

Sir,

Your letter of 28 April asking that the wages of the stevedores, quay porters, and dock labourers should be restored to the amount paid before the strike was considered at a meeting of this association held today, and in a reply, I am directed to inform you that a resolution was unanimously passed in the following words: That an offer be made to the men to leave the question to arbitration in the usual way, the question whether any and what advances should be made in the wages of stevedores, quay porters, and dock labourers; and in case the arbitrators should decide in favour of the advance, that such an advance should take effect from 10 May.

Mentioned in the letter from the representatives of the men.

Your obedient servant,
Gray Hill, secretary

The men's representatives made arrangements for the convening of special mass meetings in Liverpool and Birkenhead, inviting James Samuels to be their referee and at the same time drafting the following:

Sir,

I am instructed by my committee to acknowledge your esteemed letter of this day, and to thank your committee for the prompt consideration that they have given our circulated letter.

Amongst so vast a body of men as we represent, you will so easily understand that there should be a large number who consider themselves perfectly entitled to receive back the wages they lost last year, and who will refuse to work unless they receive back the old wages. Before therefore we can give you a definite reply to your proposal, it will be necessary for us to obtain the approval of the labourers themselves to any course we may recommend. Subject to such approval, my committee accept your offer of arbitration, it being understood that each side shall select umpires. I am to inform you that we shall be most profitably represented by an advocate to state our case.

I have the honour...

Crossing the Mersey, the steam ferry between Birkenhead and Liverpool, 1886.

On Wednesday, the officials of the incorporated unions visited the workers of the north end docks of Liverpool and Birkenhead to ascertain their views on the arbitration idea. A meeting of the stevedores, quay porters, and labourers held at Birkenhead on 6 May, Mr Baillie, the association's secretary, gave an account of the progress so far. When the opinion of the men was taken into account with regard to the question of arbitration, it was unanimously agreed to abide by the proposal of the Liverpool men; that being to subject the matter to arbitration, and in doing so, expressing their hope for a settlement by the following week at the latest. Recent arbitration results in favour of the men may have given fresh confidence in the system of arbitration. Mr J. F. Collier, a judge sitting in arbitration over the proposed master builder's reduction of joiners' wages, had been rejected.

The committee of stevedores, quay porters, and dock labourers' unions of Liverpool and Birkenhead urged the men to stay behind their initiatives. Handbills and posters were circulating:

Fellow Workmen,

Already we have issued a notice by placard announcing the names of the two gentlemen who have been chosen by yourselves and the employers to settle the wages dispute, in whose impartiality we have the most perfect confidence, and those who we feel sure will do their best to bring the matter to speedy termination. We have no doubt whatever as to the result, and we strongly advise you to remain at work until you hear their decision. Already, large numbers of you have pledged yourselves to remain at work and wait the issue. If you wish to stand well in the estimation of the general public,　　　you will take the advice already given and thus continue to retain their sympathy and respect. Otherwise, we are afraid you will bring upon yourself odium and disgrace.

By order of the united committees,
James Clark, chairman, Thomas Doogan, John Doodson, B. Reiley, Thomas Banks, Michael Blackwell, William Prosser, William Lynch, John Baillie, secretary

On 11 May, it was decided that Lord Derby be umpire and that all decisions reached should be by the evening of 12 May. The strike, which had been planned in many quarters and may have been in operation on some docks, was called off owing to fact that all employers had agreed to pay the men the old rates, at least until the arbitration rates were given.

On 13 May, the Liverpool seamen held a mass meeting on some vacant ground near Sandhills to discuss the existing wages. Mr George Fearon presided. Several men spoke and urged that now was the time for an increase in wages. The activities of the British Seamen's Protective Society were strongly condemned, and a new committee was formed to put a document before the employers. The following is an extract:

> The seamen and firemen submit that the causes that have operated towards making the dock labourers successful in their claims are applicable in a much greater degree to ourselves, and through disclaiming all attempts at obstruction and interference in a mischievous way with the trade of the port, confidently look forward to a favourable consideration of their claims at the hands of their employers.

The officers of the Amalgamated Seamen's Protective Society and the Seamen's and Firemen's Union, (which had descended from the Union of the Bowl) had called a meeting of their own members, with Mr Fairchild in the chair, ignoring those of the Sandhills' movement, which seems in fact to have been a spontaneous rank and file action without the endorsement of either 'official' body. The meeting at the Trades Hall, Duke Street, declared the purpose of obtaining an increase in wages. They also declared that they would use every method except striking to win their case.

Increased rates had in fact already been conceded by the American Line, as with Mackie and Durant, Guion, Dominion and the National lines, Richardson, Spenser & Co., Messrs Warren, Messrs Lovegrove, Owens and Cunningham, Charles Webb, Walsh, and Layland.

The Amalgamated British Seamen's and Firemen's Union based at Brunswick Street met at the Trades Hall, Duke Street, on 14 May. A Letter was read out from the secretary Mr G. Dawes. It came from the London seamen and expressed the warmest sympathy for the Liverpool men. The demands of the men were the same as those from the previous year. No news however had been received from the bulk of the shipowners. It would be tempting to draw the conclusion that the British Seamen's Protective Society was an enlarged descendant of the earlier Liverpool Seamen's Protective Society. Taplin suggests this may have been the case. I have re-read all the available material and cannot easily draw that conclusion. Eric says it was founded in London in 1872. I doubt in that case that it was anything to do with the union of Callaghan, which had a longer, well-established reputation in the port of Liverpool. Of course if this was not the same union, where had the earlier Liverpool based organisation gone? Or was it a third option operating at the port at the same time? The press often used the term, 'the Seamen's Protective Society,' presumably for shorthand, but was it short for the British Protective or the Liverpool Protective if they were not the same thing? Whatever the case, the two unions joined their efforts in this cause and held joint public meetings and deputations to the shipowners.

The Sailors Home, a controversial institution.

Meanwhile, the dock labourers were now at peace, having received their full wage rates once more.

The next meeting of seamen on 19 May announced the response from the employers that the state of trade would allow no advance on seamen's wages. Mr Dawes, chairing the meeting, said that he would require everyone's vote on what they did next. For himself, he announced that strike action must be avoided and that the question should be settled by arbitration. Mr Fairchild, a guest speaker from the Dock Labourers Association, spoke on the seamen's cause, and in so doing revealed his knowledge of the conditions endured by the seamen. He spoke of the practice of some companies to hire men described as 'pier head jumpers' rather than through the shipping offices, the problems of the advanced note, and the 'half pay system and shipping fees'. Eventually, an old seamen called Edward L. Butler proposed strike action, and much to the annoyance of the platform, it was unanimously passed amid great waving and cheering.

The following day, a great body of seamen marched from Canning Place to the sailors' home at the north end, although actually, no-one shipped that morning. A mass meeting held at Sandhills saw Mr E. Sinclair Battersley, a boarding house keeper, advising the men to hold out. He further offered to assist them by keeping a couple of men for two or three weeks free of charge, and could declare with certainty that other boarding house keepers would do the same.

Fitzpatrick, who we have come across before, earlier wrote an irate letter to the *Liverpool Mercury* blaming the agitation of the strike, the posting of unofficial notices, and the strike vote itself upon the boarding house keepers. Handbills in fact were in evidence during this struggle far more than in previous disputes, certainly as far as Liverpool was concerned. These were circulating among the seamen proclaiming that all information regarding the strike and assistance could be obtained from the seamen's union offices at No. 15 Lower Frederick Street. The possession of an established union centre for the port had long been a dream of seamen in previous disputes. At 11 a.m., a large body of men gathered and proceeded along the line of docks to Sandhills where a mass meeting was to be held. Mr Sinclair, the boarding house keeper, took the chair. Mr Butler, another boarding house keeper, stated that he had been a seamen for thirty-six years and that he had initiated the last strike, although I did not find any evidence of him in the reports I discovered.

At the mass meeting held at the Trades Hall, Duke Street, on 21 May, Mr Fairchild had been requested to take the chair. Unsurprisingly, Mr Butler condemned the letter attacking the boarding house masters, which had been written by Fitzpatrick. The vote of censure was endorsed. For themselves, the boarding house masters had been sending in pledges to house men at least for two or three weeks without charge.

Mass meetings of the railway men were also taking place, discussing hours of work and an endeavour to reduce them. On 23 May, the Operative House Painters of Liverpool announced that they too would strike unless the halfpenny per hour that had been taken off them last year was restored.

That day, another mass meeting of seamen was informed that many shipowners had granted the increase. There was much excitement around the seamen's home where the strikers gathered before setting off on a massive procession around the town. That evening, it was reported that a blackleg ship's fireman who had been preparing a fire aboard the steamer the *City of London* had been attacked by strikers and stabbed in the arm with a red hot iron, and thereby seriously injured. Meanwhile true to their promise, the house painters had struck and many employers conceded immediately, with their workers returning to work at the old, non-reduced rates.

Finally, the mass seamen's meeting of 25 May saw Mr Fairchild in the chair, proudly announcing that there had been a general advance in wages for seamen and firemen, and that the owners were now treating their men with a different attitude. The men were now receiving a 10s to £1 a month rise (the wages of firemen traditionally being 10s above that of normal ratings). The seamen's victory had been a long running campaign, but wholly successful in the end.

We end this part of the exposition with another meeting of the seamen, but one of a different complexion. As usual, the meeting was at the Trades Hall,

Duke Street. The meeting of 25 May was to hear the complaints and address the specific problems of the black seamen's fraternity. Mr E. G. Fairchild had been asked to take over the chair; this he did, saying that it was a year since he himself had addressed the question of distress among coloured seamen and laid the matter before the town mayor. He went on to outline some of the difficulties that the coloured seamen faced; the biggest one being obtaining vessels. Many were forced to go on the tramp or into the dreaded workhouse. 'You will find,' he continued, 'coloured seamen along the lines of docks sleeping among the bales of cotton, unable to get ships and starving.' They were allowed to bring ships here, but were denied ships returning to their own country. This grievance had existed for a long, long, time and now was the chance to resolve it. The following resolution was moved:

> That a committee be appointed to consider the means of giving relief to those coloured seamen presently in distress in Liverpool, and who are in a state of utter destitution, and further that the said committee be instructed to take whatever legal steps may be deemed necessary with a view to procuring legislative enactment to meet the cases of crews bringing ships safely to British ports, and who instead of being reshipped or sent to their respective homes, are discharged and left without means of returning to their own country.

Mr Jacob Cristian, a black seamen, said that when he went to the shipowners and they firmly said, '"I want no coloured man." In the country where I come from I have never seen a starving man and yet this was supposed to be a Christian country.' The committee was formed and the resolution passed. Once again we find that the boarding house keepers, on hearing of this distress, agreed to house seventeen men free of charge, and a further thirty-one were relieved from starvation and poverty, even though it was forecast it would be another three months before such men in Liverpool alone could get ships home.

The extent of racism among the seamen or the people of the port is hard to gauge. On the face of it, one would have expected seamen – men used to foreign travel and encountering different cultures and peoples – would be more cosmopolitan. Crews on the Atlantic lines seem to have been more or less integrated. Many of the Liverpool shanties incorporated 'black voices' and themes. Yet there were anti-black seamen riots around the end of the 1870s. Speaking of improved relations between black and white seamen at the sailors' home in 1884, a writer comments:

> The disposition of the seamen of all nationalities to each other has changed for the better. At one time, and not very long ago, a coloured

sailor was not regarded as a welcome person near the home. When one put in an appearance, there was not infrequently heard the cry, 'Here's a … nigger; lets go for him!' This 'anti-nigger' feeling led not long ago to a serious riot between white and black seamen at the home … When the sailors finished their meal, one fine stalwart African with a blue ribbon in his buttonhole went up to the tradesman and shook him by the hand, saying, 'Goodbye, brother!' 'Goodbye brother,' responded the tradesman: and after the coloured party had left, he assured some friends, 'That's a member of the same lodge as I am, and I am proud of him!'

(That would have remained my perception had I not chanced upon *From Ta'izz to Tyneside: An Arab Community in the North-East of England During the Early Twentieth Century*. The author Richard I. Lawless identifies the degeneration of the seamen's union after the First World War, and in particular the most appalling racist campaign against foreign seamen in general, and British Arabs shipping from Aden in particular.)

On 28 May, the result of the arbitration for the dock labourers' demands were agreed. The union has won hands down. The *Liverpool Mercury* printed the full terms of the award:

After full consideration and discussion, we have come to the conclusion that in the still unsettled state of trade, it is not in our power to fix a rate of wages that shall be accepted by both parties as permanently satisfactory. We propose therefore, that the present award shall be binding for three months only, and that at the expiration of that term we shall be ready, if called upon, to resume the consideration of the question. We award therefore that from 10 May 1880, the wages for the ensuing three months shall be: for stevedores 5*s* per day and 8*d* per hour for night work. For quay porters and dock labourers 4*s* 6*d* per day and 8*d* an hour for night work.

(Signed) Derby
James Samuelson
Richard Lowndes

The award marked a clear victory. Taplin comments, 'The strike of 1879 and the arbitration award of 1880 confirmed a basic wage rate for Merseyside dockers that was to remain unchanged until 1915.'

It also in part explains the huge gap in this chronology of struggle in the years between 1880 and 1889. These years were intense periods of depression and downward spirals of terms and conditions. That we see no further explosion of waterfront anger by either seamen or dockers during the period suggests that the level of wages and hours held, with shipowners and employers deciding to bite the financial bullet rather than press on with reductions. In this sense, 'no activity', rather than being a sign of apathy or disorganised weakness, could well be a sign of relative satisfaction enforced by latent strength.

In many ways, the struggle of 1879 carried into the following year of 1880. There was almost a conscious effort to regroup and avoid the mistakes of 1879. While it is true that trade had picked up and the margins to play with were bigger, the conduct of the strikes was the most decisive factor. The strikes of 1879 had not centralised its efforts around the trade unions, which clearly did exist. Far from providing a more participatory forum of the workers directly, the extreme decentralisation had created a vacuum into which outside liberal forces had stepped and effectively misled the movement. 1880 saw a resurgence of the movement, but one more closely linked to workers' organisations and representatives. In 1879, it was attacks upon the north end that had precipitated the all-out assault. This was possible because it was largely disorganised; the unions that existed were very small or highly selective in their membership. Secondly, at the same time it was the biggest firms that were based there. These firms not only felt the dire needs to reduce cost more sharply, but were facing a more fragmented workforce on which to impose the assault. The south end, markedly the most highly organised of the whole Mersey maritime complex, had not been subject to the reductions. In 1880, a collective Liverpool and Birkenhead Stevedores, Quay Porters, and Dock Labourers Union was able to take action directly across the whole of the waterfronts in a way in which the fragmented forces of 1879 had been unable to do.

The winters of the mid-1880s provoked riotous demonstrations by the unemployed in London. 'They also turned Liverpool dockers from hungry men into angry men.'

The Close of the Decade

As the 1880s came to an end, the dock labourers took part in a strike of a slightly different, more modern nature. The strike involved opposition to the dock 'elevator'. These had been used for the discharging of grain and had been creeping in in greater numbers as one shipping company after another adopted them. Like other such innovations before and since, its arrival meant a departure from traditional forms of work. To the shipowner, a faster discharge of vessels and a faster turnaround meant maintaining profits in the cut-throat world of mercantile marine in this period. With the use of this machine, a dozen or so men could replace fifty labourers.

Up until July 1888, there was no major action against the machine. However, things came to a head with the arrival of the SS *Roumelia*, belonging to Messrs Papayanni & Co., as she arrived at the Wellington Dock from Alexandria. Previously, the company had always employed dock labourers to discharge the grain from their holds. On this occasion however, the elevator was to be used. In response, the men declined to work. The company replied to this action by sending to the Waterloo Dock for another machine. The men responded that unless such actions were stopped, a general waterfront strike would be organised. A day later, the press reported that only 100 labourers were in fact on strike and the machine had been extensively in use on the waterfront for many years.

While no doubt this was true, in all probability the men's objection to the machines did not find a real expression owing to the vast numbers of unemployed in the port who were always ready to offer themselves at depressed wages and terms. Elsewhere, dockers had mounted opposition to this instrument, and a short time previously, the Bristol men had struck against the 'devils' as they were universally termed.

By the beginning of 1889, with renewed agitation among the seamen of the port, it is interesting to see where the seamen were in terms of their wages, and by that token to gauge how successful their earlier strike and wage movements had been. The dominant union in the port was now the National Amalgamated Sailors' and Firemen's Union. They considered that the wage rates they considered 'fair' were not only being paid, but in some cases 'considerable increases' on had been conceded to the union; in the case of the mail boats for instance, £4 10s for seamen and £5 for firemen per month. Now however, that rate of pay was being paid to all other western ocean seamen whether mail boats or otherwise.

In the ships making longer voyages to the south, the union had demanded £3 per month, and an increase of 10s had been granted. This does not seem to represent a great advance on earlier claims from a decade before. The union for its part agreed, stating that they were re-applying for wages that had been conceded some years ago. They complained that sailing ship seamen sailing southward were being paid the depressed rate of £2 10s per month, this representing less of a wage than most poor paid men can get ashore. For steamers bound to the west, a voyage of just under one month in duration, men were paid at £4 10s per month, followed by weeks of unpaid idleness ashore while awaiting new vessels. Union seamen came with the reference that members of the union were only granted credentials to *bona fide* ABs of at least four years' service, rather than the offices of those of the shark boarding house keepers and their 'off the peg' seamen. Despite this, and in response to the renewed agitation, shipowners had been making strenuous efforts to recruit men from other ports. Eighty had arrived from Scotland and thirty from Bristol, plus large numbers from Cardiff, all of whom shipped at the old rates. Cunard, as usual, had set its face against any increases and shipped large numbers of men from Belfast. The *Lake Winnipeg* of the Beaver Line sailed for Norfolk, Virginia, with a full complement of men at the rate of £4 for seamen and £4 10s for firemen.

Many of the companies, such as Inman and International, the Guion, and the White Star had for some time paid their sailors £4 and £4 10s per month, and were not at all impacted by the union's demands. Now however, with an increase of 10s being demanded, they were somewhat rattled and considered the demand 'exorbitant'. Meanwhile, the Guion Line faced something of a wildcat with the *Wyoming* crew all declining at the last minute, refusing to ship without the new rates. In this case, the owners felt obliged to concede. It was also being reported that:

> Many of the companies ... do not appear to mind paying even £5 to their firemen if they could depend upon their being thoroughly competent men. In Steamships, competent firemen are an absolute necessity and a crew of 'duffers' in the stoke hole would probably make a considerable difference in the length of a voyage across the western ocean.

Vessels were leaving the port at the increased rates. Despite public resolve to the contrary, we are informed that at the Alexandra Dock, the Inman and International Company, and the Philadelphia Company were both shipping men at the enhanced rates of pay. By the Tuesday, large numbers of concessions were taking place by the mail boat owners and owners of ordinary steamships. At the north end and in various shipping offices, eleven vessels were seeking to engage crews, including for the White Star Line steamer *Germanie*, the West India boat *California*, and the Guion Line's *Oregon*. At the Garston branch, *Auckland Castle* and *Ullswater* all shipped crews at the enhanced union rates. Companies offering less than the advance were failing to find crews and their vessels lay idle.

Meanwhile, the union had met on the Monday at the Trades Hall, Duke Street. The secretary Mr W. Nicholson reported that large numbers of seamen had joined the Union, and that two Liverpool branches, one for the north and one for the south, were in existence with a membership of 2,300. It was also reported that a rival local union had been founded in Bootle by a man named Higgins. Mr Parr urged that union seamen should stand clear of the Cunard Line for their own safety, given the calibre of the crews they were shipping instead of union seamen.

The women employed by Messrs Clarke and Son's tobacco factory of Richmond Row struck work against reductions in their wages and plans to heavily discipline them for absenteeism. About 600 women marched out

1890's advertisement; the White Star public face.

on strike. The manager was totally unprepared for this wildcat action, and since the owners were not available to advise him, he withdrew all reduction notices, at least until they returned. However, 150 hard-core women were still not satisfied and stayed out on strike.

In September, the Boilermakers and Iron Shipbuilders Society withdrew their members from work, presumably on both side of the river, in demand for 1*s* 6*d* per week increase on the time rates and five per cent increase on the piece rates. In this month, the seamen, whose demands were obviously simmering since January (and probably some years prior), decided that wages could no longer pace with prices.   A large meeting was held at the Cocoa Room, No. 75 Paradise Street, where it was unanimously agreed to press for wages in-keeping with the following: sailing ship southern voyages, £5; steamship southern voyages, £3 10*s*; sailing ship western and Baltic voyages, £3 10*s*; steamship western and Baltic voyages, £4. On the face of it, this was doubling the sailing ships sailors' wages on southern voyages and granting a higher wage than the steamship crews on the same route, while on the other route, the steamship crew would enjoy higher wages and the sail ship crews would still receive a higher rate increase on their existing wage. This seems to be an attempt to get crews' remuneration in line with the hazard level and discomfort of the work and passage rather than what shipowners felt they could pay from relative profits. A week later, printed posters bearing the seamen's demands were being stuck up outside the sailors' home.

The shipowners were in fact giving way. A ship entered the port and requested men, but the men refused to ship below the strike figure, so the

A ship's company, either the *Campania* or *Lucania*.

owners, 'on a temporary basis', gave way. Some sailors accepted 5*s* general increase, while others refused to ship at anything less than the full amount demanded. The scene was described as 'passive' by both sides.

On 22 September 1888, the *Liverpool Mercury* published 'The Boilermakers Strike: A Settlement':

The principles of the large shipbuilding yards in Liverpool yesterday conceded to the demands of the boilermakers and iron shipbuilders for an increase of wages, and in the majority of cases the men immediately resumed work. Piece workers will now receive an advance of five per cent, and smiths, platers, and riveters an advance equal to 1/6*d* per week. It is said that these terms are similar to those paid on the Tyne.

It becomes clear that between the end of the 1870s and end of the 1880s, the Seamen and Fireman's Union of the Port had passed away in one form or another. However, the National Amalgamated Sailors' and Firemen's Union of Great Britain and Ireland had sent down a delegate (Mr W. Nicholson) from Sunderland to reorganise the sailors and fireman into a branch of their union. It was said that the aim of the union was to establish a branch in every port of the kingdom, with a view to having a uniform rate of wages. By 28 December, the local papers were recording, 'Certainly it seems that the men have gained ground in their demands, as it is understood that in cases yesterday the shipowners had to give the wages asked.'

The year finished with most of the companies having given way. While others held out with their vessels idle and half their crew in the dock, others lay up their vessels in a hope of forcing defeat for the men. At the close of the year, the Port's press was speaking in very clear terms of a victory for the sailors over the shipping companies. The press was of the general opinion that such militancy was a Christmas tradition and had been a regular occurrence for many years. However, such a summary proved false as the strike spread over into January of 1889.

The tide as it were was in the seamen's favour, they being somewhat better organised this time round, as well as the number of seamen in the Port being rather low, thus adding to their bargaining power. Meanwhile, the union had prepared its case well, producing a series of pamphlets informing the seamen of the rates of pay at other ports, and demanding that they stick to union rates. On 4 January, some seventy union members paraded the streets carrying banners declaring, 'United we stand, divided we fall.' Attempts at speeches in front of the sailors' home were however frustrated by the authorities.

When the Liverpool branch of the Amalgamated Sailors' and Firemen's Union met at the Trades Hall, Duke Street, the officials were not those we have discovered in previous fights in the Port. Mr Andrew Duncan acted as chairman, Mr W. Germille as vice chairman, Mr J. Turkington as treasurer, and Mr W. Nicholson as secretary. They were to report that the Liverpool branches now had some 2,300 members. It was further announced that with regard to Mr Higgins, he had started a local union of the sort previously popular in the port. He asked people in the room to use their own judgement as to whether his union in Bootle or this national one could serve them better. This was greeted with cries of, 'National union!'

Around this time, we have an unwelcome example of some union men pursuing what seemed to be a racial agenda. The local manager of the Anchor Line Mr James Henderson received the following anonymous letter from 30 January 1889: 'If you continue shipping Manilla seamen by your Indian steamers, beware! By order of the League.' Some days previous, Mr Henderson wanted a native crew for the steamer the *Karamania*, going to Calcutta. They could not however get any such men in Glasgow. They managed to piece together a crew of Manillas at Liverpool, but these men, true to their union credentials, refused to ship below the strike demand rate. They got this, and were subsequently sent to Glasgow, but the Glasgow branch of the union, to their shame, would have nothing to do with them and consequently boycotted them.

In this particular dispute, the union showed quite advanced PR techniques, handing out leaflets to the passengers to explain the case and inform them of the fact that the shipowners were using crews of men who were not seamen at all. Crews of boot blacks had been recruited, along with bargemen and all stations in between, and it was for certain that some had never ever seen a ship before, let alone crewed one. With this information, it was hoped that passengers would refused to sail with non-union hands.

Features of the cross-trade solidarity marked in earlier disputes were also to surface in this strike. The coal heavers in the north end docks issued a statement saying that they intended to strike with the seamen unless the sailors' demands were met. It was popularly thought that such an event would be the forerunner of another general turn out. A new development came in the shape of politically-orientated class consciousness, which took the form of the Knights of Labour, who had pledged to intervene and assist the struggle in whatever way possible.

The Knights of Labour were an American organisation; some would say they had much in common with Owen's Grand National Union, while others would see them as the predecessor of the fiery industrial workers of the world, the Wobbleys. I consider that they resembled neither. In fact they were quite tame; they explicitly denounced strikes, and advocated conciliation and a balance between capital and labour. The 'Order', as it was called, had secret masonic rituals. Its leaders bore grand titles such as, 'General Master Workmen' etc. Their 'missionaries' had first come to Britain in 1884. It was during this period (1888–89) when their recruitment reached its highest recorded membership of around 10,000 members. They were however clearly very influential; at least it can be said that many of the leading characters in this tale were members of the movement or were influenced by it.

R. Bean tells us of W. A. Newcomb, a working jeweller:

[He was] indefatigable in his organising effort on behalf of tramway men, postmen, gas workers and general labourers, scavengers, seamen, and railway servants ... He belonged to the Bootle branch of the (American) Knights of Labour, which had been set up in 1889. This organisation emphasised a broad basis of recruitment by attempting to enrol all the elements in the labour force irrespective of their trade ... Arbitration, or in extreme cases, the imposition of a boycott, were felt to be preferable to strike action. In Liverpool, it was responsible for some early organisation among dockers, and for setting up the Tramways Employees Association, with Newcomb as president.

Despite the highly influential and successful leadership of many of the early Knights, their reputation was to die altogether on Merseyside as they moved into other union organisations. A meeting of the seamen's union resolved to have another procession, and that if Cunard, the key company holding out against them, did not give way, the seamen would call upon the coal heavers to be as good as their word and call them out as a prelude to generalised strike action along the dock. The procession was preceded by a huge banner bearing the words:

NATIONAL AMALGAMATED UNION OF SEAMEN AND FIREMEN OF GREAT BRITAIN AND IRELAND. UNITED WE STAND; DIVIDED WE FALL

The procession was led by a band of music, and the numbers of demonstrators swelled at every street corner as more and more people joined in. Proceeding down Strand Street, the procession halted near the dock gates and several of the leaders, mounted on a lorry, addressed the crowd. At this meeting, dense crowds of men had congregated, amongst them bodies of coal heavers, scalers, and dockers. Mr W. Nicholson assured the crowd that any scabs that boarded a western packet would be suitably dealt with by the Knights of Labour when they arrived in America. They would deal with them in a looser fashion than they could do at this side of the water, but in a fashion that he thought would one day be universal.

Meanwhile, the police were standing by in preparation, and behind them a detachment of the 9th Lancers. One can only assume such a sight would be both provocative and fearful. They were thankfully not used on such occasions.

News was just in that the sailors, stokers, and trimmers of the steamship the *Lady Woodhouse,* belonging to the British and Irish Steam Packet Company, had struck in support of the union's general rate. The strike of seamen in Dublin was developing with the halting of three cross-channel steamers, and delegates from the National Union had just arrived in Belfast. Around the coasting trade, the picture was much the same. The Glasgow shipowners were thought to be suffering worse of all.

That night in the port of London at a meeting of the seamen, 400 riggers marched with their bands and banners to join the National Union. The Cunard Company, always the most determinedly anti-union, had been reasonably successful in getting crews of sorts for their western ocean packets. However, the press was reporting:

> It seems that a good many of those men, who during the last few weeks have been put on board western ocean Steamships, have met with unlooked for difficulties on arriving at the other side of the water, owing to the deep sympathy that exists between the Knights of Labour in New York and the unionists. A great many have, from this and other causes, not returned in the ships, and this has put some of the companies to the additional trouble of securing a new crew.

Meanwhile, the strength of the union was building on all fronts. At Bristol, a crowded meeting of seamen and firemen established a new branch, as did a meeting at Birkenhead at the Grapes Hotel, Bridge Street. The boilermakers, who along with many other sectors had received a reduction in the defeat of the last strike, had now issued a demand that they were to be restored to normal on pain of strike action. By March, it was reported that their employers had conceded all demands. Around the same time, Mersey flat men asserted that unless they received a rise in their wages, they would be joining the strike and bringing 1,400 flats to a standstill.

With the seamen themselves, things seemed to have generally gone off the boil, but this was not the case. It had become the practice of the union to generally not strike the whole port, but to simply not ship with the vessels where the rate was not being paid. However on 30 March, things took a decisive turn against the sailors.

In the run up to this day, the owners of certain sailing ships had been shipping men at £2 15s per month. This was the first attempt by the sailing ship owners to do any such thing since £3 for men aboard these vessels had been secured by the union. Many of the shipping companies started to reduce the wages of the seamen back to the old rate. Mr Nicholson, on behalf of the whole union, responded that if the present trend continued, the whole, nationwide body of the union would be called out, some 46,000 in every part of the country.

The rank and file seafarer construed that this employers' re-offensive was due to the 'softly, softly' tactics of the union leadership, and that the owners could see no reason to pay the enhanced rate if certain others were getting away without doing so. It was concluded that the next step on behalf of the owners would be to try and get a rate of £2 10s per month. The boarding house masters of ill repute and certain captains had negotiated a scheme to ship men who could be worked at the very lowest of wages. Meetings of union seamen heard tales of such boarding house masters sending out runners to gather up all the tramps of the neighbourhood and ship them out at starvation wages.

Pressure for a national strike kept building, and this was reflected in certain statements from the leaders themselves, who now agreed that employers had taken advantage of their peaceful strategy. The initiative, though seeming to have passed to the owners, was not distracting the union from its recruitment strategy, which seemed to continue successfully. The local press reported that every day, more and more seamen enrolled into the union from all over Britain. The Liverpool branch secretary reported that it was only in Liverpool that the owners of shipping were mounting such resistance. Everywhere else, comparative progress seemed to have been the order of the day.

In one week in Bootle, 100 new members had been recruited. We are told these had been won to the cause during the course of a voyage. In keeping with our earlier descriptions of the dual nature of the boarding house fraternity, those sympathetic to the union – those described as 'of good character' – were not only out canvassing for the union, but bringing their boarders down to the union office to be enrolled.

On 20 April, there were reports that a slight increase had been gained for seafarers aboard south-bound steamers. Crews were shipped at £4 5s and £4 10s for a southern voyage, or 5s in advance of the demanded rate. However in most cases, sailing ships were still sticking to their £2 15s rate with one or two exceptions where the demanded rate had been accepted.

Another demonstration had been organised to protest against 'the unscrupulous conduct of the Liverpool shipowners in trying to screw down wages to a starvation rate'. Also, it was aimed against the officials of the Board of Trade who were supposed to ensure all seamen were in fact seamen; a fact far from the true situation. The protest was preceded by a brass band, and the crowd assembled in front of St George's Hall near Great George Street.

A considerable crowd had assembled to hear Mr G. Haverlock Wilson, the famous national secretary of the union, as well as the various local branch leaders from Liverpool, Birkenhead, and Bootle. The demands of the men were spelt out. It seems that the press had been totally confused as to what these were because of the various rates in operation by the companies: £4 for sailors and £4 5s for firemen in steamers going to the southward; £3 for sailing ship sailors; £3 13s for sailing ship seamen going to the westward and Baltic.

Just after Mr Wilson, the founder and national secretary of the union, finished his grand speech, an unexpected and exciting scene unfolded. The local press records:

Just before the vote of thanks to the chairman, a Mr Higgins, who for some time has been trying to form a union of his own on local principles, jumped up on the platform, and in a most abusive manner, stepping to the front, commenced to address the meeting. On a call for order, another man who was in his company commenced to abuse Mr Wilson violently, calling him 'a liar'. A Scene of considerable confusion ensued, the ultimate result being a challenge by Mr Higgins to discuss the question with Mr Wilson on a public platform. The challenge was immediately accepted, and it is arranged that Mr Higgins shall attend for this purpose at the Rotunda Lecture Hall tonight.

This is the kind of detail that labour historians become excited about when it comes to light, because it shades in the humanity and human detail that often gets lost in the record of broad historical events. It sets the imagination ablaze with speculation on the nature of the polemic. Are these local men conciliators or Merseyside rebels? Is this a brand of the religious sectionalism widely rumoured by later historians to figure in particular organisational constituents? Actually, this Mr Higgins has emerged in this tale previously; he was the founder and secretary of a local seamen's union based at Bootle.

The meeting itself had more to deal with than Mr Higgins, as the normal points of business were also to be got through. After general speeches, a delegation from the Amalgamated Society of Tailors spoke in support of the seamen. Mr J. Haslam, the miners' agent for Chesterfield, also voiced support, as did Mr W. Bailey, agent for the miners of the Nottingham coalfield. Frustratingly, the local press left it there. We do know not whether the local dissident turned up, or if in fact the debate ever took place.

On 1 May, the union issued the following circular:

To the sailors and firemen of tugboats,

We, the sailors and firemen of the National Amalgamated Sailors' and Firemen's Union of Great Britain and Ireland, earnestly request the sailors and firemen who are engaged in the tugboats on the river Mersey to take into consideration the advisability of cooperation of all parties and work together for our common welfare, and we urge upon them to form a deputation at an early date and meet our committee at the Trades Hall, Duke Street, and discuss the question.

By 8 May, the local officials of the seamen were preparing for a national strike. They were waiting for news from Wilson and his national leadership based in Sunderland as to the state of the union nationwide and attitudes toward a generalised stoppage.

A day later, things started to hot up as trade unionists on vessels ready for sailing refused to ship with non-unionists, even though the union's demanded rate was being paid. All the while, the local officials urged restraint from strike action until word arrived of the national action from Sunderland.

The union firemen on the ship the *City of Chicago* refused to sail with non-unionists, some forty-six in number. They were shipped aboard the lighter

The Floating Road , Liverpool, 1895.

(barge) *Ajax*. The captain however would not to take them ashore, but made them stay there all night without cover. The men made efforts to get aboard passing tugs, but without success. Early the following morning, fifteen men resolved to go back on board *Chicago*, but the rest resolved to remain. The rain poured down, causing great discomfort to the trade unionists. The Inman and International Company, the old anti-unionists of long standing who have featured throughout this story, then applied for summonses against the men, which were of course granted. The men were taken back by police to the landing stage. They walked with their belongings to the police buildings. In the courtyard, the local secretary Mr J. Nicholson and other secretaries were waiting.

Many other of the port's trade unionists, seeing this as a case of, 'There but for the grace of God go I,' assembled at the landing stage, expecting that maybe the brave example set by the crew of the *City of Chicago* might be followed by other crews. At noon, a number of firemen arrived with their bags on the landing stage, having been engaged by American steamers. They were requested by the crowd not to take the place of the striking men. An attempt at an impromptu public meeting was foiled by the police who moved in to disperse it.

The excitement continued until 2 p.m. when a number of men on board the steamer the *Arizona*, which was due to sail the following day, boarded a tug lying alongside. They proceeded in it to the landing stage where they were met by police, who refused permission to the men to land with strict partiality. The tug returned to the *Arizona*, but the men refused to disembark from the tug. Once again, the tug returned to the landing stage, but the force of police still prevented them from landing. A number of police went on board to try and persuade the seamen to go back to the ship, but the men refused to budge.

Finally, after sailing about the port in company with the river police, the men were allowed to come ashore. Several disputes occurred on other steamers. At that time, there was a rush of people, described as 'a very ugly rush', whenever a tender approached with firemen and sailors aboard. Another interesting scene occurred when a tender, which came from the Dominican Liner *Vancouver*, approached the landing stage. A striking seaman jumped ashore and ran along the dock. He was chased by police and then captured among scenes of great excitement. He was arrested, as were several others through the course of the day.

At the city police court on 9 May, the men appeared before the infamous Mr Raffles. Thirty-one seafarers from the steamship the *City of Chicago* stood accused with 'wilful disobedience to lawful orders, and with combining together to disobey orders'. Mr Raffles said he thought it was a monstrous thing that these men should refuse to proceed to sea simply because two 'scabs' were on board. This however, was an exceedingly unpleasant case to deal with. He had power to inflict a fine, and would impose one on each man of 10s, and costs or default of seven days imprisonment.

On 21 May, a deputation including national officials of the union met representatives of the biggest steamship companies. The union put its case, stating that the presence of union men would be a benefit to shipping since they would supply a consistent standard of workers, and discipline their own members, far better than the owners could, whenever necessary. Mr Wilson quoted from the rules of the union. He said that it was the intention of the union to provide a better class of men for the merchant service, and to see that all the members engaged for a vessel were on board at the appointed time in sober condition and ready to do their work. The union compelled all sailors to produce four years sea service before they were enrolled as able seamen. The firemen were asked to show twelve months discharges before they were enrolled as firemen. He contended that such rules would tend to improve the seamen and firemen in the merchant service. Any member of the union who neglected to join his vessel at the appointed time, or who neglected to join his work through drink, would be fined £1 for the first offence if reported to the officials of the union. For the third offence he was liable to be expelled.

The shipowners seemed not to have been overwhelmed by this display of servitude. The very same solicitor acting on behalf of the Cunard Steamship

Company applied for a summons against James Stuart, secretary of the Bootle branch of the Sailors' and Firemen's Union, for issuing a threat to stop one of the company's packets sailing if the union rate was not agreed to. The summons was granted. It was further announced that Mr Wilson himself, the national secretary of the union, had been served with two summonses in another port for intimidating certain men from shipping with non-unionists. All of the western ocean steamers were by this time carrying union crews.

Days later, the shipowners replied that they were simply unable to comply with the men's demands. The response was almost by return. A meeting of the executive at Sunderland resolved to issue a notice to the shipowners of the UK. They would seek an advance in wages in all departments, ranging from 10s to 15s per month. Should no advance be granted after 3 June, a nationwide strike (termed a general strike) would be engaged.

At the Trades Hall, Duke Street, a meeting of the men agreed not to sign early for ships and therefore allow the owners to get crews that would otherwise be held up by the strike. A further resolution that was passed agreed to distribute leaflets to the dockers not to assist in the taking of any steamer out of the dock during the struggle.

At the Alexandra Hall, Brasenose Road, Bootle, a mass meeting of dockers was organised. It was held under the auspices of the Amalgamated Dock Labourers Union of Great Britain. Like the seamen's conversion to a national union, the dockers had also been organised into a national body following visits to the port. Mr William Nicholson, the local secretary of the seamen, acted as chair.

Mr C. Kennedy, the general organiser from Glasgow, stated that the objective was to form a national dockers' union throughout the kingdom. During the course of the meeting, it was resolved that the dockers would render all assistance they could to the seamen. Many speakers from the floor recalled the other great dockers' strikes in the port, and the soldiers called in to defend the docks and the blacklegs. Others hoped that by creating a national union, they would prevent scabs being brought in from Glasgow and the like. A demonstration of labourers was organised for the following week.

Meanwhile, the *Liverpool Daily Post* was predicting dire outcomes: 'It is even possible that civil war will be the outcome of the strike, for starvation has often meant rioting, and rioting has often grown to civil war.' Four days after the strike officially began, the Union HQ reported that the union's demands had been conceded in twenty ports. A few of the firms in Liverpool also conceded to the men's demands, although the biggest were holding out. Yet despite this news, all was not well with the action, and it was announced that fifteen Western Ocean packets had sailed with full and competent crews without paying union rates. A considerable number of men arrived in the port from Yarmouth and the east coast to take the place of the Liverpool men. At the same time, shipowners in other parts of the country were being forced to lay their ships up, being unable to find blackleg crews but unwilling to pay union rates. In reply to the union's request for a further meeting with the Liverpool shipowners, they replied that sailors had been sent for from Norwegian and Danish ports, and therefore all future talks would be pointless. The union announced that it had little faith in such reports and the shipping of foreigners would results in riots in America if it happened.

The union meanwhile had organised what was described in the press as 'night and day pickets' to watch over all the rail stations and landing stages for the arrival of blacklegs. It was concluded however that the companies were finding great difficulties in finding any such men.

On 10 June, the shipping masters stepped up their attempts to sow divisions among the men. They issued leaflets along the dock announcing, 'Unless the men who are now on strike at once return to their work, they will find their places permanently filled with sailors.' The leaflets declared the strike virtually broken. The union violently denied the claims.

Meanwhile, union agents had been appointed on the continent to induce foreign seamen to stop away from English ports during their present strike. In two or three large continental ports, branches of the union had been established and were successfully enrolling members. The official organ of the union (which unfortunately is unnamed) announced that, with the exception of Glasgow and Liverpool, the strike was virtually at an end, the owners having conceded everything that was asked for. It was however reported that 150 seamen in Derry were still on strike.

On 11 June, the union initiated a long overdue 'get tough policy' on the owners. The Inman and International Company offered to pay union rates to all union crew for the ship the *City of New York*. The officials of the company even came to the union office. However, the union officials instructed that if they could pay it on one vessel they could pay it on them all. A resolution to this effect was passed at the seamen's union, in that no unionist would be allowed to sign on, regardless of the rate offered, until such time as the whole of the company conceded the demands of the men. Officials of the union toured the docks, spreading word of the new decisions.

The union then went in for a mammoth public relations campaign, with posters and leaflets addressing the seamen, firemen, and dockers, followed by the passengers and then the general public of Liverpool. It explained the case of the men and countered the arguments of the company. The *Liverpool Daily Post* commented, 'Pedestrians in many of the streets of Liverpool yesterday had the circulars from both sides showered upon them. The bills were distributed in thousands.' The address to the dockers included a call for them to put forward their own wage claim of 5s per day.

A day later, the union received a letter from the Ships' Officers Union stating that some 500 officers had determined not to ship vessels that did not have a union crew.

The next day, the seamen held another great procession through the streets. It started at noon from the Trades Hall, *en route* to Bootle along the line of docks. The Bootle members set off at the same hour from their office. The two processions converged at the Bootle timber yards to return along the line of docks to Liverpool. On the return journey, it was reported 7,000 men were marching. Large groups of dockers joined the march, and by the time it reached the Clarence Dock, some 20,000 were on it. The report continued:

> Along the line of route, the men were loudly cheered by women who were standing at the corners of the various streets. The Bootle procession numbered about 1,000 sailors and firemen, and their ranks were swelled by a similar number of dock labourers. When the two parties met at Bootle, the men indulged in great cheering. Near Sandhills on the return journey, the sailors and firemen from Birkenhead joined in the ranks. The Bootle men headed the procession with a brass band and a number of banners and flags were born by the men. Everything passed off in a peaceful manner until Dennison Street, which runs off Great Howard Street, was reached. In this street there is a boarding house keeper [who] is noted for supplying hands to the shipping companies at the old rates during the strike. Word was passed along the ranks a short time previously that it was the intention of the leaders to march through the street, and this order gave immense satisfaction to the men. When the head of the procession reached Dennison Street at the dock end, it was found that a line of police was drawn up across the roadway for the purpose of preventing the men passing along it. A short argument took place between the leaders and the police while cries were raised of 'break through'. The police, seeing the thousands of men in the procession, at once gave way, and the men marched through the street without offering the slightest violence to the boarding house keeper. After leaving Dennison Street, the procession went down Old Hall Street and the Exchange, where a large number of merchants left their business for a few minutes in order to watch the demonstration.

The march then did a tour of various shipping lines before dispersing to separate meetings, although most men took off for their dinners.

The purpose of the demonstration was to show the town that the strike was a long way off finished or lacking in support, and this was most surely proven. In the meantime, the men themselves were starting to take a more militant turn. It was announced that several crews had signed on both at the sailors' home and on board the steamers at below the union rates. The men were starting to feel frustrated at the 'sit back and watch' attitude counselled by their higher officials. In the afternoon, a large number of cattlemen went to the sailors' home to sign articles for the steamer *Virginia*, not to go as members of the crew but to obtain their customary free passage back to Boston. At this precise time, about 1,000 seamen and firemen were congregated around the home. They concluded that these men were shipping in as scabs under false colours. A man, who we are told wore a rosette and was a union delegate, stirred the men to action, saying that they would prevent anyone from signing on at the home. They then occupied the waiting room of the home, and the cattlemen beat a hasty retreat until the police intervened and cleared the seamen out.

Meanwhile, the union was continuing with its 'night and day pickets', watching over all the railway stations and landing stages for the arrival of blacklegs.

At the concert hall, Lord Nelson Street, Mr Wilson addressed a meeting of the seamen and their wives. We are told there was a great attendance of sailors, firemen, women, and families. Wilson was greeted with a great cheer. He told them that the shipowners were telling the public that it was he who was bringing ruin not only to the seafarers, but to the wives and families too. He had taken the opportunity to call the wives and families to this meeting and ask them their verdict on the owners' claim. Cries of, 'You are not!' resounded from the women folk amongst prolonged cheering. Wilson accused the shipowners of not paying the allotment notes to the men's wives in many cases, and this was greeted well by the crowd, with the women shouting, 'That's true!' He could picture these women and the miseries and starvation they were likely to entail during the strike, and asked them if they were prepared to face it. Cries of, 'Yes!' were heard from the women, alongside more cheering.

Whatever the leader's subsequent short comings, Wilson here showed great perception in seeing the wives and families of the strikers as part of the movement, and their involvement as crucial to its success. They after all probably comprised two-thirds of the maritime community of the port.

At the same time as the owners were boasting of their supplies of labour from the continent, a communication was received from the seafarers of Denmark. It stated that the seamen, firemen, and sailors of Copenhagen had formed a branch of the union, calling themselves the Free Seamen's Federation of Denmark. The union had only been formed for one week, but had in that time built up a membership of 550 members, who would demand the same rate of pay as the British sailors. Telegrams were being freely exchanged between the leaders of both the unions.

Locally too, we see glimpses of sympathy strikes and 'knock on' strikes etc., for example, the strike of 300 to 350 'scalers' (actually de-scalers) at Bootle. They stated that the owners could not get the vital tubes of their ships' boilers cleaned, and that ships therefore could not get out of the docks. The scalers proceeded to Birkenhead with the object of calling out their brothers in support of the seamen and firemen. About 100 dock labourers at the north end turned out in support of the seafarers. The element of pure 'solidarity' here should not be lost; it is a common identity with fellow workers, which we witness across 'trades' throughout the period of this research – an identification that, in my view, transcends simple economic self-interest, and certainly must have instigated class and political conclusions to have been drawn.

On 19 June, a morale and fund raising concert was held at the Rotunda Lecture Hall, William Brown Street. A very large audience assembled, and songs and recitations, together with a brass band, provided the entertainment. Two days later, the shore gangs came out, both for the seamen and in support of an advance for themselves of 6d per day to fix a rate of 5s per day.

Meanwhile, the flow of blacklegs into the port continued. The press reported such men as seamen, tall and healthy, while the union maintained that such people had never seen a ship before. What is clear is that the shipowners by all means were managing to get enough crews to sail their vessels. Watching strangers take their places, the strikers' tempers were becoming frayed. The steamer *Fritera* was lying in the Wapping basin, being made ready for sea. The crew, who were now ashore from the previous voyage, are alleged to have told the press that they would have returned, but were afraid of the union men. Consequently, the company hired new men. On the night of their concert, the men and boys engaged in scaling the boilers turned out in support for the seamen. A day later, the blackleg crew joined the ship. A number of union men went on board to try and talk them out of their work; more and more men boarded the vessel. An officer who had tried to repulse the men was himself assaulted and the blackleg crew, expecting similar treatment, fled the ship. The press reported that the steamer was under the complete charge of the union men for some time.

A day or two later, the crew of the *Tenerife* were signing articles for the vessel that was lying in the Coburg Dock. Several crew had signed and others were lined up to do so. A crowd of union men suddenly appeared on the dock quay yelling 'scabs' at the top of their voices and urging them to join the strike and come ashore. Ultimately, the whole crew did so and mingled with the strikers. The police that were present were faced with many hundreds of shouting union men and were unable to prevent the disaffection.

One feature that must have driven the authorities to apoplexy was the possible political overtones seen in the disaffection of naval reserve crews, with all the comparatively recent memories of mutinies and challenges to the realm. The spectre of revolution might well have haunted some local Tories.

A mass demonstration of seamen and firemen taking place on 27 June saw 300 Royal Navy Reserve ratings leave off their drill on the *Eagle*, laying in the

Kings Dock, and join the demonstration. They took their place at the head of the demonstration, which marched along the Wapping and Goree docks while flags and banners waved and a band played. The demonstration was greatly swelled by RNR men, together with sailors and firemen from Bootle. In all, some 900 RNR ratings joined the demonstration, many in the uniform of the King's Navy.

A probable crisis of confidence was also obviously apparent. A meeting of the Liverpool branch decided to challenge the shipowners to arbitration. Arbitration, as we have seen before, takes control and direction away from the strike movement and the strikers. It places its fate in the notion of independent 'fairness', which in class terms, is problematic. The call for arbitration is usually made by the weakest side; in previous disputes, the shipowners and masters made the call. Such a call at this stage from the strikers could only send a sign to the owners not to weaken. On 3 July, the owners decided there was nothing to arbitrate about and unanimously rejected such a course of action.

July opened with 700 timber carriers coming out and marching through the town in support of a claim for increased wages. Certain of their masters conceded right away, but it had not been sufficient to satisfy the workers, who marched in procession through the streets of Bootle. The demonstration caused great dismay to the local shopkeepers, who could see still further hardships to trade. In Bootle, some 3,000 seamen of all sorts were on strike, plus 750 scalers and 250 shore gang men.

All of the docks and boarding houses were laid under special police guard in case of attack. Large bodies of seamen marched up and down great Howard Street and Waterloo Road in the afternoon. Several times, the police made sorties to disperse the men when they gathered toward Dennison Street, a sources of rogue boarding house masters who were the recruiting pimps for blacklegs. On 4 July, a huge body of trade unionists marched to Bootle, while others congregated throughout the day near Dennison Street. All sides reported assaults by their various protagonists in the course of that day.

It was these boarding house 'rouges' that became the centre of union demonstrations in Dennison Street and the infamous Great Howard Street. The strikers had learned between forty and fifty non-unionists were housed in these streets in readiness to ship out on stricken vessels. But before the strikers could exert any powers of persuasion to the contrary, they had already been taken out under strong police guard toward the river, together with a cart carrying their luggage. Despite this, the strikers believed that many more potential scabs were still in the houses. The *Liverpool Post* reported:

> According to arrangements made the previous night, Dennison Street was made the assembly place of two processions of the sailors out on strike.

One which started from Bootle, and the other from headquarters at the Trades Hall, Duke Street. The men began to gather about ten o'clock, and shortly after eleven, the procession arrived in full force. They took their stand in Dennison Street and the neighbouring streets, and gave three cheers for the union and groans for the 'scabs' and the shipowners, and generally appeared in a very excited condition. There were at that time but few police on the ground, but a messenger was dispatched for immediate aid. In the meantime, the men had been told they must not block the street altogether, and to a certain extent amenable to order, they commenced marching down one side of the street and up the other, forming a complete, circular procession. Soon however, the more rowdy spirits were unable to restrain themselves and attacks began to be made on the various obnoxious boarding houses in the vicinity. Marching up Gibraltar Row, a body of men attacked the house of a man named Doyle, whom they suspected of harbouring 'scabs'. The Gibraltar Arms was also attacked, the windows completely knocked out of their frames, and the landlords hooted – dubbed as a crimp, and on being got hold of by some of the men, they were considerably mauled and otherwise maltreated. The police now had become somewhat reinforced. The head constable had arrived accompanied by Chief Superintendent Hancox, Superintendent Parkinson, Detective Inspector Irvine, and inspectors Hassal, Macaulay, Edmondson, and M'Conchie. Order were given for the police to march down the street and clear the houses of all but the residents. Considerable difficulty was found in this, and the men, although they did not attack the police, resisted every effort to dislodge them. A request was sent for further aid, and shortly after twelve o'clock, the mounted police rode up under Inspector Sales.

By this time however, the demonstration had already moved off. The police were mobbed by frightened boarding house masters of the 'rouge' variety, pleading for protection. As a result of this, they mounted a guard at the end of the streets to prevent any but business traffic passing through it.

Good and bad news was received on 4 July. The timber carriers' employers had all given way to the demands of the workers, so this column of labour would be leaving the front, albeit victorious. A rumour began to circulate that certain men were breaking away from the union ranks and slipping aboard vessels at night time. The union accordingly posted 750 pickets, and half patrolled Regent Road between the Alexandra docks. One shift of pickets finished their shift at midnight, whereupon another shift took over. The men made a good job of it and stopped everyone from going through unless they could make good account of themselves. Cabs attempting to pass through had their passengers questioned as to their business. In several instances, we are told that scab seamen were badly treated. The police, although present, were unable to cope with the vast crowds of striking seamen. Reinforcements of police from Bootle were roused from their beds to clear the streets. Repeated attempts were made by the police to do so, but the crowds were too great; the seamen were offering great resistance to the police, who drew their truncheons and charged the men. Several were severely injured. A number of boarding masters and runners who were familiar with using such hours of the morning to transact their business were captured, and were later seen returning to their homes bearing the scars of their encounters. Many of the skirmishes through the course of the night resulted in combatants being conveyed to Bootle Hospital.

In the middle of such valiant scenes came news that branches of the union elsewhere were against the strike. Dundee and Glasgow both passed resolutions condemning the current strike, although we are not told on what grounds.

Perhaps such criticism prompted the announcement of 8 July that a general ballot of the membership would be held. It would ask whether they were to stop out on strike, but curiously only for the coming week. This was passed with a great majority in favour. In the Birkenhead and Liverpool branches, it had been more than ten to one in favour.

Despite what appears a great vote of confidence in the strike on Merseyside, the *Liverpool Post* then headed its 13 July piece on the labour question with the headline, 'Collapse of the Sailors' Strike.' It was then reported that the strike was virtually finished, with even the local leadership admitting to the press that the union had not the remotest chance of winning the struggle now. The men were deserting in their hundreds to join ships. At the same time, Mr Wilson was away in Cardiff. The local leaders were asking in amassment why the men had not voted to terminate their strike when they had been given such wise council from themselves to do so. To put a brave face on it and pull some spuds from the fire, the leaders claimed the strike to have been victorious. This was so, because the seamen would not need to strike again for a long time and the shipowners would never again refuse arbitration.

The strike was never publicly, or from what I can see, constitutionally ended. We are left with a heroic tale of struggle, and a pitiful and probably unnecessarily premature end. Even the press conceded however, that the failure of the strike did not mean the end of union; far from it. The week prior to the reported end of the strike, large numbers of new members had been recruited at Liverpool and Birkenhead. Entrance fees were raised from 5s 4d to £1 in what can only have been a bureaucratic stroke in anticipation of the strike ending and advances being paid. It could be a way of now honourably going to work, having joined the union, while the union would see its membership and funds grow. So the strike *de facto* ended. Little more can be gleaned of the mechanics of this sudden turn, although maybe history will turn up an answer in the future. Certainly, a key element in the employers' strategy was the pivotal position of the reactionary boarding house keepers and their ability to recruit crews of all descriptions, seaworthy and not at all. Their role ensured that they would be forever immortalised in the seamen's work songs the globe over, and come back down to us in history via the folk song revival of the 1960s and 1970s. Few of the bearded, thumbs-in-belts folk singers of those decades, singing of 'hanging Paddy Doyle for his boots' for example, would know that these were real actors in a very bitter play. That the Board of Trade chose to turn a blind eye to the non-suitability of the crews was also somewhat fortuitous to the owners. Modern struggles in the 1980s saw many official blind eyes turned in favour of employers during crucial strikes, so we cannot perhaps be too retrospectively outraged.

As the seamen's strike was ending, the strike of the waterfront labourers was beginning. Perhaps this was not the beginning, as we have seen throughout the course of the seamen's strike that various sections of the dock labour force launched joint actions in support of their own wage claims.

The London dockers were already on strike in a great battle for 'the dockers' tanner'. It was perhaps one of the most famous strikes in English labour history and many historians and their students have seen it as a watershed. I have never really understood why, for the London dockers were fighting for the rate of wages already fought for and paid to the Liverpool dock labourers. Henry Hyde Champion, a middle class member of the London Dock Strike Committee, tells us of his comrades: '... The Dockers – a class hitherto disorganised and helpless – had formed a combination...' Given the Liverpool history of constant organisation, such an observation seems unlikely to be true, although he draws a distinction between the 'stevedores' who he says had been organised for many years, and the 'labourers'. He tells us their union had been formed by 'a handful' only two years prior. Regarding the seamen of that port, he tells us that having failed many previous attempts at organisation, they 'have quite recently established a union which is said to number 70,000 members'. He further tells us that it was the seamen and 'stevedores' who 'really formed the backbone of the strike'. A short time afterwards, the Liverpool men saw this as an opportunity to launch their own strike and increase their wages still further.

On 3 September, a gang of 100 grain porters at the Harrington Dock struck in support of a claim for 1s per day increase on their 5s per day rate, plus an increase of from 8d to 1s for overtime. This was followed by movements of workers on other vessels. Grain porters were incredibly hard working teams, often carrying as much as 45 tons of wheat per man per day. It seems that mainly the south end was involved with this action, with some participation in the north. The action was brief in many south end locations, with settlements being conceded at once.

That afternoon, the press reported that grain porters in the south end were still out to the number of 200 or so. Other porters were out in solidarity. The press reported that no organisation existed among the grain porters at this time, although this did not stop them mounting pickets and patrols of the docks.

In the afternoon, a meeting of the strikers took place in front of the Harrington café. About 1,000 men gathered; forming a ring with a space left in the middle, thus declaring an open platform and agenda. After some time however, no-one had stepped forward and it looked like the spontaneous meeting, together with the spontaneous strike, might collapse. Nobody felt prepared to assume the role of leader or spokesman.

Then a labourer called Richards stepped forward. He said that although he was not a bag carrier, he had come on strike in support of their demands for 6s per day. He believed they deserved their money. 'They do!' came the response from the crowd. If it was not worth 6s a day to carry 45 tons, he should like somebody to tell him what it was worth. He expressed regret that no bag carrier had the courage to come forward to speak for them. 'Hear, hear!' said the crowd, suggesting that many were sympathy strikers. Lots of them who had struck work that day, he said, were not actual bag carriers, yet not one bag carrier would come forward and say what it was that they wanted. 'Bravo!' came the response. He went on to say that he could see bag carriers round him who wanted others to help them fight their battles, so why would they not come forth and speak. Next, a labourer called J. Hooker addressed the meeting, and although he too was not a bag carrier, he thought their work was terrible, arduous, and that they deserved their money. He stated that he would leave the ship he was working on if the carriers did not get their money. But he asked, considering a different tactic, if there was a ship on which no bag carriers were working, why should a man leave work on that ship? The reply from the crowd was, 'To uphold the men who are carrying bags.' This was greeted by applause. It was drawing close to starting time, and if they took his honest opinion from his heart, they would go back to work but carry no bags. 'Hear, hear!' was heard from the crowd. Richards said that since no bag carrier would come forward, his advice was for them to look for a job. A voice in the crowd shouted out, 'Let the bag carriers stick out for themselves and let those who can get a job.' The question was put to the vote as to whether they would stand out with the carriers, and this was carried in favour of a solidarity strike with one or two dissenters. We see here a feature of workers' meetings, which often baffles outside observers and sometimes leaders, whereby the meeting votes in favour of an unexpressed feeling rather than the logic of the spoken direction of debate.

The following day, the corn porters struck work in support of the grain porters.

The *Liverpool Mercury*, after stating that considerable interest and influence was passing between London and Liverpool dockers, went on to tell us that by 7 September, the grain carriers had won their advance and were back to normal working.

Meanwhile in this period, the Liverpool dockers who had in the past been sorely plagued by blacklegs were being equally unprincipled to their London comrades. London dockers had never traditionally scabbed on any striking port in any numbers. Yet here we had ships diverted to Liverpool from London being worked on, and hundreds of Liverpool men flooding London to take the Londoners work with their eyes wide open.

On 12 September, it was announced that the Birkenhead branch of the National Union of Dock Labourers of Great Britain and Ireland, which had been established during the seamen's strike, were holding a meeting at the Queens Hall, Claughton Road. The meeting discussed the state of their union nationally, which they viewed to be very strong, and also the London dockers strike, which they were supporting financially. The following month, they announced that they themselves would strike if their wage demand was not met and that this strike would commence in 1890. The 1889 struggle ended with a short sharp strike of forty dockers on the *City of Dublin* steam packet.

The Missing Strike

Despite the well respected and authoritative writing of Sir James Sexton in his great book about his life as a militant dockers' agitator of the period, I have found no reference whatever to the great strike of 1889 to which he refers. Readers will see the scope of local newspapers used in this research, yet I can find no reference to any such strikes either here or in the national press. The leaders of which he speaks of are certainly seen to be in the official capacity of officers of the Dock Labourers Union. Yet despite the obvious importance of the strike he refers to, I can find no reference to it. There are three possible explanations: either the fickleness of the press, or my own failure to discover it. These first two explanations are unlikely; the press in Liverpool abounds with detailed reports of the seamen's strike, and coverage of meetings of associations great and small. Why ignore a related action on the docks? The range of sources I have used makes missing a report in the papers highly unlikely. Which leads me to reluctantly draw a third conclusion, at the risk of bringing a labour historian's *'fatwah'* upon my unworthy, blasphemous head, that Sir James seems to have got his dates mixed up. The leaders, events, trials, and failings of the strike he describes as 1889 in fact take place in 1890. Readers will easily see this to be the case. Talking of the strike leaders, Sexton says:

> These men were Richard McGhee and Edward McHugh, both hailing from the north of Ireland. McGhee was a commercial traveller, McHugh

was a printer. They were ardent reformers, friends, and students of Henry George, and the founders of the dockers' union in Glasgow...

In an interview with the *Liverpool Daily Post*, M'Hugh (it is clear the press of those days did not employ the lower-case 'c'), acting as general secretary, says that the idea of forming a National Union of Dock Labourers 'first originated among a number of men employed in coasting steamers in Glasgow in the early part of [1889]'. 'He was himself a follower of Henry George.'

Leaders of the 1890 strike include E. McGhee, and E. McHugh (M'Hugh). Sexton claims that the union button, designed by McGhee, was used to identify members in good standing, and was a tactical disaster and the cause of defeat of the 1889 strike. In fact, the battle over the badge and the employers' response to it occurred in the 1890 strike. Sexton says of the strike (which he cites as 1889), 'The effort ended strangely enough through the intervention of an ex-convict, Michael Davitt – with some small concessions to the men, but with bitterness indeed to the leaders.'

Actually Mr Davitt, a famous Irish leader, makes his surprise appearance during the strike of 1890, on 25 March to be exact, and intervenes to find a solution to the dispute, albeit not one sanctioned by the union at any level. While it is true that history can repeat itself, such a fusion and duplication of events and personalities tests credulity. It is clear that Sexton mixed up a minor strike and the union's general agitation toward the end of 1889 with the actual launch of the strike movement in 1890.

The year 1890 had marked a woeful defeat of a dedicated strike by the seamen. The Seamen's Union however, prevailed and prospered. In November, after recurrent walk-outs by crews obeying the union rule not to ship with non-members, the Inman and International Company, one of the most entrenched and belligerently anti-union firms in the port, granted the Seamen's Union a closed shop, although other companies, while on negotiating terms with the union, refused to grant it recognition as such.

The new decade began with the formation of the Mersey Quay and Railway Carters Union, with branches opening in Bootle, Liverpool, and Birkenhead and a collective membership of 2,000. Paul Smith's recent paper gave me a greater depth of understanding of this section of the port's workforce than I had otherwise obtained. I had considered the highly strategic role of this group and their obvious skills with numerous big horses and vehicles, coupled with their less than high profile turn out in the preceding forty years of struggle. I concluded that such a specialist group must have been able to demand and receive prime wages. I also had concluded that many of the port's carters must have been owner-drivers who simply passed on increased charges to the shipping company or buyers. Smith however, concluded that most where in fact wage labourers, and that although skilled, it was not a skill that was rare or uncommon. Many carters and potential carters would have come from the farms, well used to driving big horses in large sets and hauling large farm vehicles. Smith explains that in 1891:

> Some 11,000 carters were in casual employment, taken on when required from 'stands', which in Liverpool were on public view. This later became important in enforcing union preference and the closed shop. An unknown proportion of carters held permanent posts. Carters (as with dockers) were segregated by customary distinctions within occupations, ethnicity, and locality, and employers' and workers' preferences.

He presents a complex picture; at the north end, the carters would be Catholic, while at the south end, Protestant. He suggests that there was some sectarian indulgence in employers' choice of carter biased by religion and origin. Organisations among the respective work forces would also reflect this bias and sectarianism, although probably not to the point of total separation. It would, however, reflect in the capacity and inclination for independent workplace organisation. Interestingly, Paul Smith tells us that early sources suggest the united decision of the carters in the previous year not to support the strike (which was presumed to be a dock strike, although as I have demonstrated, one that does not seem to feature in any of the local or national papers) of 1889. Perhaps if true, this would not be too surprising, since the same paper tells us that their union was not founded until November of that year. Certainly, there had been wide spread agitation by the newly formed Liverpool Amalgamated Scavengers and Ashmen's Union. The build-up to action against the 'corporation' as part of a general wages offensive failed, and later we hear the union complaining that they were 'sorry to hear that the carters and wharfmen had not thrown in their lot with the others and agitated for an increase'. I think it fair to assume *this* was the strike they actually had decided not to support. Even more interesting, Smith says of the carters:

> In this environment and among workers who lacked a 'habit of association', the construction of trade union organisation was a daunting task. Any success was fragmented and ephemeral: for example, the failure of a strike by Liverpool carters in 1872 was followed by the collapse of a newly-born union.

If true, this seems an odd outcome if we recall from earlier in this work the carters' strike of 1872, which after the intervention of Mr Simpson and the result of arbitration, was a total success. Indeed, it had stimulated his stature in the wider dockers' strike movement.

Paul Smith's paper also contradicts this press report insofar as it asserts that the union was actually founded some three months earlier in the previous year. '... The MQRCU was formed in November 1889 at a meeting called by William Almond, a carter. It was an occupational union of carters engaged in transport to docks and railways ...' Just to add a bit more spice to the debate, we might recall that carters were in strike action in 1866. One of the strikers appeared in court for attacking a blackleg, and the clear implication was that they had a union back then. Leaving the precise date of formation aside, the papers start to report a strike on the horizon within the first days of January, despite the offer by many employers to cut the time worked by two or three hours and pay a higher overtime premium.

Prior to this, it seems that a carter had no defined working hours:

Rising at 4.30 a.m., he would arrive at the stable at 5.15 a.m., attend to the horses, have breakfast, and then leave before 7 a.m. for the docks or rail depots so as to be early in any queue for loading. Several trips carrying goods might be made in a day, each requiring heavy labour in loading and unloading ... in practice, about half an hour was available for dinner. In the evening, an hour's stable duty was necessary. The overall working day could amount to 15 hours.

On 9 January, the carters engaged by Messrs Thompson, M'Kay & Co., refused to work unless they conceded something with regard to overtime payment. The carters were told that their demands would be met if they returned. This action then set the scene for others to contemplate action.

By 11 January, five big employers of carters had conceded to the demands. The union quickly spread with 5,000 members. Thirty-five companies (employing 1,000 men) agreed to its pay and hours demands.

The grain carriers restarted their agitation this month at the north end docks. They demanded 6d per day increase. It was predicted that they would win outright. At the Langton Dock, nearly 100 men went out on strike, the bushellers taking the lead for an advance of about 1s per day. They were working on a highly dusty grain called kurraches. When this demand was not met, they walked out. All the other men dependent upon them were then thrown out of work.

Near the end of the month, it was reported that the strike at the south docks was over, with the grain carriers returning. The north end weighers however were still out and ships were being moved to different docks for unloading. This report seems to have been untrue unless the strike restarted, since the day after, the same paper reported, 'At the south docks there are several cargoes of wheat remaining undelivered owing to the strike, and the same state of affairs exists at the north docks.'

Quietly, the strike movement was spreading, and to forestall this, certain employers were pre-emptively raising their rates. At the same time, some owners introduced scabs from Cheshire to unload 300 bags of wheat. At this time, there were five cargoes in the docks awaiting unloading due to the strike. The grain weighers were holding a meeting in support of their strike and demand for a 5s to 6s per day increase. The scalers joined the action and marched about 100 strong along the line of docks. Despite the wildcat nature of the action, and its apparent buoyancy, by 24 January it was being widely reported that the strike of grain carriers, bushellers, and labourers was over. It had lasted a week and most returned on their old terms.

At the Huskisson Dock the same day, a circular was being distributed:

Dock Labourers: Desperate struggle going on in Belfast, Steamship the *Bangore Head* at present stopped in Brunswick Dock; *Lord Londonderry* expected, of same line. Fellow workers of Liverpool, we appeal to you on no account to work the above steamers until such times as the men of Belfast have received their just rights – By Order.

The steamship the *Bangore Head* of Belfast arrived in the river and docked at the Brunswick. A number of men were taken to discharge her cargo, but before they could commence work, a representative of the National Dockers' Union appeared on the scene. He informed the men of the dispute in Belfast and the way the companies were trying to get Liverpool men acting in ignorance to break the strike. He told them the union was supporting the Belfast men's struggle and as such they should not touch the cargo. As a result, 200 men went on strike and no other crews could be found to discharge the steamer.

The carters also then refused to have anything to do with Belfast vessels. The ship in question was moved to the Albert Dock where the employees of the Mersey Docks and Harbour Board, always the weakest link in the dock chain, set to work discharging her. Meanwhile, the *Lord Londonderry,* lying in the Alexandra Dock, was similarly blacked, and no docker would touch her.

This solidarity action demonstrated an immense maturity of organised labour in Liverpool. The Belfast dispute was not over wages; the owners had granted the demanded rates, and indeed the Belfast wages were better than those of Liverpool. Rather, the dispute was about union power. The company had merely hired a freight clerk who was not in the dockers union. The Belfast men were holding the line for solid union organisation and a *de-facto* closed shop. To impose this level of job control at such an early year, and be able to call upon and receive almost total solidarity action, cannot be overstated.

On the same day that saw the carters join the action, the Langton Dock came out. They stated that their wages had only been paid up until the Saturday morning instead of up until 4 p.m. as per agreement. The press reported that the employers had conceded and would make the money up on the next weeks' wages.

At the Wellington Dock, a group of men engaged in discharging the steamer the *Ganoese* refused to carry on unloading the cargo of sulphur unless they received a 1s per day rise. This was obviously a one off or day-to-day dispute based on this specific cargo, as had been the earlier action at the Langton Dock. In this case, the demand was also conceded at once.

The overall wage demand that the dockers had submitted, having been considered by all the docks masters, was rejected. At once, the leadership of the union issued a statement saying that they did not envisage a stoppage because they were not strong enough. The membership in the port was estimated by the union at 7,500 members.

The Liverpool Grain Storage Company had their warehouses opposite the Alexandra Dock. The men here worked in choking clouds of grain dust. This dust, like coal dust, scarred the lungs, producing serious injury and presumably death. The men were demanding an increase of 6d per day on their existing 4s. The owners refused, and at once tried to find scabs. The regular workforce of 100 walked off the job.

Meanwhile, the Birkenhead dock labourers put forward their claim for an increase in wages. The shipowners refused. In this case, the labourers struck work. The grain porters who were still on strike were meeting in the Cocoa Rooms, Derby Street. The directors of the firm had agreed to pay the advance, but wanted full rights to decide which rooms to place men in and which work was done by whom. We see again in this instance that high levels of job control were clearly in the hands of the workers. The main point of issue here was centred around the class of workers called 'bandsmen'. Two out of seven such workers had been removed and replaced by boys. Objecting to this, the men had the boys removed, but the two men were still not re-engaged. Some of the boys were present at the meeting and amid cheers announced that they would not do the work of the bandsmen. It was subsequently resolved that the men would go back to work for the increases, but if boys were again employed on men's work, they would recommence the strike.

Knights of Labour *v.* the National Dock Labourers Union

A very confusing and bitter dispute had arisen between the Knights of Labour, mentioned briefly earlier, and the National Dock Labourers' Union. Both these organisation seem to have lived alongside one another and acted in concert. Quite a number of the influential leaders of the dockers' union had come from their ranks. It seems likely that members of the Knights would also have been members of the dockers union, although this may not have been the case, and could conceivably have been the source of the strife.

Some of the dockers were engaged in discharging a vessel when they encountered workers similarly engaged, whom they perceived to be non-unionists. These men were asked to join the union, and when they refused, the men, in accordance with their customs and rules, walked off the job. We are then told that the Knights of Labour offered to discharge the vessel, an offer that the employers enthusiastically took them up on.

A noisy meeting of the Knights, convened with others of the port's unions, saw the seamen's union secretary Mr Connery take them to task for becoming scabs. For their part, the Knights denied that this had been 'officially' done. I gather that the non-unionists were themselves members of the Knights of Labour. The seamen's secretary tried to address the meeting. The press reports:

[The secretary] was ordered to sit down by the chairman. Most disorderly scenes then occurred. Several violent altercations taking place between men belonging to the rival organisations, in different parts of the room.

Mr Higgins again rose to speak, and after comparative quiet had been restored, he made an abusive attack on a man in the audience. Upon this there were groans from the majority of the audience, several of whom denounced the speaker as a coward and a 'mean man' and threatened to pull him off the platform and 'go for him'.

One of the members of the Knights of Labour shouted that such language should not be used, and said he was sorry to see their organisation dragged in the dirt (loud cheers and groans).

The meeting ended in disorder with fifty labourers in the audience selecting an opponent each and carrying on a furious verbal battle for ten minutes, which flowed over into the street for a considerable time. The scars from this dispute went deep and the matter would resurface later.

Over at Birkenhead, the strike rumbled on. Although an official action, it seems to have been rather localised. Fifty scabs had been brought in and were being housed in sheds at the Morpeth Dock, which were guarded by a detachment of police.

This particular dispute again had its roots in union organisation and the extent to which the owners granted the union its due. The union had some 5,000 members, who had set up a fund to provide welfare benefits for sickness and accidents. (We have seen little of accidents and industrial disease in this work, but clearly they must have been endemic in the industrial *mêlée* of ships, water, moving vehicles, horses, cranes, and cargoes many of toxic and hazardous materials, swaying planks, and overhead yards.) The ordinary subscriptions were at first 3*d* weekly then the second one of 2*d* per week thereafter. The men had invited the employers to join any set-aside funding they might have to the union funds in order to make a better single fund. Most masters fell in line with this and agreed to hand over substantial moneys to the fund.

A minority refused. In retaliation the men refused to handle their cargoes, while it was being reported that Liverpool men were being brought in to break up this action.

By 1 February, it was reported that the Belfast strike was over and the blacking could be lifted on the stranded vessels.

The sophistication of union organisation on both sides of the river was demonstrated by a joint meeting of scalers, dockers, and seamen from Birkenhead, Liverpool, and Bootle. Its task was to establish a closed shop in all port and maritime trades both sides of the river; no mean task for 1890. In the chair was Mr W. Winterburn, president of Liverpool United Trades Council.

Mr Nicholson of the Sailors' and Firemen's Union tabled a motion calling on all union men of the port not to work with non-unionists. He advised them to wait until their coming business meetings before voting on it. He advised that the scalers ought not to strike for better wages, but as a start to any future campaign, not to work with any non-unionists. He outlined a plan whereby, if the coming meeting was well attended and all classes of workers pledged themselves not to work with non-unionists, a joint committee would be formed. Likewise, an early move to launch a dock labourers' strike in the port was felt premature. With too many divisions in the work force, such an endeavour would be held over until March.

The joint meeting consisted of dockers, sailors, firemen, flatmen, scalers, coal heavers, quay porters, quay carters, and various other trades. William Winterburn of the Trades Council acted as president. He moved the initiating resolution to support mutual cooperation of all the bodies. He stated that if bringing non-unionists into the struggle was coercion, it was time they had more of it. He also pointed to the failure of individual societies and urged amalgamation.

Mr McKeown, vice president of the dockers' union and secretary of the Birkenhead branch, ascended the stage. The famous Ben Tillet of London was cheered when he mounted the platform and spoke in support of amalgamation. The resolution was unanimously carried.

Markedly, representatives of the gas workers' union were not on the platform. R. Bean tells us, 'The gas workers and general labourers organised into nine occupational branches on the Mersey and elsewhere under socialist influence, deplored the Liverpool dock strike, and adopted a policy of neutrality toward the dispute.' The gas workers as an important group in organisational terms do not feature in this work, largely because it is strike driven. The gas workers did not favour strike action in principle, but had nonetheless 'softly, softly,' achieved levels of organisation that were noteworthy. We do not find them however in the pages of the local or national press slogging it out with their employers in general terms. Despite their policy, an employers' offensive in Liverpool 'resulted in a total of £1,800 strike pay being granted during the first four years of the branches existence'.

A further mass meeting of dock labourers, implementing the spirit of the previous joint meeting, agreed now to try and recruit all unskilled workers into the union, not simply those working on the waterfront. On 19 February, the Wellington Dock workers struck in support of a claim for 6s instead of 5s 6d per day to unload a cargo of 350 tons of emery stone. This resulted in the vessel being moved to the enclosed Stanley Dock where outside labourers were brought in to unload her. Most of these men were brought in from the south end, and upon their arrival were informed by a union delegate that the vessel was blacked. They obviously respected this boycott, as the vessel was eventually discharged by dock board men, who worked right through the night to achieve that end. The dock board employees, as we have shown before, were the hardest to organise due to the nature of their employers and their isolation. Early attempts at joining general turn outs always ended in failure and the blacklist.

The action however was ultimately a success and the company agreed to pay such rates in the future. The men returned to work with kindly words for their employers (Messrs Papavanni).

A few days later, the steamer the *Cameroon*, carrying the Royal Mail, was detained owing to a dockers' strike involving the workers engaged to stow the cargo. They refused to carry on their work unless the owners immediately discharged non-union men working in the ship. The owners refused, and so the men left the ship. Later, the employers were able to introduce more non-unionists and fill their places. The steamer however was still delayed on leaving. Another steamer going into the Graving was a further casualty of the workers going on strike.

At this time, there was great dissatisfaction at the north end. Many were in favour of launching a general port strike there and then. As the men were leaving the Alexandra Dock where they had been working one of the lake steamers, they stated their intention of coming on strike if either non-union men or members of the Knights of Labour were employed in the same occupation. This would seem to confirm my earlier suspicions that the cause of the earlier conflict with the Knights was that they were not generally members of the conventional dockers union, but saw themselves as an independent ally of it. The members of the dockers' union however, believed that if you were not in their organisation, you were a non-unionist and would be treated as such. This would be particularly so given the fact that they actually scabbed earlier, albeit 'unofficially'.

The grain carriers were again 'grist to the mill'. Those employed on the

George's Dock, 1881.

steamer *Guide* in the Huskisson Dock struck for an advance in wages. They demanded 7s per day. This was refused and they left the dock in a body. The dispute had started among a few men who were trimming to the elevators in the hold. Next, the men proceeded to the steamer the *Flaminian*, owned by Messrs Leyland & Co., also discharging grain. She was lying alongside in the same dock, and in a moment the strikers had called her workers out with them. They then numbered 150.

Another steamer in the dock, the *Caroline*, also contained grain. When the strikers approached her, they found she was being unloaded by the crew, mostly Spaniards, who proved unsympathetic to joining the strike, although a further fifty men employed in the vessels left off work. The wildcats were to get no applause from the official union leadership however, who condemned their actions and said that it would weigh heavy against the union cause. The call for higher wages had obviously been prompted by the dire conditions in the grain holds.

By afternoon, the employers were offering to take the elevators out of the holds and thereby reduced the terrible clouds of dust. Instead, the men could bushel the corn at the old rates of piece rates prices. Some of the men wanted to accept this right away, but the majority wanted a written guarantee from the employers to the effect that they would never again use elevators in the future. The employers, obviously looking for a short term solution to the immediate problem, would give no such future guarantee. A day later, 1,000 men were on strike, gathered around the north docks.

Meanwhile, the union's central strategy of building 100 per cent union membership was proceeding apace. Large numbers of men were joining the Dock Labourers' Union, and those seeking employment wore a small metallic badge, the object being to distinguish those who wore them from non-unionists who did not.

James Sexton explains in his book *Agitator* that this union button was designed by McGhee after he became president of the dock workers' union. The shape and colour of the badge were changed quarterly and was issued only to those in good standing. It bore on its face a figure donating its date, the wearer's number on the branch roll, and on the back, a figure indicating the branch to which the individual belonged. It therefore gave quite a lot of information about the wearer to those who knew how to read it.

The union leadership had all along been against grain porters taking strike action and had said so. The committee of the Dock Labourers Union at Bootle appointed three delegates to visit the Huskisson Dock to advise the grain men to return to work. When these delegates reached the workers gathered around, they refused to listen to them, instead threatening to throw them into the dock if they did not clear off with their unwelcome message. A man who stated he was a delegate of the central branch urged the men on his own advice not to resume work. They had no intention of doing so.

All along the line of docks, dissension railed against the leaderships' refusal to sanction strike action, with the officials declaring that they would not sanction any body of men who struck. Meanwhile, unofficial meetings of the workers were being held around the docks.

The officials could not hold back the swelling tide and all along the docks men were going on strike in support of higher wages. Others wearing their union badges refused to work unless everyone had one. Mass meetings were being held, at which the men resolved not to work below union rates. Meanwhile the employers, seeing which way the wind was blowing, started to import the scabs and non-unionist from other areas.

At the north end, it was said that by 4 March, every dock labourer was wearing his union badge, and at the union's office in Derby Road, men were joining in their hundreds. At a mass meeting at the north end, Mr McHugh of Glasgow and the general secretary of the union urged all men to combine. A resolution was passed pledging the grain men not to return to work unless union terms were granted, nor to work on elevators at less than 7s per day.

McHugh was thirty-six when he became general secretary. He had been born in Ireland, but lived in Scotland since childhood. By trade he was a compositor, working in Glasgow since 1869. He was a follower of Henry George, and had a history of support for dissident causes, including that of the crofters in the Highlands. He was regarded as a passionate speaker.

Richard McGhee was national president, having been elected for the position when he was thirty-eight. Also Irish, he had lived in Glasgow since the age of twenty-one. He had been an engineer, but then a commercial traveller in stationary and cutlery. He had been politically involved in Irish and Scottish agitation. He was, like his comrade and friend McHugh, a follower of Henry George. He was also deeply influenced by Michael Davitt, the Irish radical land reformer. In the 1880s, he had been active in the West Midlands supporting agitation by the nail and chain makers organised by the Knights of Labour. He had in fact been commissioned by them to act as their organiser in Glasgow. Both men therefore would have come with the highest of fiery credentials; Irish nationalists, Scottish radicals, with links to the American radical philosopher Henry George, who was an advocate of land nationalisation as a means of a single tax, which overlaps with the outlook of the Knights of Labour. Nobody on the docks could ever throw the term 'gaffer's men' at these two. This was not however, to ultimately save them from messy compromise.

The Knights of Labour may not have seen the arrival of the NUDL as completely welcome. Indeed, they may have seen them as rivals. In Liverpool, they had played a role in establishing the Tramway Men's Union with the assistance of the seamen's union, and were quite entrenched at Bootle. A clash was on the cards, although given the previous involvement of NUDL leaders with the organisation and the nature of the collision, when it came, it was to be along unexpected lines.

On the employers side, 1,000 non-unionists were being introduced from Manchester, and they stated that they would import many thousands more to break the union. 4 March saw the following mysterious manifesto appear along the docks, signed with the names of dock union leaders:

NATIONAL UNION OF DOCK LABOURERS
STRIKE! STRIKE! STRIKE!
Down with tyrants and non-unionists!

On and after this day [4 March], no member of this union must work with any man who is not a member of this union, nor accept employment unless he is paid union rates as laid down in the old rules issued two months ago. Stand by your Union – the hope of all who suffer: the dread of all who wrong! No federation nor trade council advisers or assistance wanted. Strike money 13s per week will be paid to unionists and non-unionists alike in this struggle. Apply at branch office next Saturday 8 March.

Signed on behalf of the executive,
E M'Ghee, M. M'Keown, F. Kennedy. E. M'Hugh, Patrick

Hughes, J. Power. J. Fitzharris.
Boundary Street branch, Liverpool.

However, this strange turn to getting the gloves off was quickly denied by the leadership, who reported in the press that the poster had not in fact been issued by the union and the names of the officials were forged. McHugh and McKeown, denying the authenticity of the poster, said that they were getting a detective to investigate the matter. They wished to stress that the decisions of the executive committee would be communicated to the members at public meetings.

In the meantime, there was another partial victory, with shipowners, merchants, and master stevedores granting the 7s per day demand to workers trimming the elevators. The following union meeting agreed that they should work for any employer who had granted the union's demands. Then McHugh stated that the executive committee would decide whether it was to be peace or war. The crowd roared in defiance, 'War!' The decision was to be arrived at that evening. He suggested to the meeting that it was in fact the employers who had posted the controversial call to action, that the union were not fools and would fight on their own ground in their own time. He ended up by saying that he wished the policemen that he could see among the crowd were in one great union with the dockers, sailors, and firemen.

One can see that the leadership is trying the whole time to hold back action until a later, perhaps stronger, time, and why from their point of view premature action would be counter-productive and therefore of advantage to the employers. However, to believe the posters were posted by employers' agents, as a provocative action, seems less likely than a group of militants reminding the executive committee of the demands and suggesting the course of action that should be taken, even perhaps hoping to jump start action prematurely by forging the posters with an authority they did not actually possess. The suggestion of lavish strike pay was obviously a bit of tongue in cheek sarcasm.

A day later, it was estimated that 7,000 men were out on the north end docks, and all those engaged at the Alexandra and Langton docks had joined the turn out. This time, authentic notices had been posted calling upon no man to work below union rates. The owners scoured the country looking for labourers to import. One man had actually been introduced from just three miles short of Lands End. It was estimated that some 4,000 to 5,000 men were already in the port to break the strike.

700 labourers marched in procession from Liverpool town hall in order to lay certain matters in connection with the strike before the mayor. 350 of them were importees. The mayor would not see them, so they marched off in single file to the workhouse for the purpose of seeking relief. They were all refused assistance.

Later, when the mayor was told the means of the men's inducement to the town, of the deception and the promise that no strike was in progress, he decided to take action, writing to the Employers Labour Association. He demanded these men's fares be paid home. He criticised the way in which they had been deceived. Great numbers of imported men, refusing to scab, were seen in starving conditions hanging about the docks. Some of these men were in fact stone masons who had been in regular employment at home in Cornwall. They had been told a new dock was under construction and that would be their work. They marched to the police court to seek redress, but were told there was nothing anyone could do for them.

Then, news came that the fruit porters had joined the strike, with a demand for 6d per day increase on their wage of 4s 6d.

By 7 March, 30,000 men plus were out, no response to their general demands having been forthcoming from the employers. Thousands of workers assembled at the Alexandra and Harrington docks. The two bodies converged towards the centre of the city, joining at South John Street. The united streams swelled into a mighty torrent rolling on toward the south, where a monster demonstration was held.

Messrs R. P. Houston & Co. sent a letter to the union conceding everything asked for, and consequently his employees were allowed to return to work. This was not the overall trend however, and most employers were digging in to fight it out.

The scene on the docks, as imported men and non-dockers tried to undertake the tasks, presented the strikers with a comic opera every day, and knowing the Liverpool wit, one can only imagine the comments and mockery that must have greeted the sight as large groups of strikers watched the performances. Clerks, time keepers, and foremen were seen struggling with crates, while most of them being rather feeble, undertook everything very slowly. While unloading a ship at the Alexandra Dock, several of the new arrivals did not let go of the bales and packages in time as the experienced men would do, and were dragged down the slides or shot over the sides of ships, or else fell headlong into the piles of goods being unloaded. Police patrolled from north to south in dock buses, while inside the Huskisson Dock, a party of armed soldiers stood on guard. At the Seaforth barracks, the Lancers stood in readiness for the call. The *Liverpool Mercury* of 8 March reports, 'The strike of dock labourers in Liverpool is assuming alarming proportions!' The movement had spread to all districts of the Mersey, Bootle, Birkenhead, and Cheshire etc.

There were processions of the unemployed. One such procession comprised several thousand members of the union, headed with a brass band and a number of banners. The Union Jack held a prominent place, but there was also a tricolour (presumably Irish), and the stars and stripes. The band played stirring anthems to heighten the men's hopes and inspiration. A day later, some

40,000 men paraded their membership of the union. The chief objection of the employers was the question of the closed shop and the affront to their rights to employ who they wanted, unionist or non-unionist.

That same day, 1,300 new men arrived to start work. On the docks, these men were beyond the sphere of the union's influence, housed and fed behind the guarded gates of the dock. However, several vessels still left the river with their cargoes unloaded their destinations unstated.

It was reported that the coal heavers were joining the turn out and thus adding their great weight to the strike cause. The carters too were in deep consideration as to whether to join in solidarity action. Such sections would unlikely be easily replaced by strangers.

A depot ship was being used by employers for feeding, housing, and deploying blacklegs. 300 London men, like most having been promised that no strike was in progress, had been carried into the port. However, the men got wind of the strike before they left Euston, and on the train, the agent who had hired them got severely treated, with his watch and gold chain taken by way of compensation. Several unionists had got among the men, a well know delegate named Harry Orbell being among them. The importees, upon arriving at the Alexandra Dock Station, were secretly joined by several well-known labour representatives from the port. They, along with the others, succeeded in getting aboard the *City of Richmond*, which must have taken quite some degree of courage. Among these was none other than Mr McHugh, general secretary of the union. The agent, it seems, was not the brightest of men. Breakfast was served to them all, which we can be sure the strikers among the company thoroughly enjoyed. Upon being called upon to go to work, 143 refused point blank. They then broke out of the ship amid scenes of great excitement. The men then approached the ship's masters and officials, and told them they had been brought on false pretences. The men received half the price of their fares home from the masters. The men joined the strikers' procession in the afternoon and then boarded the train home.

There is not the space here to adequately describe the monster demonstration that these Londoners participated in. It was a mass parade of colour and strength, numbering some 59,000, 'From the town hall down to the dock being packed by one dense moving mass of humanity' as the *Daily Post* put it. The same paper tells us that the 1,300 coal heavers had joined both the strike and the procession. They were easily recognisable by their 'attire and the general griminess of their appearance'.

The seamen and firemen, while having no wish to take up any extreme measures, had held meetings with the shipowners regarding the wages and employment of non-union labour. It was announced that the dock labourers of Hamburg had formed a trade union to fight for higher wages and reduced hours.

A path meanwhile was being beaten to the door of the mayor with constant delegations of imported men complaining of the trickery and falsehoods being employed to get them to the city.

On 11 March, Messrs W. H. Stott & Co. agreed to the union's rules and wage demands. In consequence, the men restarted work. Subsequently however, a letter was passed on to Mr McHugh saying that the company had agreed to pay the rates, but the workmen had refused to take notice of the union's instructions to recommence work while the others were still out. The company therefore had immediately withdrawn its offer. This was a tactical error on behalf of the men perhaps, albeit for a principled reason.

However, more success was being had, both with companies giving way, and men actually going back to work under the new agreements. Companies that gave way included Messrs Thompson, Tedcastle & Co., master stevedore John Copeland, and the Sligo Steam Navigation Company Ltd.

On 10 March, the cotton porters struck in support of their fellow dockers, as did the dock board's men. On the same date, the grain men who had just won their own increases at the Waterloo and neighbouring docks rejoined the strike, obviously in solidarity, leaving some fifty or sixty vessels idle. In some cases, vessels were being worked by bosses themselves trying to fulfil certain orders.

The meetings between the seamen's and firemen's representatives and the shipowners resulted in the latter conceding everything that the former had demanded. Doubtless, the on-going dockers' action gave an added incentive for them to do so, rather than face the joint action of both groups.

Another vast demonstration was held, which according to the press, had good effect upon the ordinary citizens of the town. Each marching man wore his union badge. The young lads of the docks also showed their solidarity by marching, and a few bands accompanied the march. These played the death march when passing the owners territory, which must have been an amusing sight for the crowds. Meanwhile, three more employers gave way to the union's demands.

On 11 March, a crowd of more than 200 strikers tried to get into the north docks by way of the Canada Dock timber yards in order to call out the timber workers. A large force of police however held back the men from the timber workers, who had thus far refused to join the strike. At the same time, between 100 and 150 labourers at Seaforth threatened to attack the people of the locality who would not join the turn out. These must have been local dockers away from the main thrust of the action. A large force of police however prevented any such action.

Then the men employed by Liverpool Grain Elevator Company, that is the workers who actually make the machines that the grain workers found so objectionable, went on strike in support of the dockers. One can only imagine the impact this must have had on the strikers, especially the grain workers. Furthermore, the flatmen who led the barges on the river decided not to work for anybody other than union crews.

Despite such spectacular demonstrations of solidarity, the shipowners were confident that victory was close to hand because of their apparent ability to import strangers, some 6,000 of whom we were told were now at work. Plus, the employers scented a major shift of ground in the union's leadership's position. The original demand was that *no* union man should work with a non-union man. Yet now, the leadership was saying it was only preventing unionists working with *imported* non-unionists.

As a result, the employers did some fancy footwork and announced that their principle was one of selecting the best men for the job, and of course, they conceded that the union men were the best men for the job. Presumably they would whisper, '*Usually.*'

Meanwhile, the carters of the port had made use of the local papers to voice their complaints against their secretary who had refused to call a meeting; the rank and file feeling being that they ought to be out in support of the dockers, while the secretary, like many of his type, wished to maintain the peace and was quite prepared to use his authority to do so.

Paul Smith tells us: 'The MQRCU ensued any language of class war it did not want any of the doctrines of John Burns, of Ben Tillet, or of Mr Cunningham Grahame (MP), and they did not call the masters "bloodsuckers" or any other names.' He goes on to describe the battle within the carters' union:

> The dock strike of February–March 1890 opened a fissure within the union. Many carters were laid off and some 10 per cent of members wanted to strike in support. Almond defended the union's policy: 'As a union, we have never interfered in trade quarrels outside our immediate calling.'

The Bootle branch of the dockers' union posted the following in its offices:

> Dear Friends, I hope you will be wise,
> And from disturbance shall forebear:
> Do not come here to raise a noise,
> To talk aloud or curse or swear,
> But to the union show respect
> And this advice do not neglect.
> To raise disturbance in this place;
> But no – it plays the traitors part,
> And on the union brings disgrace
> That's pleasing the union, let them see

That we can live in unity.
For union men, we should be friends,
And stand together like a wall,
Each man whereby his help he lends
To keep good order in this hall
Likewise and prudent business men
We'll fight the case with head and pen.

The men decided to reject any notion of arbitration in this dispute and to fight their corner to the very bitter end as the press put it. 'No surrender' was the watchword of the men; 'No arbitration' its brother.

On 14 March, the union took up a dubious tactic; they would call out all their members from all employers, even those who agreed the union terms and rates of pay. At the labourers' headquarters in Mill Street, the following notice was written on a blackboard: 'Stop everything. Knock off everybody. A general lock out.'

A day later the grain porters, who had already been out, in, and then out again, decided to go back again on the same the terms they had, which indeed were terms they had just improved. They stated that they only came out to demonstrate solidarity with the other labourers.

Meanwhile, to prevent any further stimulant to trouble, the magistrates decided to close all pubs and beer houses in Bootle for various periods of time, although it was well agreed that very few cases of drunkenness or even normal drinking was being engaged in by the labourers on strike. The effect of this endeavour was that thousands of labourers flooded over the boundaries into Liverpool itself. Most of the surrounding districts experienced the same thing; a welcome boost to trade in troubled times no doubt.

The struggle within the carters was now becoming crucial to the result of the strike overall. This led to some extraordinary events. At a mass meeting, Mr McHugh urged the carters to forget about their rules and their officials and turn out on strike with the labourers. They, it was said, held the key to the struggle. Paul Smith tells us of the carters' leadership in its first full year of existence:

Close personal and organisational links with local business men and professionals were evident from the beginning. The MQRCU's first president was the brewer, Orangeman, and Conservative councillor John Houlding, and in its first decade, the union was identified with the Conservative Working Men's Association.

As a result of such urging, and indeed the discontent of many carters at not being involved, many, albeit mostly 'irregular' workers, *did* turn out the following day. They joined the biggest, most impressive demonstration of union strength yet seen in the city. 500 troops were sent to the city to protect property in case the men should become disorderly. Between 600 and 1,000 carters led the demonstration, easily distinguished by their peculiar dress. This great demonstration, as luck would have it, had fallen on St Patrick's Day. '... A large number of men carried the emblem of the patron saint of Ireland in their caps and coats.'

A very authoritative leaflet was being circulated to the carters. One must remember that this is a distinctive and independent trade union. It is not at all clear who was instructing who at first. One presumes that many workers would have found the leaflet very objectionable and counter-productive, putting more backs up by its instruction, rather than fraternal requesting. It read:

National Union of Dock Labourers in Great Britain and Ireland
To the Mersey Quay and Railway Carters' Union

Fellow Workers,

At a mass meeting of the above union held on Saturday night 15 inst., it was carried by an overwhelming majority that you assist the dock labourers in their present struggle.

You are therefore required to pledge yourselves that you shall not cart to or from the dock estate until this dispute is settled.

By order of the majority of the Carters' Union.
NB: This applies to or from the docks only.

Among the carters themselves, the treasurer of the union issued a long address to the members, pointing out rules and regulations and how they were breaking everything that they had agreed to previously. He urged them not only to stay at work, but to vote to do so when they were balloted on the question. The rule on strike action required a two-third majority in the affirmative; a well-nigh impossible task in any union. The police were drafted in to protect the carters who were still at work, for fear they would be molested.

Both the flatmen and the coal heavers, strong allies of the labourers, were said to be strongly of the opinion that the matter should now be put to arbitration. Many of the rank and file, seeing no ready solution, were also coming round to this view. While the rank and file started to search around for an amicable solution, the employers resolved to starve the men back to work. Meanwhile however, the fight was still very much on. At Birkenhead, a large number of men gathered at the Morpeth Dock, and as soon as the one o'clock gun sounded, they made a move for the *Deucalion*, on which about 100 men were engaged in loading. They had intended to call out the workers.

The latter refused to respond, and after arguments began, the police moved in and shifted the pickets. These did not disperse and moved on instead to the *Clan Sinclair*, which was loading in the next birth. They called on the men working to leave, which these men did without hesitation. The whole party next revisited the *Deucalion,* and this time the workers left the ship right away. The numbers so enlarged, they moved off around the dock to several other vessels, one of which was the *Ruby.* Seeing the pickets approaching, the labourers on this ship left. Pickets were then placed on all the stricken vessels, while the remainder of the strikers marched into Price Street and round the town. Owing to the joint action by the majority of carters, very few goods were being transported anywhere.

At the mass meeting of strikers at Bankhall, great dissatisfaction was voiced by men and there was very little unity of direction. The two factions emerging were those wanting to stand out together until all achieved victory, and those who preferred the previous tactic of allowing work to recommence for employers who were prepared to pay union rates and agree to union terms. This latter, on the face of it a sound strategy of systematically weakening the employers while relieving the pressure on the workforce overall, was abandoned by the union earlier, the reason being that most employers who were giving way were doing so simply to fulfil outstanding orders and relieve the most dire effects of the strike on their businesses. They had no intention of keeping to the agreements after the short period of advance and relief had passed. They were 'making hay while the sun shone'. The other flaw in the strategy was that it confronted crucial solidarity action being taken by the coal heavers and carters. Why then should those unaffected by the dispute strike, while the labourers whose dispute it was went back to work?

Meanwhile, the feud with the carters' leaders raged. Mr McHugh stated that the secretary of the carters' union had given him an undertaking that he would call out all of his men, but instead, he had issued a circular telling them to go to work. Next on the platform was Mr Houston, a shipowner who had always been friendly to the union. Mr McHugh asked the men if they were willing to go to work for such gentleman, who had never been an enemy of the union? He would leave it to the meeting to decide. The great difference of opinion regarding the union's strategy was then let loose. The majority tide was for all stopping out. One of the carters in the crowd shouted, 'Let's go in if we get terms, lads.' He was immediately knocked down by a burly unionist, and kicked on the ground, his nose completely smashed. He was then hustled to the outside of the crowd.

The shipowner next addressed the crowd. He said that all the other employers had forecast that the men would turn on them. He was not with them, but the men. He asked would they work on his ships? to which the men cried out, 'No' and continued to voice the opinion that nobody should work while other comrades were on strike.

Mr McHugh told the meeting that the coal heavers had come on strike on the understanding that they would work for employers who had granted the union's terms. He was afraid the meeting had been poisoned by the owners. The crowd all the while was shouting out its demands, 'We don't go in at all; all hands or none!'

The secretary then suggested that if they worked for the good employers, they could do so in relays so that all might get a turn. This was greeted with shouts of 'no surrender!' He suggested that it was suicide to refrain from working for the men who were their friends, which produced angry cries of both 'hear hear' and 'don't give in!' He then said that if such a lack of reason was to prevail he would resign. He then asked them if they would leave the full running of the campaign in his hands and those of McKeown. This being somewhat of a coup, the crowd had no real choice but to agree in unanimity.

Mr Kennedy, who represented the carters on strike, next addressed the men. He strongly condemned the attitude of their own secretary for not obeying the wishes of the membership. He was loudly cheered, and it was clear the carters were determined not to return to work until a satisfactory condition had been reached for the dockers.

McHugh next said that he was going to call a meeting of the various executives and consider the whole question. This was met by approval by the crowd. However at this stage, several people mounted the platform and carried on arguments with others in the crowd. The general view, regardless of McHugh's ultimatum, was that they would not return until all returned.

Shortly after the meeting, a lorry laden with grain was seen proceeding along by the warehouses. A number of boy scalers halted the horses and others mounted the cart and started throwing them into the road. It did not take long before six mounted police and 100 in cabs were seen charging toward the scene. However, on judging the scale of trouble to be very small and no doubt the crowd very large, they turned around amid cheers from the crowd and a shower of grain from the youngsters. The press stated that had there been serious trouble the mounted police would have had little impact since the carters had no fear of horses. The cart was later reloaded by the strikers and the driver allowed to proceed along his way.

At the south end, it was reported:

The Liverpool police have reason to believe that a number of the hands on strike belonging to the rowdy class who have seen a good deal life in the Far West have for some days been in possession of firearms. The matter is now engaging the attention of the authorities.

Throughout the dispute, the south end had been relatively quiet. The

Liverpool South End Dock Labourers Association had been serving its members faithfully for some twenty-four years, and had similar perspectives in terms of work and wages as the National Dock Labourers Union. They held a meeting in rooms at Fontenoy Street. The south end workers had been working under the hours that were being demanded elsewhere, namely nine hours on nights. The union was at this present time out on strike with the other labourers. They resolved that they would remain so until all the employers gave way.

The flatmen however, decided to resume work and expressed their disappointment at the labourers in not working for owners who had conceded. They also set themselves the perspective of trying to persuade the labourers to go to arbitration.

Collapse of the Carters' Solidarity Action

At the meeting of the carters, the militants were badly routed. Their meeting held at the Albert Hall, Carnean Street, heard the results of their ballot on strike action. Total recorded votes 2,593, of which 2,163 were against a strike and 430 for a strike, leaving the majority of 1,733 against strike action.

It was later said that the role of the carters' secretary Almond had been pivotal: 'It was solely through [Almond's] efforts and the confidence the men have in him, that a general strike of carters was avoided.' A year later, it is said he had done a runner with the funds. The loss of the carters was a crucial blow, followed by the announcement that the coal heavers would return to work on their own unless the other labourers agreed to arbitration.

A meeting of the dock labourers' executive committee at the Toxteth Hall considered the position of the strike. Outside the hall, crowds of strikers expressed dissatisfaction with the leaders' actions, with the men, 'Appearing to be in a state of suppressed revolt.' Such discontent was not simply one way. A manifestation from the other side appeared on the morning of 19 March in the form of a large poster:

Fellow Dock Labourers, What Are We Doing?

1) Starving our wives and children
2) Pawning our goods
3) Giving our permanent jobs to scabs
4) We are hesitating so long that the scabs are learning our work
5) Ships are being stopped off port and sent elsewhere
6) Our delegates have three good meals a day, while we and our families

are hungering

7) About ten ships a day are going to sea. This shows that the scabs are learning our work.

8) Vote by ballot, not by hand, where we dare not act contrary to our delegates

9) Let us work at once, and the scabs will dissolve away of themselves, as no stevedores will employ them as permanent men, they being paid by piece work.

10) Join in numbers of twenty. Then you will be safe from brutal attack

11) When shall the delegates be paid and we be tranquil?

12) Let us arbitrate, and be equally represented masters and men, but in the meantime go to work, so as to stop the scabs learning our business. Otherwise, many of us will be sacked for ever.

A fellow sufferer

Campania leaving her landing stage, 1907.

One could speculate on the true source of the poster. Meanwhile, the joint executives of the union had met, and as a result, it was reported that the bulk of the shipowners had practically given away, and that all of the smaller ones were anxious to come to terms with the men. The union stated that financially it would win the day, but the owners would get concessions.

At a mass meeting following another mammoth procession, which we are told was buoyant and showed no signs of poverty, McHugh stated that the coal heavers in fact had *not* gone back to work and the men should not believe stories in the newspapers unless they knew them to be true. He wanted all to know on the authority of the coal heavers' secretary that no coal heavers had gone back to work; that the coal heavers were present at that very meeting.

Tom Mann was welcomed onto the stage to great cheers. He brought greetings and congratulated them on the handling of the strike while the crowd expressed its determination to stick it out.

In the meantime, more anti-strike posters were appearing, reading much the same as the others, but adding that the leadership was afraid of arbitration and that the men should go back to work at once. In fact, all of the leaders were now talking in terms of some form of arbitration or committee of enquiry to resolve the problem. A letter from the employers dated 21 March asked the union if they the employers conceded to everything that the union asked for, would they then certify to work in harmony with the imported men? This is somewhat of a conundrum, since one of the chief union rules was that they would *not* work with non-union men. They side-stepped the question by responding that they would work on those terms 'with' the Liverpool non-union men, and even the imported men, if the employers kept them all from the union men. In other words, they still would not work with them, but would work while they were working elsewhere.

Meanwhile, the combativity of the men did not seem in any way weakened. It must be said that neither did it seem to be among the leaders. McHugh appears to have warned the employers of the revolutionary consequences of waiting too long to appease the men. He asked the crowd if they knew the meaning of 'ca-canny', the northern pit term for 'go slow', which it seems, they knew well. He advised them to adopt the ca-canny tactic whenever they returned to work.

The employers now responded to the executives, asking for five principle points to be the basis of an agreement. They responded that no negotiations could be opened upon such points. Furthermore, no more communications would be held with the union.

The famous Irish Nationalist leader and founder of the Irish Land League Mr Michael Davitt visited both sides of the river, one would presume to express his support for the men, although his contribution cannot be said to have added much. He advised the men either to go back or to stop out, but that they should keep the peace. He further offered to act as a go-between for the men and masters if that was desired. Michael Davitt, who James Sexton clearly disliked (he calls him a criminal in his autobiography *Agitator*), was it seems, much respected. Born in Ireland in 1846, he was like many other families, evicted in 1852. In 1856, he began work in the Lancashire cotton factories, lost his right arm in machinery, and then entered the printing trade. By politics a Fenian, he was imprisoned in 1870 for seven years, and was later the founder of the Irish Land League. In 1881, he was sentenced to a further three years in prison, and was later elected MP for County Meath (his sentence was quashed by special vote of Parliament).

As the mass meeting at which Mr Davitt spoke proceeded, the crowd was cheering the arrival of Mr Tillett of the London Dockers Union when suddenly alarm was raised. In the crowd were two fully equipped soldiers, one of whom had his bayonet fixed for action. The other probed his way through the crowd with the butt end of his rifle. However, nothing came of the incident and the platform urged this to be considered as deliberate provocation.

The union was obviously under pressure and in need of assistance from some other strategic quarter. On 25 March, they approached the seamen and firemen to throw in their lot in with the dock labourers. At the same time, they issued the following leaflet among the strikers:

The employers association now refuses all negotiations with your union. The strike has become a lock out.

> When thugs garrotte
>   Combine
> Why should you not
>   Combine
> Let sickly slaves
> Fill paupers graves –
> When persecutions tempest raves
>   Combine
> For Holy right
>   Combine
> You have the pow'r
> This very hour
> To make the heartless tyrants cow'r
>   Combine

New York is helping. Pickets are to be strengthened! A strong effort will now be made to get imported men out of bond. Men stand firm! Keep outside the public house! Maintain the peace!

Edward M'Hugh, general secretary
No. 98 Derby Road

Davitt meanwhile, true to his promise, had gone around the town visiting shipowners. As a result, he arranged for them to meet a delegation from the union. It finished almost as soon as it started. The employers now insisted that the strikers would not be taken on at once, only as they were required, and the strangers would be given priority. There would be no guarantee against victimisation.

Needless to say, the union representatives walked out and reported the brief encounter to the workers, who greeted their rejection with cheers and cries of condemnation against the masters and scabs. Despite this, a further meeting was convened between the two sides. The union's representatives then reported back to a mass meeting at the pier head. Mr McKeown reported that from now on, the employers would employ men for the week with a week's notice either way. Each man would work for 53 hours per week and overtime would be given according to rates laid down. This was on the understanding that although the man was working in overtime, it would not count as such until he worked the full 53 hours. The crowd laughed out loud at this. They were also insisting that the union should in no way interfere with the men who were desirous of entering into an engagement with them on the basis laid down by them; a forerunner of individual contracts and an end of collective bargaining, one would have thought. If they could find sufficient men to work at 30s per week on that basis, they would do so. They would require that each man would sign an agreement to this effect. At this stage, the crowd burst into cries of, 'Let them go to hell!' It was pointed out however, that these rules were still under consideration and the men could discuss it all in greater detail, to which many in the crowd responded, 'No! No! … Never! … Burn them!' No 'day' agreement would cover night work; the men would be employed and paid by the hours at nights.

In the face of this mass declaration to fight to the bitter end, McHugh again put to them that they must work for employers who had recognised the union and granted them their terms. These men, he said, had not employed a single scab during the whole course of the dispute. This time when put to the vote, the men voted in favour. He said, to the men who break away and go in, and those who eventually would go to work for the employers of the Employers' Labourers Association, do as little as possible for them; to harass, embarrass, and ruin them if they could. He wished them to restrict their output. He asked them what was the watchword when the strike was over? To which they all replied, 'Ca-canny!' Overall, although the crowd was reported as being disheartened and critical of the strike management, some were talking of going back regardless of what had been said. A troop of soldiers marching nearby the meeting were being followed by a crowd of hooting strikers, one can imagine with great hilarity. Such occasions would not suggest that a sense of dejection was general.

The mass meeting at Birkenhead decided that they too would go to work for employers paying the union rates and terms. The local press headline of 31 March loudly proclaimed, '*RESUMING WORK AT DOCKS & THE RUSH FOR EMPLOYMENT.*' In fact, the men were merely implementing their decision to work for those employers who had conceded their demands. In the Harrington Dock, there was bother. One of Messrs Harrisons' boats was being worked by 'knobsticks' as the Liverpool men called the strangers. On entering, the Liverpool men had made a rush to sweep the scabs out. The police however intervened and made one arrest for attacking them. It was said that many union men were finding work along the docks.

Finally on 1 April, a date which will not have been lost on the Liverpool natives' wits, the great Merseyside dock strike was over, after three weeks of glory and bitterness. The men began returning to work that morning. It was said the Mr Davitt had been the chief figure working behind the scenes. He went off his own bat to get what terms he could for the men. The results of these negotiations were put to the men at a mass meeting at Bankhall. He believed that he had obtained certain conditions from the masters that they did not find palatable, but had ultimately accepted. It was my own conclusion that Davitt would never have come to these terms without the nod and the wink from his friends in the leadership. They were on a hook and he was to get them off it, and also take the rap for any bad feeling about the settlement. That at least, is my view. Taplin was later able to confirm what had been my gut feeling. He tells us, 'As a last gesture, McHugh invited Michael Davitt ... close friend of McGhee ... to seek a settlement,' After persistence, Davitt had succeeded.

Under the terms he had negotiated, they would get paid for a dinner hour, or if they had to work it, they would be paid two hours. On the night shift, men would not be compelled to work more than nine hours. If they volunteered to work beyond that, they would be paid in accordance with the scale of overtime issued on the last occasion. Thirdly, union men and non-union men would work harmoniously together. Fourthly, there would be weekly labour and weekly notice on either side. The union was not to object to allowing men and employers to come to an agreement on these points if they wished, which is to say they were not forced to go on these terms; the union would not force them upon these points at all. They could agree to weekly labour, or not. If they did, they would have to deposit one week's wages in instalments. It was also a condition that union men, in the interests of peace, would not wear their union badge at work.

The final condition was that the union was not to boycott the Liverpool shipowners in other ports in connection with a quarrel in which Liverpool shipowners or Liverpool dockers were not involved. This is obviously a reference to the solidarity action with the Belfast vessels. While these terms were being read out, the crowd gave forth derisive laughter. Davitt, for his part, urged them to think of their wives and children and go back on the terms offered.

McHugh spoke in favour with the rest of the leadership and the men in turn almost unanimously agreed to accept the terms. One would expect that this was done with great reluctance, and they resolved to maintain a strong union.

The dispute had ended; the union was intact, although this was a major defeat. Many felt the owners had set them up in order to smash the union. It had started when the Employers' Labourers Association had issued a manifesto initiating that working conditions and hours would be altered. This was not entirely the case. The strike had started with the issue of the grain elevators and the grain men who wanted an advance in wages owing to increased danger from the machines. This, plus the employers' notices, had been the joint catalyst of the strike. The grain workers had got their rise, and this had stimulated other sectors into taking action quite unofficially. In fact, the employers' new terms would force certain of their colleagues to extend working night shift hours from nine to ten hours. It also required that stevedores who had been receiving 13s per night be reduced to 12s. The employers had issued their bill; the union demanded its withdrawal and the preservation of the status quo. The employers, in course of their negotiations, demanded a copy of the union rules. Being so armed, they could then select a suitable rule to breach, for example, the one forbidden working with non-unionists, thus throwing down the gauntlet that they knew the men were bound to pick up. That at least, was the analysis of the union's leadership.

James Sexton claimed that was McGhee's badge that had caused all the trouble, and the insistence of the union that no man be allowed to work on the dock who was not wearing the badge. In his book *Agitator* he says:

This had the most disastrous consequences for the union, causing an instant drop of 50 per cent in membership. We did not improve the position by issuing an official announcement that in future members would not be required to wear the badge, though they were advised to be able to produce it at any moment.

It was a weak-kneed, wishy-washy plan, of which I for one most heartily disapproved, and of course, it did nothing to check the rush of the rats from an apparently sinking ship. Indeed, it increased it by causing some to depart in sheer disgust at such a gutless decision.

A strange sequel came at the end of the strike, a strike by non-unionists

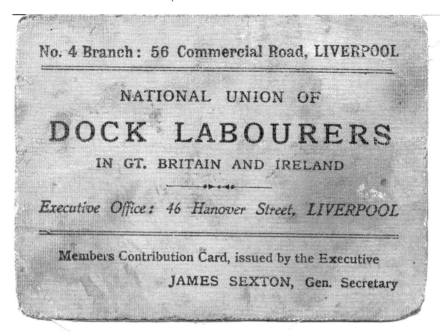

Union Card front cover: Sexton's, Dock Labourers Union.

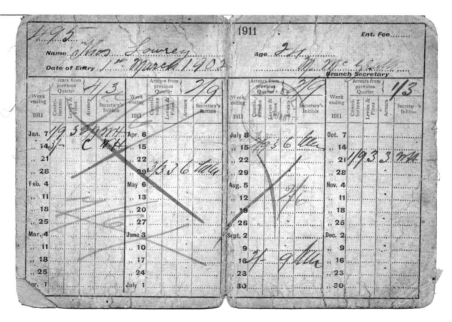

Union Card inside: Highly prized Dockers union card, this man joined in 1902.

against the re-employment of unionists at the north end. They refused to work with union men and struck. After a while, the employers paid them off. About 1,000 men chartered a train and left the port.

Of course, nothing was settled by the ending of the strike. Many went back to work, then came right back out again over the non-operation of the night shift agreement. At Birkenhead, the men were back in dispute over the working of Saturday, and for a short time, the coal heavers struck against having to sign 'the pledge'.

Just toward the end of March, the shop assistants had been seizing the initiative of engaging in dramatic direct action. Throughout much of the docks agitation, shop workers had been holding processions and demonstrations of their own. These were actions aimed at causing their fellow workers to walk out of the shop and thus force an earlier closing of the premises. Posters had been widely posted around Everton and Kensington telling of a grand demonstration that would begin at half past eight from Heyworth Street. Similar demonstrations had taken place previously, 'In various parts of the city, and considerable damage to property having resulted.' Broken windows and other damage was wrought upon tradesmen unsympathetic to the cause. The head constable Captain Nott-Bower, decided to adopt strong measures to prevent such disturbances. This he would do by dispersing any such demonstration of shop assistants, and to stop them forming up. A large body of police was assembled. About eight o'clock, a large crowd had collected in Northumberland Terrace and Heyworth Street, and a spring cart loaded with torches arrived along with two floats loaded with shop assistants. The police then intervened and demanded who was in charge. Mr A. Johnson of Mill Street and Mr Cormack of Victoria Street admitted that they organised the demonstration. They were then told that the head constable had banned it, and such processions were now illegal. 'They were to be stopped at all costs.' More carts began arriving, one with a band of music. While the organisers tried to call off the demonstration, others sought means of continuing. Meanwhile, a large crowd of 8,000 or 10,000 had assembled.

The processions were upon this peremptorily ordered to stop, and having refused to do so, as all were now in a considerable state of excitement, Superintendent Wood ordered a body of police to form themselves in a cordon across the street, and this carried out at once, the waggonette was brought to a summary standstill, and a considerable number of the crowd were at the same time dispersed by the actions of the police who wheeled about in all directions as the crowd pressed upon them. The occupants of the waggonette, in spite of this display of force on behalf of the police, persisted in their endeavour to carry out their programme, and seeing this, Superintendent Wood at once took prompt action to

Highland Monarch, 1896, F. W. Hawks.

prevent it by seizing the horses ... The populace again began to swarm round the scene of conflict between the police and shop assistants.

During the ensuing turmoil, the superintendent threatened to take the horses from the wagon, he also ordered the band to disperse and warned the bandmaster not to play, and that if he did so, the crowd would reassemble. The bandsmen were forced to disperse individually, all transport having been seized by the police.

At the north end, the labourers were up in arms about the fact that many employers had not acceded to the conditions that had been agreed. Two rules were involved; one referred to 'half day' and 'half night' work. The union's rule No. 6 read as follows: 'The half day be on Saturday from 7 a.m. until 12 p.m.

Except in cases where members are not required in the afternoon, the break for the half day must be at 11.30 a.m.

The masters at the north end were insisting that the 'half day' shall in all cases be from 7 a.m. until 12 noon. The union's rule for the half night followed:

The first half night shall begin at 6 p.m. and end at 10.30 p.m. Any members required to work any time after that hour without supper shall be entitled to a full night's wages, the night under such circumstances to end at 11 p.m.; the second half night shall begin at 11.30 p.m. and end at 4.a.m.

In this case, the bosses were saying that the first half night shall terminate at 11 p.m., and that the second half night would commence at 12 p.m. and conclude at 5 a.m.

As it stood, the executive committee were instructing their members to strike only at places where the terms of the agreement were not being carried out. The South End Dock Labourers Union, still alive and kicking, reported that they were only having difficulty at one firm. Meanwhile, the whole of the National Dockers Union was being reorganised.

Elsewhere at the north end, about 350 men employed by Messrs J. T. Fletcher & Co. went on strike in accordance with the union rate of 5s 6d per day for their class of work. The employers however had graded them with lotters, weighers, scribers, and sack holders, who were due only 5s per day.

A poster next appeared all along the Liverpool and Birkenhead docks, an extract of which reads:

To the dock labourers of Liverpool And Birkenhead

Fellow workmen,

The employers association struggled to garrotte the National Union in its infancy. Our organisation is stronger today than when the fight was forced upon us. One of the monsters of the employers association said he would 'starve the men into subjection'. Had the dastardly declaration been made by a Turk or Russian instead of a Christian shipowner of Liverpool, the hypocrites in high places would yell and shout their denunciations throughout the land. But we are only dock labourers. We now see how essential it is to develop a manly spirit of self reliance and to utilise the combined strength of all for the benefit of each.

Signed by order of the general committee

At Birkenhead, the coal heavers working on one of the largest steamers discovered that some of the imported men were at work. They therefore left the ship in one body and called out the men from another large steamer under the same master stevedore. Seeing these developments, the dock labourers began to gather. A short time previously, the labourers refused to work for anybody except the Clan Line, which had accepted union's terms. The labourers were incited by the question of the half days and half nights. Many hundreds gathered around the coal heavers and all gave vent to a wide range of grievances. At length, it was resolved to work for nobody but the Clan Line and the China boats that had come to their terms. The men stood in hundreds in groups about the docks and gates talking angrily about one of the master stevedores. Later, the work on one of the steamers was transferred to a different master. As many men as could be employed went in for this other man.

Unrest was far from over. At a meeting of the Bootle branch of the dock labourers' union, McHugh told the men they should not sign the employers' contracts. He said that Monday next would be an important day. Between 4 o'clock and seven o'clock in the morning, no member must work. By that method they would find out which employers were going to stand by the terms agreed. On Saturday, everyone had to knock off at eleven in the forenoon, go for their dinners, and return at noon. Saturdays had to be an eight hour day. They had to insist on the nine hour night.

To help win support, McHugh was up and about the docks in the morning agitating and talking to the men in little groups, and earnestly addressing them to force the agreement. It was being reported that in the north, the men generally worked on the old terms and not the agreed ones. At the south end, the men who adhered to the agreement did so with the consent of the employers. Whenever the unionists did force the issue and left off work, they were replaced right away by the importees.

The general attitude of the union was that the men would be advised to make do with it until they felt themselves strong enough to take any dynamic action. However, the workers found themselves in a powerful position; with a ship in a hurry to get to sea, they could encroach their Saturday demands and the nine hour night.

The 'ca-canny' system seems to have been imposed as far as possible by the union officials, not always with the approval of the rank and file, for whom it can be a great trial. At Birkenhead, three pieces of equipment called 'falls' were being used for the speedy departure of a vessel. A union official insisted that according to their rules, only two were allowed. The gang working on one of the falls had then to withdraw from the job. In other places, the union implemented a rule concerning the hoisting of bales of cotton on steam cranes, with two instead of four being hoisted in accordance to rules. The press complained that there were Indian bales and not American, and as such, they were much smaller. The union official had his way however, and two bales were hoisted instead of four. The vessel of course took twice as long to clear. Other classes of workers complained loudly at the idea of the Saturday half day being 11 o'clock, markedly the carters, railway men, and flatmen. In all, the men felt that a period of stability and wages, despite the conditions, might be welcome, whereas the militants and union officials saw the continuation of the union as being inextricable from the continuation of the struggle by these reduced means.

If anything, the position of the union seemed to be hardening, but the renewed toughness was breaking hardest on the door of the worker himself, who had not yet had time to recover from the extremes of hardship just endured.

A meeting of the union agreed for two representatives from each firm and company to delegate system based upon each place of work. It was agreed that any man who worked for a weekly wage, and even offered himself for work under a weekly hire system, would not be enrolled into the union. Any members disregarding this rule would be 'hunted from the docks'. All men were again to start wearing their union buttons at work.

To the members who had been led to expect that the end of the strike would bring sanction from the union to commence work again and earn a little money, that prospect seemed to be in jeopardy due to the renewed campaign and re-hardening of the union's stance. Had the leadership called upon the men to stand their ground earlier, I have no doubt they would have done so. But they were urged to go back intact and make the best of the deal. Now the leadership seemed to be changing its mind. The patience of the members was under trial.

In addition, the union was now adopting a sectarian attitude to other smaller dock unions. The Clarence Dock Labourers Association had been around quite some time. Their membership was largely confined to the coastal steamers. The union was making a bid to poach its members, but such overtures were strongly resisted. Their attitude to The National Gas Workers and General Labourers Union was somewhat worse. This union was perhaps only slightly older than the National Dock Labourers, and had a fair amount of support in the port, but as we have seen from this history, it had not featured greatly in dock organisation and disputes. By increasing degrees, members of the dock union were refusing to work with members of the general union, and began boycotting them. This seemed an odd time to open up an inter-union dispute, particularly since the general union had kept its members well clear of the docks and the dock work during the course of the strike. However, as suggested earlier, there may be some evidence that the gas workers' leadership had been critical of the strike.

On 25 July, the National Seamen's Union, or at least their leadership, who had done the dockers no great favours in this last dispute, issued the most fantastic international strike notice. It stated to the shipowners that a general strike of seamen in the UK would take place until the seamen of Denmark had their demands for parity with Britain acceded to.

Meanwhile on the docks, in response to discrepancies, uneven actions, and responses and complaints from the four branch secretaries, the National Union called a mass meeting of all its members to discuss their problems and where they now were. It was decided that no member should work after 5 p.m. on 21 July unless union rates were paid; these were cited as working on without tea to 7 p.m. three hours; to 9 p.m., half nights with tea hour to 10.30 p.m. Half night with supper hour; 4 a.m. twelve hours. Members ordered out at twelve midnight to receive not less than half night. No member to start overtime work when not employed during the day, other than at 6 p.m. and twelve midnight.

The sequel to the momentous struggle was that McHugh was deposed as secretary of the union in 1893 in favour of James Sexton. McHugh subsequently went to the USA where he organised the longshoremen in the principle ports.

Despite the clarion call to a strike of international seamen's labour when they met at their union meeting on 9 August, no mention was made of any international brotherhood, nor even any situation in Denmark. Perhaps these issues had already been resolved without putting to the test a national strike in international solidarity. Instead, they argued for the need for an amalgamation

The Landing Stage, 1901.

of all labouring classes into a single federation.

Would that such noble aims prevailed. Instead, the union enters a thoroughly reactionary period in the years between the Great Wars. The dock struggle again re-emerged with news that the south end had struck because the foreman over them was not in the union. A ship came along to the north end, but the word from London was that she was blacked and they would not touch it.

I think it wise to end by taking the temperature of trade unionism in Liverpool at the close of this book. It can be nowhere better judged than in the monster demonstration of workers held in September of 1893.

A grand procession of trades took place, over 50,000 persons representing 56 trades unions, assisted in what may be considered one of the most imposing demonstrations ever seen in the provinces ... Trade processions are practically the modern counterpart of the medieval processions in which the workmen's guilds of the olden times took a historic part, and they have the effect of creating on the public mind some impression of the power and the number of the vast army of horny-handed toilers on whom the trade and commerce of the country in so large depend ... The vast procession was divided into four sections, and their order (decided by ballot) and estimated members were as follows:

1: Shipping (including five branches of the Dock Labourers Union and Coal Heavers Union, sailors and firemen, mast and block makers, shipwrights, watermen and sail makers), 50,000.
2: Building Trades, 4000.
3: Miscellaneous, including railway servants, brush makers, carters, printers, St Helens plate glass workers, tobacco operatives, 10,000
4: Engineering, 10,000.

Each section was headed by a mounted marshal. Mr Joseph Peters, the president of the Liverpool Trades Council, was distinguished by a spotless white sash, as he rode along majestically. A small pioneering section chosen to lead the way was composed of members of the Trades Congress Parliamentary Committee, congress delegates, members of Liverpool and Vicinity United Trades Council, wearing red rosettes and the female bookbinders and the tailors unions, the latter wearing ribbons and sashes ... The dock labourers numbering 14,000 formed outside the Custom House, while another important body representing the port of Liverpool – the seamen and firemen – met in front of Malakoff Hall, Cleveland Square ... A touching incident occurred as the dock labourers passed up Mount Pleasant into Oxford Street. The inmates of the Brownlow Hill workhouse has assembled at the windows overlooking

James Greig's *Cooperage*; 23 Virgil Street, off Scotland Road, Liverpool, *c.* 1890.

the street and cheered the labourers as they passed. The latter rested for
a few seconds and then returned the compliment with three loud cheers.
As the rear of the dock labourers passed, the Mersey riggers, sheet metal
workers, and Mersey watermen who had formed in James Street and
Hanover Street fell into line. At the top of Duke Street, the Mersey
shipwrights and coopers massed along Cornwallis Street and Kent Street
fell in, and the now extensive gathering was further augmented at St
James Mount by boiler scalers, sail makers, and the old dock labourers'
unions ... The front of the banners bore pictures illustrative of the scenes
of daily toil, while on the other side the representations indicated that
one chief feature of trades societies is the alleviation of the sick and the
helping of the widows and orphan. To take two typical examples. A fine
banner carried in the midst of the bricklayers suggested the nature of
their association with the motto 'industry is the source of prosperity',
the reverse side containing several small pictures denoting philanthropic
aid. The plumbers possessed two beautifully painted banners. On the
front of one of them, two plumbers were represented standing with
hands grasped by the side of a fountain, while on the other side four
sketches indicated the humanitarian aspect of the societies work – one
representing a plumber visiting a sick brother, the inscription at the base
being, 'I was sick and ye visited me.'
The display by the Dock Labourers Union, a body recently formed,

was considered a feature of the shipping faction. The banners included several sent by London branches, and all of them containing pictures of ships in dock with labourers busily engaged in discharging them. On the lorry, which conveyed the Toxteth branch banner, stood an elderly man of sable colour, and as he grasped the hand of a local member, he formed a living illustration of the motto on the banner, 'All men are brothers,' a motto whose enunciation at the Trade Congress by a London delegate was received with applause when he discussed the proposal of working men's federation for the whole world. The members of the Mersey Ships Scrapers, Accident and Burial Society indicated the character of their calling by carrying brushes and scrapers, and neat specimens of the brush making handicraft were carried by members of that body. The sail makers had a model of a fully rigged ship ... Several of the coopers carried models of casks and other trade productions, some amusement was created by a working model showing a couple of coopers preparing their tools on a grindstone. The Mersey flatmen and watermen's show of banners and flags was very noticeable, and among the mottoes were, 'unity is strength', 'succour the widows and orphans', and that associated with odd-fellowship, 'friendship, love and truth'. The operative House painters, 1,200 in number, gained high praise for their soldier-like marching. They were headed by three brass bands ... A unique figure among the carpenters and joiners was a piper in Highland costume ... The coach makers society preceded by the Akbar boy's band and small wooden models of carriages was favoured with four banners, one having been sent by the Glasgow branch, and this explained to spectators the reason of the motto on it: 'Let Glasgow Flourish'... Hairdressers have little time to demonstrate on a Saturday being occupied with their tonsorial art, and accordingly, few members of the recently formed society paraded. Two of their order bore a banner with the inscription 'The Hairdressers of Liverpool appeal to the public to support union shops, meaning thereby the shops that closed each Thursday afternoon in order to afford assistants a well-earned half holiday.

A new round was set; the unions remained. The spirit of Merseyside workers was as strong as ever. In the following decade, general unrest on the docks in the summer of 1911 saw dockers in Liverpool and Manchester strike on 1 August. They had won within eleven days, but then the carters came out and pickets took hold of the port again. The shipowners responded with a general lock out on 14 August.

Most trouble was expected in Liverpool where Tom Mann was organising the Dockers. 200 troops of the Yorkshire regiment were already stationed

Campania at her Liverpool berth, 1907.

in the city. Two naval gunboats were ominously anchored in the Mersey. Such a display of state power did not intimidate the strikers, and on 13 August a meeting of transport workers in front of St Georges Hall turned into a riot. Police lines were showered with missiles, several baton charges were made on the crowd, and the troops fired several volleys over their heads. Around 200 people were injured on both sides. The following day, the lockout began and affected 25,000 workers. The strike committee retaliated by calling out 75,000 more.

Tom Mann was something of a one-man revolution in the eyes of the employers throughout Britain. He had stared work down the mines as a trapper at the age of nine at the Victoria Colliery, near Coventry. The pit closed after a series of deadly accidents, roof falls, and explosions. At fourteen, he started as an engineering apprentice in Birmingham. Out of his time, he moved to London where he became involved with early socialist movements, and became attracted to the ideas of Marx. He fused the earlier ideas of Christianity that had influenced him with revolutionary Communism and a

Mass Meeting, St George's Plateau, Liverpool, 13 August 1911 during the general transport strike.

belief in direct working class action rather than parliamentary solutions. In 1888, the decisive London dock strike saw him and his comrade Ben Tillett organising international solidarity and support alongside the dockers unions. The London dockers won a decisive victory. 1894 saw him elected as general secretary of the Independent Labour Party. From 1901 to 1910, he lived and organised in Australia, where he helped form the Australian Socialist Party. He was twice put on trial for sedition, but they failed on either occasion to get a conviction.

On his return, he became an organiser for the dockers union, and moved sharply towards ideas of industrial syndicalism and industrial unionism, which was everywhere making its stamp on the working class movement, particularly on the railways and mines. He formed the Industrial Syndicalist Education League and the Syndicalist Railwayman.

1911 Liverpool General Transport Strike

The Liverpool General Transport Strike was to rock the British state, spreading panic of an impending workers' revolution. For the first time ever, transport workers in Britain were now organised into a single industrial union. The Transport Workers Federation was formed under the leadership of Mann and Tillett. Reminiscent of many earlier disputes, the action was joined by other central workers adding their own demands. The seamen had seen their wages drop by around ten per cent compared with the 1890s. The seamen's strikes had started in 1910. In May, the TWF organised a massive demonstration in the city, with thousands of transport workers marching through the city centre.

They were at once joined by dockers walking off the job and joining the demonstration. As the mood in the city took on a general turn out, the Shipping Federation brought in the army and locked out its workers on 14 August.

On 15 August, prison vans transporting arrested insurgents were attacked by a large crowd. '... The prison convoy cavalry escort opened fire. Vauxhall Road became a bloody battlefield.' Two workers were shot to death and a policeman was kicked to death. Violence spread throughout the city, and infantry launched repeated bayonet charges while workers responded with barricades and wire entanglements. Liverpool chief constable informed the Home Office, 'The object was purely and simply to attack the police, whom they tempted into side streets ... The mob pursued the same tactics, stoned troops and police from windows and house tops ...'

The Royal Navy cruiser HMS *Antrim* was sent to the Mersey to back up a flotilla of gunboats, while armed marines took over the Mersey ferries. HMS *Warrior*, another big cruiser, was positioned in readiness off the Isle of Man. The King telegraphed Churchill to inform him that the situation in Liverpool was more like a revolutionary struggle than a strike, and that troops should be given a free hand, and not be half-heartedly deployed.

The King's observations began to look accurate as local insurrections spread across Britain. On 18 August, the four national rail unions called the first national rail strike. Ostensibly in solidarity action with the dockers, it had also been propelled by the refusal of the railway companies to recognise the unions. Troops moved to the rail depots and camped out in major parks across the northern cities and London. 200,000 workers were now on strike or locked out. Industrial production across Britain came to a halt. 'The worse stoppages where within the rough geographical square marked by Newcastle, Liverpool, Coventry and Hull, and South Wales.'

In the end, with riots and live ammunition issued to troops, and hand-to-hand fighting with police, the union moderates, fearful of the revolutionary trajectory of the movement, imposed their influence and control to call off the strike wave together with the labour movement moderates. For his part, and writing a leaflet aimed at the troops being brought into the city titled 'Don't Shoot', Mann was arrested and charged with sedition, receiving a sentence of six months. A widespread labour movement campaign, which promised to restart the action and wrest back control from the sell outs, ensured that he was out in seven weeks.

In August 1919, gunboats return to the Mersey. Troops marched through the streets with their bayonets fixed; another worker would die on the streets of Liverpool, shot by British soldiers. This time, it would not be the dockers who launched the rebellion, but the police. Merseyside became the storm centre and strongest focus of resistance in the national police strike.

We leave the scene set at the entrance of the new century, a step too far in scope for the parameters of this history perhaps. But sufficient to say, the workers of Merseyside were entering it with a full head of steam and no lack of vision, rooted firmly in more than sixty years of determined class struggle against all odds.